SOFTWARE ENGINEERING FOR SCIENCE

Chapman & Hall/CRC
Computational Science Series

SERIES EDITOR

Horst Simon
Deputy Director
Lawrence Berkeley National Laboratory
Berkeley, California, U.S.A.

PUBLISHED TITLES

COMBINATORIAL SCIENTIFIC COMPUTING
Edited by Uwe Naumann and Olaf Schenk

CONTEMPORARY HIGH PERFORMANCE COMPUTING: FROM PETASCALE
TOWARD EXASCALE
Edited by Jeffrey S. Vetter

CONTEMPORARY HIGH PERFORMANCE COMPUTING: FROM PETASCALE
TOWARD EXASCALE, VOLUME TWO
Edited by Jeffrey S. Vetter

DATA-INTENSIVE SCIENCE
Edited by Terence Critchlow and Kerstin Kleese van Dam

THE END OF ERROR: UNUM COMPUTING
John L. Gustafson

FROM ACTION SYSTEMS TO DISTRIBUTED SYSTEMS: THE REFINEMENT APPROACH
Edited by Luigia Petre and Emil Sekerinski

FUNDAMENTALS OF MULTICORE SOFTWARE DEVELOPMENT
Edited by Victor Pankratius, Ali-Reza Adl-Tabatabai, and Walter Tichy

FUNDAMENTALS OF PARALLEL MULTICORE ARCHITECTURE
Yan Solihin

THE GREEN COMPUTING BOOK: TACKLING ENERGY EFFICIENCY AT LARGE SCALE
Edited by Wu-chun Feng

GRID COMPUTING: TECHNIQUES AND APPLICATIONS
Barry Wilkinson

HIGH PERFORMANCE COMPUTING: PROGRAMMING AND APPLICATIONS
John Levesque with Gene Wagenbreth

HIGH PERFORMANCE PARALLEL I/O
Prabhat and Quincey Koziol

PUBLISHED TITLES CONTINUED

SOFTWARE ENGINEERING FOR SCIENCE

Edited by

Jeffrey C. Carver
University of Alabama, USA

Neil P. Chue Hong
University of Edinburgh, UK

George K. Thiruvathukal
Loyola University Chicago, Chicago, Illinois

CRC Press
Taylor & Francis Group
Boca Raton London New York

CRC Press is an imprint of the
Taylor & Francis Group, an **informa** business
A CHAPMAN & HALL BOOK

CRC Press
Taylor & Francis Group
6000 Broken Sound Parkway NW, Suite 300
Boca Raton, FL 33487-2742

© 2017 by Taylor & Francis Group, LLC
CRC Press is an imprint of Taylor & Francis Group, an Informa business

No claim to original U.S. Government works

Printed on acid-free paper
Version Date: 20160817

International Standard Book Number-13: 978-1-4987-4385-3 (Hardback)

Library of Congress Cataloging-in-Publication Data

Names: Carver, Jeffrey, editor. | Hong, Neil P. Chue, editor. |
Thiruvathukal, George K. (George Kuriakose), editor.
Title: Software engineering for science / edited by Jeffrey Carver, Neil P.
Chue Hong, and George K. Thiruvathukal.
Description: Boca Raton : Taylor & Francis, CRC Press, 2017. | Series:
Computational science series ; 30 | Includes bibliographical references
and index.
Identifiers: LCCN 2016022277 | ISBN 9781498743853 (alk. paper)
Subjects: LCSH: Science--Data processing. | Software engineering.
Classification: LCC Q183.9 .S74 2017 | DDC 005.1--dc23
LC record available at https://lccn.loc.gov/2016022277

Visit the Taylor & Francis Web site at
http://www.taylorandfrancis.com

and the CRC Press Web site at
http://www.crcpress.com

Printed and bound in the United States of America by
Edwards Brothers Malloy on sustainably sourced paper

Contents

*Roscoe A. Bartlett, Anshu Dubey, Xiaoye Sherry Li, J. David Moulton,
James M. Willenbring, and Ulrike Meier Yang*

List of Figures

List of Tables

About the Editors

Dr. Jeffrey C. Carver is an associate professor in the Department of Computer Science at the University of Alabama. Prior to his position at the University of Alabama, he was an assistant professor in the Department of Computer Science at Mississippi State University. He earned his PhD in computer science from the University of Maryland. His main research interests include software engineering for science, empirical software engineering, software quality, human factors in software engineering, and software process improvement. He is the primary organizer of the workshop series on Software Engineering for Science (http://www.SE4Science.org/workshops). He is a Senior Member of the IEEE Computer Society and a Senior Member of the ACM. Contact him at carver@cs.ua.edu.

Neil P. Chue Hong is director of the Software Sustainability Institute at the University of Edinburgh, which works to enable the continued improvement and impact of research software. Prior to this he was director of OMII-UK at the University of Southampton, which provided and supported free, open-source software for the UK e-Research community. He has a masters degree in computational physics from the University of Edinburgh and previously worked at Edinburgh Parallel Computing Centre as a principal consultant and project manager on data integration projects. His research interests include barriers and incentives in research software ecosystems and the role of software as a research object. He is the editor-in-chief of the *Journal of Open Research Software* and chair of the Software Carpentry Foundation Advisory Council. Contact him at N.ChueHong@software.ac.uk.

George K. Thiruvathukal is a professor of computer science at Loyola University Chicago and visiting faculty at Argonne National Laboratory in the Math and Computer Science Division and the Argonne Leadership Computing Facility. His research interests include parallel and distributed systems, software engineering, programming languages, operating systems, digital humanities, computational science, computing education, and broadening participation in computer science. His current research is focused on software metrics in open-source mathematical and scientific software. Professor Thiruvathukal is a member of the IEEE, IEEE Computer Society, and ACM.

List of Contributors

Daniel P. Ames
Department of Civil &
  Environmental Engineering
Brigham Young University
Provo, UT, USA

Katie Antypas
National Energy Research Scientific
  Computing Center
Lawrence Berkeley National
  Laboratory
Berkeley, CA, USA

Satish Balay
Mathematics and Computer Science
  Division
Argonne National Laboratory
Argonne, IL, USA

Roscoe A. Bartlett
Sandia National Laboratories
Albuquerque, NM, USA

Jed Brown
Department of Computer Science
University of Colorado Boulder
Boulder, CO, USA

Laura Christopherson
RENCI
University of North Carolina at
  Chapel Hill
Chapel Hill, NC, USA

Ethan Coon
Computational Earth Sciences
Los Alamos National Laboratory
Los Alamos, NM, USA

Alva Couch
Department of Computer Science
Tufts University
Medford, MA, USA

Pabitra Dash
Utah State University
Logan, UT, USA

Anshu Dubey
Mathematics and Computer Science
  Division
Argonne National Laboratory
Argonne, IL, USA

Daniel Hook
Software Group
ESG Solutions
Kingston, ON, Canada

Jeffery S. Horsburgh
Department of Civil &
  Environmental Engineering
Utah State University
Logan, UT, USA

Ray Idaszak
RENCI
University of North Carolina at
  Chapel Hill
Chapel Hill, NC, USA

Arne N. Johanson
Department of Computer Science
Kiel University
Kiel, Germany

Upulee Kanewala
Computer Science Department
Montana State University
Bozeman, MT, USA

Matthew Knepley
Department of Computational &
    Applied Mathematics
Rice University
Houston, TX, USA

Xiaoye Sherry Li
Computational Research Division
Lawrence Berkeley National
    Laboratory
Berkeley, CA, USA

Lois Curfman McInnes
Mathematics and Computer Science
    Division
Argonne National Laboratory
Argonne, IL, USA

Brian Miles
CGI Group Inc.
Fairfax, VA, USA

J. David Moulton
Mathematical Modeling and Analysis
Los Alamos National Laboratory
Los Alamos, NM, USA

Andreas Oschlies
GEOMAR Helmholtz Centre for
    Ocean Research
Kiel, Germany

Matthew Patrick
Department of Plant Sciences
University of Cambridge
Cambridge, United Kingdom

Katherine Riley
Argonne Leadership Computing
    Facility

Argonne National Laboratory
Lemont, IL, USA

Barry Smith
Mathematics and Computer Science
    Division
Argonne National Laboratory
Argonne, IL, USA

Spencer Smith
Computing and Software
    Department
McMaster University
Hamilton, ON, Canada

Calvin Spealman
Caktus Consulting Group, LLC
Durham, NC, USA

Michael Stealey
RENCI
University of North Carolina at
    Chapel Hill
Chapel Hill, NC, USA

David G. Tarboton
Department of Civil &
    Environmental Engineering
Utah State University
Logan, UT, USA

Dali Wang
Climate Change Science Institute
Oak Ridge National Laboratory
Oak Ridge, TN, USA

James M. Willenbring
Sandia National Laboratories
Albuquerque, NM, USA

Frank Winkler
National Center for Computational
Sciences
Oak Ridge National Laboratory
Oak Ridge, TN, USA

Boris Worm
Biology Department
Dalhousie University
Halifax, NS, Canada

Ulrike Meier Yang
Center for Applied Scientific
Computing
Lawrence Livermore National
Laboratory
Livermore, CA, USA

Zhuo Yao
Department of Electrical Engineering
& Computer Science
University of Tennessee
Knoxville, TN, USA

Hong Yi
RENCI
University of North Carolina at
Chapel Hill
Chapel Hill, NC, USA

Acknowledgments

Jeffrey C. Carver was partially supported by grants 1243887 and 1445344 from the National Science Foundation. Any opinions, findings, and conclusions or recommendations expressed in this material are those of the author(s) and do not necessarily reflect the views of the National Science Foundation.

Neil P. Chue Hong was supported by the UK Engineering and Physical Sciences Research Council (EPSRC) Grant EP/H043160/1 and EPSRC, BBSRC and ESRC Grant EP/N006410/1 for the UK Software Sustainability Institute.

George K. Thiruvathukal was partially supported by grant 1445347 from the National Science Foundation. Any opinions, findings, and conclusions or recommendations expressed in this material are those of the author(s) and do not necessarily reflect the views of the National Science Foundation.

MATLAB® is a registered trademark of The MathWorks, Inc. For product information, please contact:

The MathWorks, Inc.
3 Apple Hill Drive
Natick, MA 01760-2098 USA
Tel: 508 647 7000
Fax: 508-647-7001
E-mail: info@mathworks.com
Web: www.mathworks.com

Introduction

General Overview

Scientific software is a special class of software that includes software developed to support various scientific endeavors that would be difficult, or impossible, to perform experimentally or without computational support. Included in this class of software are, at least, the following:

- Software that solves complex computationally- or data-intensive problems, ranging from large, parallel simulations of physical phenomena run on HPC machines, to smaller simulations developed and used by groups of scientists or engineers on a desktop machine or small cluster

- Applications that support scientific research and experiments, including systems that manage large data sets

- Systems that provide infrastructure support, e.g. messaging middleware, scheduling software

- Libraries for mathematical and scientific programming, e.g. linear algebra and symbolic computing

The development of scientific software differs significantly from the development of more traditional business information systems, from which many software engineering best practices and tools have been drawn. These differences appear at various phases of the software lifecycle as outlined below:

- Requirements:
    - Risks due to the exploration of relatively unknown scientific/engineering phenomena
    - Risks due to essential (inherent) domain complexity
    - Constant change as new information is gathered, e.g. results of a simulation inform domain understanding

- Design
    - Data dependencies within the software

- The need to identify the most appropriate parallelization strategy for scientific software algorithms
- The presence of complex communication or I/O patterns that could degrade performance
- The need for fault tolerance and task migration mechanisms to mitigate the need to restart time-consuming, parallel computations due to software or hardware errors

- Coding

  - Highly specialized skill set required in numerical algorithms and systems (to squeeze out performance)

- Validation and Verification

  - Results are often unknown when exploring novel science or engineering areas and algorithms
  - Popular software engineering tools often do not work on the architectures used in computational science and engineering

- Deployment

  - Larger node and core sizes coupled with long runtimes result in increased likelihood of failure of computing elements
  - Long software lifespans necessitate porting across multiple platforms

In addition to the challenges presented by these methodological differences, scientific software development also faces people-related challenges. First, educational institutions teach students high-level languages and programming techniques. As a result, there is a lack of developers with knowledge of relevant languages, like Fortran, or low-level skills to handle tasks like code optimization. Second, the dearth of interdisciplinary computational science programs is reducing the pipeline of graduates who have the experience required to be effective in the scientific software domain. Furthermore, the lack of these programs is reducing the motivation for graduates to pursue careers in scientific software. Third, the knowledge, skills, and incentives present in scientific software development differ from those present in traditional software domains. For example, scientific developers may lack formal software engineering training, trained software engineers may lack the required depth of understanding of the science domain, and the incentives in the science domain focus on timely scientific results rather than more traditional software quality/productivity goals.

The continuing increase in the importance and prevalence of software developed in support of science motivates the need to better understand how software engineering is and should be practiced. Specifically, there is a need to understand which software engineering practices are effective for scientific software and which are not. Some of the ineffective practices may need further refinements to fit within the scientific context. To increase our collective understanding of software engineering for science, this book consists of a collection of peer-reviewed chapters that describe experiences with applying software engineering practices to the development of scientific software.

Publications regarding this topic have seen growth in recent years as evidenced by the ongoing *Software Engineering for Science* workshop series[1] [1–5], workshops on software development as part of the *IEEE International Conference on eScience*[2,3] conference, and case studies submitted to the *Working towards Sustainable Scientific Software: Practice and Experiences* workshop series[4,5]. Books such as *Practical Computing for Biologists* [6] and *Effective Computation in Physics* [8] have introduced the application of software engineering techniques to scientific domains. In 2014, *Nature* launched a new section, *Nature Toolbox*[6], which includes substantial coverage of software engineering issues in research. In addition, this topic has been a longstanding one in *Computing in Science and Engineering* (CiSE)[7], which sits at the intersection of computer science and complex scientific domains, notably physics, chemistry, biology, and engineering. CiSE also has recently introduced a Software Engineering Track to more explicitly focus on these types of issues[8]. EduPar is an education effort aimed at developing the specialized skill set (in concurrent, parallel, and distributed computing) needed for scientific software development [7][9].

In terms of funding, the United States Department of Energy funded the Interoperable Design of Extreme Scale Application Software (IDEAS) project[10]. The goal of IDEAS is to improve scientific productivity of extreme-scale science through the use of appropriate software engineering practices.

Overview of Book Contents

We prepared this book by selecting the set of chapter proposals submitted in response to an open solicitation that fit with an overall vision for the book.

---

[1]http://www.SE4Science.org/workshops
[2]http://escience2010.org/pdf/cse%20workshop.pdf
[3]http://software.ac.uk/maintainable-software-practice-workshop
[4]http://openresearchsoftware.metajnl.com/collections/special/working-towards-sustainable-software-for-science/
[5]http://openresearchsoftware.metajnl.com/collections/special/working-towards-sustainable-software-for-science-practice-and-experiences/
[6]http://www.nature.com/news/toolbox
[7]http://computer.org/cise
[8]https://www.computer.org/cms/Computer.org/ComputingNow/docs/2016-software-engineering-track.pdf
[9]http://grid.cs.gsu.edu/ tcpp/curriculum/?q=edupar
[10]http://ideas-productivity.org

The chapters underwent peer review from the editors and authors of other chapters to ensure quality and consistency.

The chapters in this book are designed to be self-contained. That is, readers can begin reading whichever chapter(s) are interesting without reading the prior chapters. In some cases, chapters have pointers to more detailed information located elsewhere in the book. That said, Chapter 1 does provide a detailed overview of the Scientific Software lifecycle. To group relevant material, we organized the book into three sections. Please note that the ideas expressed in the chapters do not necessarily reflect our own ideas. As this book focuses on documenting the current state of software engineering in scientific software development, we provide an unvarnished treatment of lessons learned from a diverse set of projects.

General Software Engineering

This section provides a general overview of the scientific software development process. The authors of chapters in this section highlight key issues commonly arising during scientific software development. The chapters then describe solutions to those problems. This section includes three chapters.

Chapter 1, *Software Process for Multiphysics Multicomponent Codes* provides an overview of the scientific software lifecycle, including a number of common challenges faced by scientific software developers (note readers not interested in the full chapter may find this section interesting). The chapter describes how two projects, the long-running FLASH and newer Amanzi, faced a specific set of these challenges: software architecture and modularization, design of a testing regime, unique documentation needs and challenges, and the tension between intellectual property and open science. The lessons learned from these projects should be of interest to scientific software developers.

Chapter 2, *A Rational Document Driven Design Process for Scientific Software* argues for the feasibility and benefit of using a set of documentation drawn from the waterfall development model to guide the development of scientific software. The chapter first addresses the common arguments that scientific software cannot use such a structured process. Then the chapter explains which artifacts developers can find useful when developing scientific software. Finally, the chapter illustrates the document driven approach with a small example.

Chapter 3, *Making Scientific Software Easier to Understand, Test, and Communicate through Software Engineering* argues that the complexity of scientific software leads to difficulties in understanding, testing, and communication. To illustrate this point, the chapter describes three case studies from the domain of computational plant biology. The complexity of the underlying scientific processes and the uncertainty of the expected outputs makes adequately testing, understanding, and communicating the software a challenge. Scientists who lack formal software engineering training may find these challenges especially difficult. To alleviate these challenges, this chapter reinterprets two testing techniques to make them more intuitive for scientists.

Software Testing

This section provides examples of the use of testing in scientific software development. The authors of chapters in this section highlight key issues associated with testing and how those issues present particular challenges for scientific software development (e.g. test oracles). The chapters then describe solutions and case studies aimed at applying testing to scientific software development efforts. This section includes four chapters.

Chapter 4, *Testing of Scientific Software: Impacts on Research Credibility, Development Productivity, Maturation, and Sustainability* provides an overview of key testing terminology and explains an important guiding principle of software quality: understanding stakeholders/customers. The chapter argues for the importance of automated testing and describes the specific challenges presented by scientific software. Those challenges include testing floating point data, scalability, and the domain model. The chapter finishes with a discussion of test suite maintenance.

Chapter 5, *Preserving Reproducibility through Regression Testing* describes how the practice of regression testing can help developers ensure that results are repeatable as software changes over time. Regression testing is the practice of repeating previously successful tests to detect problems due to changes to the software. This chapter describes two key challenges faced when testing scientific software, the oracle problem (the lack of information about the expected output) and the tolerance problem (the acceptable level of uncertainty in the answer). The chapter then presents a case study to illustrate how regression testing can help developers address these challenges and develop software with reproducible results. The case study shows that without regression tests, faults would have been more costly.

Chapter 6, *Building a Function Testing Platform for Complex Scientific Code* describes an approach to better understand and modularize complex codes as well as generate functional testing for key software modules. The chapter defines a *Function Unit* as a specific scientific function, which may be implemented in one or more modules. The *Function Unit Testing* approach targets code for which unit tests are sparse and aims to facilitate and expedite validation and verification via computational experiments. To illustrate the usefulness of this approach, the chapter describes its application to the Terrestrial Land Model within the Accelerated Climate Modeling for Energy (ACME) project.

Chapter 7, *Automated Metamorphic Testing of Scientific Software* addresses one of the most challenging aspects of testing scientific software, i.e. the lack of test oracles. This chapter first provides an overview of the test oracle problem (which may be of interest even to readers who are not interested in the main focus of this chapter). The lack of test oracles, often resulting from the exploration of new science or the complexities of the expected results, leads to incomplete testing that may not reveal subtle errors. Metamorphic testing addresses this problem by developing test cases through metamorphic relations. A metamorphic relation specifies how a particular change to the input should change the output. The chapter describes a machine learning approach to automatically predict metamorphic relations which can then serve as test oracles. The chapter then illustrates the approach on several open source scientific programs as well as on in-house developed scientific code called SAXS.

Experiences

This section provides examples of applying software engineering techniques to scientific software. Scientific software encompasses not only computational modeling, but also software for data management and analysis, and libraries that support higher-level applications. In these chapters, the authors describe their experiences and lessons learned from developing complex scientific software in different domains. The challenges are both cultural and technical. The ability to communicate and diffuse knowledge is of primary importance. This section includes three chapters.

Chapter 8, *Evaluating Hierarchical Domain-Specific Languages for Computational Science: Applying the Sprat Approach to a Marine Ecosystem Model* examines the role of domain-specific languages for bridging the knowledge transfer gap between the computational sciences and software engineering. The chapter defines the Sprat approach, a hierarchical model in the field of marine ecosystem modeling. Then, the chapter illustrates how developers can implement scientific software utilizing a multi-layered model that enables a clear separation of concerns allowing scientists to contribute to the development of complex simulation software.

Chapter 9, *Providing Mixed-Language and Legacy Support in a Library: Experiences of Developing PETSc* summarizes the techniques developers employed to build the PETSc numerical library (written in C) to portably and efficiently support its use from modern and legacy versions of Fortran. The chapter provides concrete examples of solutions to challenges facing scientific software library maintainers who must support software written in legacy versions of programming languages.

Chapter 10, *HydroShare — A Case Study of the Application of Modern Software Engineering to a Large, Distributed, Federally-Funded, Scientific Software Development Project* presents a case study on the challenges of introducing software engineering best practices such as code versioning, continuous integration, and team communication into a typical scientific software development project. The chapter describes the challenges faced because of differing skill levels, cultural norms, and incentives along with the solutions developed by the project to diffuse knowledge and practice.

Key Chapter Takeaways

The following list provides the key takeaways from each chapter. This list should help readers better understand which chapters will be most relevant to their situation. As stated earlier, the takeaways from each chapter are the opinions of the chapter authors and not necessarily of the editors.

Chapter 1

- The development lifecycle for scientific software must reflect stages that are not present in most other types of software, including model development, discretization, and numerical algorithm development.

- The requirements evolve during the development cycle because the requirements may themselves be the subject of the research.

- Modularizing multi-component software to achieve separation of concerns is an important task, but it difficult to achieve due to the monolithic nature of the software and the need for performance.

- The development of scientific software (especially multiphysics, multi-domain software) is challenging because of the complexity of the underlying scientific domain, the interdisciplinary nature of the work, and other institutional and cultural challenges.

- Balancing continuous development with ongoing production requires open development with good contribution and distribution policies.

Chapter 2

- Use of a rational document-driven design process is feasible in scientific software, even if rational documentation has to be created post hoc to describe a development process that was not rational.

- Although the process can be time consuming, documenting requirements, design, testing and artifact traceability improves software quality (e.g., verifiability, usability, maintainability, reusability, understandability, and reproducibility).

- Developers can integrate existing software development tools for tasks like version control, issue tracking, unit testing, and documentation generation to reduce the burden of performing those tasks.

Chapter 3

- Scientific software is often difficult to test because it is used to answer new questions in experimental research.

- Scientists are often unfamiliar with advanced software engineering techniques and do not have enough time to learn them, therefore we should describe software engineering techniques with concepts more familiar to scientists.

- Iterative hypothesis testing and search-based pseudo-oracles can be used to help scientists produce rigorous test suites in the face of a dearth of a priori information about its behavior.

Chapter 4

- The complexity of multiphysics scientific models and the presence of heterogeneous high-performance computers with complex memory hierarchies requires the development of complex software, which is increasingly difficult to test and maintain.

- Performing extensive software testing not only leads to software that delivers more correct results but also facilitates further development, refactoring, and portability.

- Developers can obtain quality tests by using granular tests at different levels of the software, e.g., fine-grained tests are foundational because they can be executed quickly and localize problems while higher-level tests ensure proper interaction of larger pieces of software.

- Use of an automated testing framework is critical for performing regular, possibly daily, testing to quickly uncover faults.

- Clearly defined testing roles and procedures are essential to sustain the viability of the software.

Chapter 5

- Use of regular, automated testing against historical results, e.g., regression testing, helps developers ensure reproducibility and helps prevent the introduction of faults during maintenance.

- Use of regression testing can help developers mitigate against the oracle problem (lack of information about the expected output) and the tolerance problem (level of uncertainty in the output).

Chapter 6

- The use of a scientific function testing platform with a compiler-based code analyzer and an automatic prototype platform can help developers test large-scale scientific software when unit tests are sparse.

- The function testing platform can help model developers and users better understand complex scientific code, modularize complex code, and generate comprehensive functional testing for complex code.

Chapter 7

- The oracle problem poses a major challenge for conducting systematic automated testing of scientific software.

- Metamorphic testing can be used for automated testing of scientific software by checking whether the software behaves according to a set of metamorphic relations, which are relationships between multiple input and output pairs.

- When used in automated unit testing, a metamorphic testing approach is highly effective in detecting faults.

Chapter 8

- Scientists can use domain-specific languages (DSLs) to implement well-engineered software without extensive software engineering training.

- Integration of multiple DSLs from different domains can help scientists from different disciplines collaborate to implement complex and coupled simulation software.

- DSLs for scientists must have the following characteristics: appropriate level of abstraction for the meta-model, syntax that allows scientists to quickly experiment, have tool support, and provide working code examples as documentation.

Chapter 9

- Multi-language software, specifically Fortran, C, and C++, is still important and requires care on the part of library developers, benefitting from concrete guidance on how to call Fortran from C/C++ and how to call C/C++ from Fortran.

- Mapping of all common C-based constructs in multiple versions of Fortran allows developers to use different versions of Fortran in multi-language software.

Chapter 10

- Use of modern software engineering practices helps increase the sustainability, quality and usefulness of large scientific projects, thereby enhancing the career of the responsible scientists.

- Use of modern software engineering practices enables software developers and research scientists to work together to make new and valuable contributions to the code base, especially from a broader community perspective.

- Use of modern software engineering practices on large projects increases the overall code capability and quality of science results by propagating these practices to a broader community, including students and post-doctoral researchers.

Chapter 1

Software Process for Multiphysics Multicomponent Codes

Anshu Dubey, Katie Antypas, Ethan Coon, and Katherine Riley

1.1   Introduction

Computational science and engineering communities develop complex applications to solve scientific and engineering challenges, but these communities have a mixed record of using software engineering best practices [43, 296]. Many codes developed by scientific communities adopt standard software practices when the size and complexity of an application become too unwieldy to continue without them [30]. The driving force behind adoption is usually the realization that without using software engineering practices, the development, verification, and maintenance of applications can become intractable. As more codes cross the threshold into increasing complexity, software engineering processes are being adopted from practices derived outside the scientific and engineering domain. Yet the state of the art for software engineering practices in scientific codes often lags behind that in the commercial software space [16, 36, 52]. There are many reasons: lack of incentives, support, and funding; a reward system favoring scientific results over software development; limited understanding of how software engineering should be promoted to communities that have their own specific needs and sociology [22, 35].

Some software engineering practices have been better accepted than others among the developers of scientific codes. The ones that are used often include repositories for code version control, licensing process, regular testing, documentation, release and distribution policies, and contribution policies [21, 22, 30, 32]. Less accepted practices include code review, code deprecation, and adoption of specific practices from development methodologies such as Agile [9]. Software best practices that may be effective in commercial software development environments are not always suited for scientific environments, partly because of sociology and partly because of technical challenges. Sociology manifests itself as suspicion of too rigid a process or not seeing the point of adopting a practice. The technical challenges arise from the nature of problems being addressed by these codes. For example, multiphysics and multicomponent codes that run on large high-performance computing (HPC) platforms put a large premium on performance. In our experience, good performance is most often achieved by sacrificing some of the modularity in software architecture (e.g. [28]). Similarly lateral interactions in physics get in the way of encapsulations (see Sections 1.3 and 1.4 for more examples and details).

This chapter elaborates on the challenges and how they were addressed in FLASH [26, 33] and Amanzi [41], two codes with very different development timeframe, and therefore very different development paths. FLASH, whose development began in the late 1990s, is among the first generation of codes that adopted a software process. This was in the era when the advantages of software engineering were almost unknown in the scientific world. Amanzi is from the "enlightened" era (by scientific software standards) where a minimal set of software practices are adopted by most code projects intending long term use. A study of software engineering of these codes from different eras of scientific software development highlight how these practices and the communities have evolved.

FLASH was originally designed for computational astrophysics. It has been almost continuously under production and development since 2000, with three major revisions. It has exploited an extensible framework to expand its reach and is now a community code for over half a dozen scientific communities. The adoption of software engineering practices has grown with each version change and expansion of capabilities. The adopted practices themselves have evolved to meet the needs of the developers at different stages of development. Amanzi, on the other hand, started in 2012 and has developed from the ground up in C++ using relatively modern software engineering practices. It still has one major target community but is also designed with extensibility as an objective. Many other similarities and some differences are described later in the chapter. In particular, we address the issues related to software architecture and modularization, design of a testing regime, unique documentation needs and challenges, and the tension between intellectual property management and open science.

The next few sections outline the challenges that are either unique to, or are more dominant in scientific software than elsewhere. Section 1.2 outlines the possible lifecycle of a scientific code, followed by domain specific technical challenges in Section 1.3. Section 1.4 describes the technical and sociological challenges posed by the institutions where such codes are usually developed. Section 1.5 presents a case study of FLASH and Amanzi developments. Sections 1.6 and 1.7 present general observations and additional considerations for adapting the codes for the more challenging platforms expected in the future.

1.2   Lifecycle

Scientific software is designed to model phenomena in the physical world. The term *physical* includes chemical and biological systems since physical processes are also the underlying building blocks for these systems. A phenomenon may be microscopic (e.g. protein folding) or it can have extremely large or multiple scales (e.g. supernovae explosions). The physical characteristics of the system being studied translate to mathematical models that describe their essential features. These equations are discretized so that numerical algorithms can be used to solve them. One or more parts of this process may themselves be subjects of active research. Therefore the simulation software development requires diverse expertise and adds many stages in the development and lifecycle that may not be encountered elsewhere.

1.2.1   Development Cycle

For scientific simulations, modeling begins with equations that describe the general class of behavior to be studied. For example, the Navier–Stokes equations describe the flow of compressible and incompressible fluids, and Van der Waals equations describe interactions among molecules in a material. More than one set of equations may be involved if all behaviors of interest are not adequately captured by one set. In translating the model from mathematical representation to computational representation two processes go on simultaneously, discretization and approximation. One can argue that discretization is, by definition, an approximation because it is in effect sampling continuous behavior where information is lost in the sampling interval. This loss manifests itself as error terms in the discretized equations, but error terms are not the only approximations. Depending on the level of understanding of specific subphenomena and available compute resources, scientists also use their judgment to make other approximations. Sometimes, in order to focus on a particular behavior, a term in an equation may be simplified or even dropped. At other times some physical details may be dropped from the model because they are not understood well enough by the scientists. Or the model itself may be an approximation.

The next stage in developing the code is finding appropriate numerical methods for each of the models. Sometimes existing methods can be used without modification, but more often customization or new method development is needed. A method's applicability to the model may need to be validated if the method is new or significantly modified. Unless a reliable implementation is already available as third-party software (stand-alone or in a library), the method has to be implemented and verified. At this stage the development of a scientific code begins to resemble that of general software. The numerical algorithms are specified, the semantics are understood, and they need to be translated into executable code. Even then, however, differences exist because scientific code developers work iteratively [51] and requirement specifications evolve through the development cycle. Figure 1.1 gives an example of the development cycle of a multiphysics application modeled by using partial differential equations.

1.2.2   Verification and Validation

The terms verification and validation are often used interchangeably, but to many scientific domains they have specific meaning. In their narrow definition, validation ensures that the mathematical model correctly defines the physical phenomena, while verification makes sure that the implementation of the model is correct. In other words, scientists validate a model against observations or experiments from the physical world, while developers verify the model by other forms of testing [46]. Other definitions give broader scope to verification and validation (e.g. [50]). For example, validation of a numerical

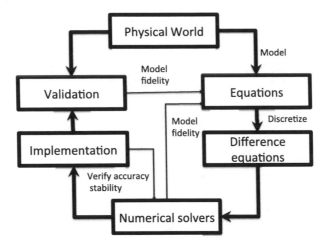

Figure 1.1: Development cycle of modeling with partial differential equations.

method may be constructed through code-to-code comparisons, and its order can be validated through convergence studies. Similarly, the implementation of a solver can be validated against an analytically obtained solution for some model if the same solver can be applied and the analytical solution is also known [45]. Irrespective of specific definitions, correctness must be assured at all the stages from modeling to implementation.

The process of deriving a model involves many degrees of freedom as discussed earlier, therefore, the scientific experts carefully calibrate model validation. Similarly, in addition to correctness, applied mathematicians verify numerical methods for stability, accuracy, and order of convergence. Many numerical methods are themselves objects of ongoing research, so their implementation may need modifications from time to time. Whenever such modifications happen, the entire gamut of verification and validation needs to be applied again. This represents a particular challenge in scientific software where no amount of specification is enough to hand the implementation over to software engineers or developers who do not have domain or math knowledge. A close collaboration among various experts is necessary because the process has to be iterative, with scientific judgment applied at every iteration.

One other unique verification challenge in scientific software is caused by finite machine precision of floating-point numbers. Any change in compilers, optimization levels, and even order of operations can cause numerical drift in the solutions [40]. Especially in applications that have a large range of scales, differentiating between a legitimate bug and a numerical drift can be difficult [155]. Therefore, relying on bitwise reproducibility of the solution is rarely a sufficient method for verifying the continued correctness of an application's behavior. Robust diagnostics (such as statistics or conservation of physical quantities) need to be built into the verification process. This issue is discussed in greater detail in Chapter 4.

Testing of scientific software needs to reflect the layered complexity of the codes. The first line of attack is to develop unit tests that isolate testing of individual components. In scientific codes, however, often dependencies exist between different components of the code that cannot be meaningfully isolated, making unit testing more difficult. In these cases, testing should be performed with a minimal possible combination of components. In effect, these minimally combined tests behave like unit tests because they focus on possible defects in a narrow section of the code. In addition, multicomponent scientific software should test various permutations and combination of components in different ways. Configuring tests in this manner can help verify that the configurations of interest are within the accuracy and stability constraints (see Section 1.5.1.2 for an example of testsuite configuration for FLASH).

1.2.3 Maintenance and Extensions

In a simplified view of the software lifecycle, there is a design and development phase, followed by a production and maintenance phase. Even in well-engineered codes this simplified view is usually applicable only to infrastructure and APIs. The numerical algorithms and solvers can be in a continually evolving state reflecting the advances in their respective fields. The development of scientific software is usually responding to an immediate scientific need, so the codes get employed in production as soon as they have a minimal set of capabilities for some simulation. Similarly, the development of computational modules almost never stops through the code lifecycle because new findings in science and math almost continuously place new demands on the code. The additions are incremental when they incorporate new findings into an existing feature; and they can be substantial when new capabilities are added. The need for new capabilities may arise from greater model fidelity or from trying to simulate a more complex model. Sometimes a code designed for one scientific field may have enough in common with another field that capabilities may be added to enable it for the new field.

Irrespective of the cause, coexistence of development and production/-maintenance phases is a constant challenge to the code teams. It becomes acute when the code needs to undergo major version changes. The former can be managed with some repository discipline in the team coupled with a robust testing regime. The latter is a much bigger challenge where the plan has to concern itself with questions such as how much backward compatibility is suitable, how much code can go offline, and how to reconcile ongoing development in code sections that are substantially different between versions. FLASH's example in Section 1.5.1.3 describes a couple of strategies that met the conflicting needs of developers and production users in both scenarios. Both required cooperation and buy-in from all the stakeholders to be successful.

1.2.4   Performance Portability

Performance portability is an important requirement of multiphysics scientific software that need HPC resources. HPC machines are expensive and rare resources, and in order to achieve high application performance, codes need to be optimized for the unique HPC architectures. However, the lifecycle of a multiphysics application may span many generations of HPC systems, which have a typical lifespan of about 4 to 5 years. Depending on the size of the code, optimization for a specific target platform can take a significant fraction of the platform lifecycle with corresponding loss in scientific productivity. Therefore, developers must consider the trade-offs and advantages of a highly optimized code for a single platform versus designing their software using constructs that perform modestly well across a range of platforms.

1.2.5   Using Scientific Software

Users of scientific software must have a basic understanding of the models, the approximations, and the numerical methods they are using to obtain valid scientific results. They must know and understand the valid regimes for applicability of numerical algorithms, as well as their accuracy and stability behavior. For example a numerical method that can resolve a smooth fluid flow only will fail if there are discontinuities. Similarly, in order to use the fast Fourier transform method, users must ensure that their sampling interval resolves all modes. Failure to do so may filter out important information and lead to wrong results. Sometimes equations have mathematically valid but physically invalid solutions. An inappropriately applied numerical scheme may converge to such a nonphysical solution.

At best any of these situations leads to a waste of computing resources if the defect in the solution is detected. At worst it may lead to wrong scientific conclusions. Some people in the scientific community even argue that those who have not written at least a simplistic version of the code for their application should not be using someone else's code. Although that argument goes too far, it embodies a general belief in the scientific community that users of scientific codes have a great responsibility to know their tools and understand the capabilities and limitations. These are some of the factors that play a role in the tendency of scientific code developers to do strict gatekeeping for contributions.

Key Insights

- Several stages of development precede software development in science, including translation of physical processes into mathematical models, discretization, convergence, and stability testing of numerics.

- Many of these stages may be undergoing research, which makes verification and validation both important and challenging.

- Performance portability is important for HPC scientific software.

- Software users must understand their tools and also the limitations of the tools well.

1.3   Domain Challenges

Multiphysics codes, by definition, solve more than one mathematical model. A typical code combines 3 to 4 diverse models, and in extreme cases codes may employ many more. Rarely, all models work with the same discretization using a similar algorithmic approach (for instance, stencil computations in explicit PDE solvers). Models with diverse discretizations and algorithms are more common. In such cases, each operator has its own preferred data layout and movement that may differ from those needed by other operators. Different models may also need different developer expertise. Therefore, when designing scientific software, creating modular components wherever possible is especially important. The reason is that different expertise may be required to understand each component, and a modular design allows application developers to focus on the areas they know best. For example, mathematics expertise is needed to develop and implement numerical algorithms associated with physics operators, while software engineering expertise is needed to design code architecture. In addition, modular code allows various components to interface with each other in a clearer way.

Although desirable, modularization can also be difficult to achieve in multimodel codes. Normally challenges related to different data layout and memory and communication access patterns can be mitigated through encapsulation and well defined APIs. The outer wrapper layers of the operators can carry out data transformations as needed. Two factors work against this approach in scientific codes, however. One is that scientific simulation codes model the physical world, which does not have neat modularization. Various phenomena have tightly coupled dependencies that are hard to break. These dependencies and tight couplings are transferred into the mathematical models and hinder the elimination of lateral interactions among code modules. An attempt to force encapsulations by hoisting up the lateral interactions to the API level can explode the size of the API. And if not done carefully this can also lead to extra data movement. The second is that the codes are performance sensitive and wholesale data movement significantly degrades performance. The module designs, therefore, have to be cognizant of potential lateral interactions and make allowances for them. Similarly, the data structures have to take into account the diverse demands placed on them by different operators and carefully consider the trade-offs during software design. Considerations such as these are not common in software outside of scientific domains. Section 1.5 describes how these challenges have been met by FLASH and Amanzi.

Multiphysics multiscale codes often require tight integration with third-party software, which comes in the form of numerical libraries. Because multiphysics codes combine expertise from many domains, the numerical solvers they use also require diverse applied mathematics expertise. It can be challenging for any one team to assemble all the necessary expertise to develop their own software. Many, therefore, turn to third-party math libraries for highly optimized routines. As mentioned in Section 1.2.5, the use of third-party software does not absolve them from understanding its appropriate use. Additionally, information about appropriate use of third-party software within the context of a larger code must also be communicated to the users of the code.

Key Insights

- Multiphysics codes need modularization for separation of concerns, but modularization can be hard to achieve because of lateral interactions inherent in the application.

- Codes can use third-party libraries to fill their own expertise gap, but they must understand the characteristics and limitations of the third-party software.

1.4 Institutional and Cultural Challenges

Many adaptations in software engineering for scientific applications described in the preceding section pertain to software design and testing. A number of challenges also arise because of the kind of organizations and the research communities where these codes are developed. The most crippling and pervasive challenge faced by scientific codes in general, and multiphysics codes in particular, is that funding for software development and maintenance is difficult to attain. Evidence from projects that secured funding for software infrastructure design indicates that when software is designed well, it pays huge dividends in scientific productivity. Examples include community codes such as NAMD [49], Amber [23], and Enzo [53], which are used by a significant number of users in their respective communities. A more persuasive case can be made by a handful of codes such as FLASH [26, 31], Cactus [19], and Uintah [18, 48], which were built for one community, but have expanded their capabilities to serve several other communities using a common infrastructure.

Even with this evidence it remains difficult to obtain funding for investment in software engineering best practices. Available funding is most often carved out of scientific goal-oriented projects that have their own priorities and timeline. This model often ends up shortchanging the software engineering. The scientific output of applications is measured in terms of publications, which in turn depend on data produced by the simulations. Therefore, in a project driven purely by scientific objectives, the short-term science goals can lead to situations where quick-and-dirty triumphs over long-term planning and design. The cost of future lost productivity may not be appreciated until much later when the code base has grown too large to remove its deficiencies easily. Software engineering is forcibly imposed on the code, which is at best a band-aid solution.

Another institutional challenge in developing good software engineering practices for scientific codes is training students and staff to use the application properly. Multiphysics codes require a broad range of expertise in domain science from their developers, and software engineering skill is an added requirement. Often experts in a domain science who develop scientific codes are not trained in software engineering and many learn skills on the job through reading or talking to colleagues [43,296]. Practices are applied as the scientists understand them, usually picking only what is of most importance for their own development. This practice can be both good and bad: good because it sifts out the unnecessary aspects of SE practice and bad because it is not always true that the sifted out aspects were really not necessary. It might just be that the person adopting the practice did not understand the usefulness and impact of those aspects.

Institutional challenges also arise from the scarcity and stability of resources apart from funding. Deep expertise in the domain may be needed to model the phenomenon right; and that kind of expertise is relatively rare. Additionally, domain and numerical algorithmic expertise is rarely replicated in a team developing the multiphysics scientific application. Then there is the challenge of communicating the model to the software engineer, if one is on the team, or to team members with some other domain expertise. Such communications require at least a few developers on the team who can act as interpreters for various domain expertise and are able to integrate the ideas. Such abilities take a lot of time and effort to develop, neither of which is easy in academic institutions where these codes are typically organically grown. The available human resources in these institutions are postdocs and students who move on, leaving little retention of institutional knowledge about the code. A few projects that do see the need for software professionals struggle to find ways of funding them or providing a path for their professional growth.

These institutional challenges are among the reasons that it is hard and sometimes even undesirable to adopt any rigid software development methodology in scientific application projects. For example, the principles behind the agile manifesto apply, but not all the formalized processes do. Agile software methods [9] are lightweight evolutionary development methods with focus on adaptability and flexibility, as opposed to waterfall methods which are sequential development processes where progress is perceived as a downward flow [11]. Agile methods aim to deliver working software as early as possible within the lifecycle and improve it based on user feedback and changing needs. These aims fit well with the objectives of scientific software development as well. The code is developed by interdisciplinary teams where interactions and collaborations are preferred over regimented process. The code is simultaneously developed and used for science, so that when requirements change, there is quick feedback. For the same reason, the code needs to be in working condition almost all the time. However, scarcity of resources does not allow the professional roles in the agile process to be played out efficiently. No clear separation exists between the developer and the client; many developers of the code are also scientists who use it for their research. Because software development goes hand in hand with research and exploration of algorithms, doing either within fixed timeframe is impossible. This constraint effectively eliminates using agile methods such as *sprints* or *extreme programming* [22]. The waterfall model is even less useful because it is not cost effective or even possible to have a full specification ahead of time. The code has to grow and alter organically as the scientific understanding grows, the effect of using technologies are digested, and requirements change. A reasonable solution is to adopt those elements of the methodologies that match the needs and objectives of the team, adjust them where needed, and develop their own processes and methodologies where none of the available options apply.

Because of the need for deep expertise, and the fact that the developer of a complex physics module is almost definitely going to leave with possibly no replacement, documentation of various kinds takes on a crucial role. It becomes necessary to document the algorithm, the implementation choices, and the range of operation. The generally preferred practice of writing self-explanatory code helps but does not suffice. To an expert in the field who has comprehensive understanding of the underlying math, such a code might be accessible without inline documentation. But it is not to people from another field or a software engineer in the team (if there is one) who may have reasons to look at the code. For longevity and extensibility, a scientific code must have inline documentation explaining the implementation logic and reasons behind the choices made.

Key Insights

- The benefits of investment in software design or process are not appreciated, and the funding model is not helpful in promoting them either.

- Development requires interdisciplinary teams with good communication, which is difficult in academic institutions.

- Methodologies get better foothold if they are flexible and adapt to the needs of the development team.

- Developer population is transient; detailed inlined documentation is necessary for maintenance.

1.5   Case Studies

FLASH and Amanzi are the codes from two different eras that we use as case studies.

1.5.1   FLASH

The FLASH code [13, 26] has been under development for nearly two decades at the Flash Center at the University of Chicago. The code was originally developed to simulate thermonuclear runaways in astrophysics such as novae and supernovae. It was created out of an amalgamation of three legacy codes: Prometheus for shock hydrodynamics, PARAMESH for adaptive mesh refinement (AMR) and locally developed equation of state and nuclear burn code. It has slowly evolved into a well-architected extensible software with a user base in over half a dozen scientific communities. FLASH has been applied to a variety of problems including supernovae, X-ray bursts, galaxy clusters, stellar structure, fluid instabilities, turbulence, laser-experiments design and analysis, and nuclear reactor rods. It supports an Eulerian mesh combined with a Lagrangian framework to cover a large class of applications. Physics capabilities include compressible hydrodynamics and magnetohydrodynamics solvers, nuclear burning, various forms of equations of state, radiation, laser drive, and fluid-structure interactions.

1.5.1.1   Code Design

From the outset FLASH was required to have composability because the simulations of interest needed capabilities in different permutations and combinations. For example, most simulations needed compressible hydrodynamics, but with different equations of state. Some needed to include self-gravity, while others did not. An obvious solution was to use object-oriented programming model with common APIs and specializations to account for the different models. However, the physics capabilities were mostly legacy with F77 implementations. Rewriting the code in an object-oriented language was not an option. A compromise was found by exploiting the Unix directory structure for inheritance, where the top level directory of the unit defined its API and the subdirectories implemented it. Metainformation about the role of a particular directory level in the object oriented framework was encoded in a limited domain-specific language (configuration DSL). The metainformation also included state and runtime variables requirements, and dependencies on other code units. A *setup tool* parsed this information to configure a consistent *application*. The setup tool also interpreted the configuration DSL to implement inheritance using the directory structure. For more details about FLASH's object-oriented framework see [26].

FLASH is designed with separation of concerns as an objective, which is achieved by separating the infrastructural components from physics. The abstraction that permits this approach is well known in scientific codes, that of decomposing a physical domain into rectangular blocks surrounded by halo cells copied over from the surrounding neighboring blocks. To a physics operator, the whole domain is not distinguishable from a box. Another necessary aspect of the abstraction is not to let any of the physics modules own the state variables. They are owned by the infrastructure that decomposes the domain into blocks. A further separation of concern takes place within the units handling the infrastructure, that of isolating parallelism from the bulk of the code. Parallel operations such as ghost cell fill, refluxing, or regridding have minimal interleaving with state update obtained from applying physics operators. To distance the solvers from their parallel constructs, the required parallel operations provide an API with corresponding functions implemented as a subunit. The implementation of numerical algorithms for physics operators is sequential, interspersed with access to the parallel API as needed.

Minimization of data movement is achieved by letting the state be completely owned by the infrastructure modules. The dominant infrastructure module is the *Eulerian* mesh, owned and managed by the *Grid* unit. The physics modules query the *Grid* unit for the bounds and extent of the block they are operating on and get a pointer to the physical data. This arrangement works in most cases but gets tricky where the data access pattern does not conform to the underlying mesh. An example is any physics dealing with Lagrangian entities (LEs). They need a different data structure, and the data movement is dissimilar from that of the mesh. Additionally, the LEs interact with the mesh, so maintaining physical proximity of the corresponding mesh cell is important in their distribution. This is an example of unavoidable lateral interaction between modules. In order to advance, LEs need to get field quantities from the mesh and then determine their new locations internally. They may need to apply near- and far-field forces or pass some information along to the mesh or be redistributed after advancing in time. FLASH solves this conundrum by keeping the LE data structure extremely simple and using argument passing by reference in the APIs. The LEs are attached to the block in the mesh that has the overlapping cell - an LE leaves its block when its location no longer overlaps with the block. Migration to a new block is an independent operation from everything else that happens to the LEs. In FLASH parlance this is the Lagrangian framework (see [29] for more details). The combination of Eulerian and Lagrangian frameworks that interoperate well with one another has succeeded in largely meeting the performance-critical data management needs of the code.

1.5.1.2　Verification and Validation

FLASH instituted a rigorous verification program early in its lifecycle. The earliest versions of FLASH were subjected to a battery of standard hydrodynamics verification tests [33]. These verification tests were then used to set up an automated regression test suite run on a few local workstations. Since then the test suite has evolved into a combination of tests that aim to provide comprehensive coverage for verifying correct operation of the code [20, 27]. Because FLASH is in a constant state of production and development, verification of its correctness on a regular basis is a critical requirement. The testing is complicated both by the variety of environments in which FLASH is run and by the sheer number of ways in which it can be configured.

Testing is an area where the standard practices do not adequately meet the needs of the code. Many multiphysics codes have legacy components written in early versions of Fortran. Contrary to popular belief, a great deal of new development continues in Fortran because it still is the best HPC language in which to express mathematical algorithms. All of solver code in FLASH is written in F90, so popular unit test harnesses aren't available for use. Small-scale unit tests can be devised only for infrastructural code because all the physics has to interact with the mesh. Also, because regular testing became a part of the FLASH development process long before formal incorporation of software engineering practices in the development process, FLASH's designation of tests only loosely follows the standard definitions. Thus a unit test in FLASH can rely on other parts of the code as long as the feature being tested is isolated. For example, testing for correct filling of halo cells uses a lot of AMR code that has little to do with the halo filling, but it is termed a unit test in FLASH parlance because it exclusively tests a single limited functionality; we refer to such tests as *FLASH unit-test* from here on. The dominant form of regular testing is integration testing, where more than one code capability is combined to configure an executable. The results of the run are compared with preapproved results to verify that changes are within a specified acceptable range. Because of a large space of possible valid and useful combinations, selection of tests is challenging. FLASH's methodology for test design and selection is described below; for more details see [155].

FLASH's testsuite consists of about a dozen FLASH unit-tests and roughly 85 multipurpose composite tests. A composite test runs in two stages and has a comparison *benchmark* for each stage. A benchmark in FLASH testsuite is a full state checkpoint. Composite test benchmarks are checkpoints at two distinct timesteps M and N, where $M < N$. Both are analyzed and approved by a domain expert. If there is a legitimate cause for change in the results (e.g. an improvement in an algorithm), benchmarks have to be reapproved. The first stage of a composite test verifies that no errors have been introduced into the covered code units and their interactions, by comparing with the benchmark at time M. The second stage restarts the execution from checkpoint at M and runs up to time N. This stage of the test verifies that the covered code can correctly start from a checkpoint without any loss of state information. The FLASH testsuite configures and builds each test every time it is run; therefore, build and configuration tests are built-in. Progress of a test is reported at every stage, the final stage being the outcome of the comparison. Because FLASH has many available application configurations whose union provides good code coverage, the task of building a test suite is simplified to selection among existing applications. In many applications the real challenge is picking parameters that exercise the targeted features without running for too long. We use a matrix to ensure maximum coverage, where infrastructure features are placed along the rows and physics modules are placed along columns. For each selected test all the covered features are marked off in the matrix. Marking by the same test in two or more places in the same row or same column represents interoperability among the corresponding entities. The following order is used for filling the matrix:

- Unit tests

- Setups used in science production runs

- Setups known to be sensitive to perturbations

- Simplest and fastest setups that fill the remaining gaps

FLASH's testing can be broadly classified into three categories: the daily testing, to verify ongoing correctness of the code; more targeted testing related to science production runs; and porting to and testing on new platforms. Daily testing is performed on multiple combinations of platforms and software stacks and uses the methodology described above. In preparing for a production schedule, testing is a combination of scaling tests, cost estimation tests, and looking for potential trouble spots. Scientists and developers work closely to devise meaningful weak-scaling tests (which can be difficult because of nonlinearity and adaptive mesh refinement), and tests that can exercise the vulnerable code sections without overwhelming the test suite resources. Sample smaller scale production runs are also performed on the target platform to help make informed estimates of CPU hours and disk space needed to complete the simulation. For more details on simulation planning see [27]. For porting the code to a new platform, a successful production run from the past is used as a benchmark for exercising the code on a new platform, along with a subset of the standard test suite.

FLASH has had some opportunities for validation against experiments. For example, FLASH could model a variety of laboratory experiments involving fluid instabilities [25, 38]. These efforts allowed researchers to probe the validity of models and code modules, and also bolstered the experimental efforts by creating realistic simulation capabilities for use in experimental design. The newer high-energy density physics (HEDP) initiative involving FLASH is directed at simulation-based validation and design of experiments at the major laser facilities in the United States and Europe. Other forms of validation have been convergence tests for the flame model that is used for supernova simulations, and validation of various numerical algorithms against analytical solutions of some known problems. For example, the Sedov [12] problem, which is seeded by a pressure spike in the center that sends out a spherical shock-wave into the domain, has a known analytical solution. It is used to validate hydrodynamics in the code. Several other similar examples exist where a simple problem can help validate a code capability through known analytical solutions.

1.5.1.3 Software Process

The software process of FLASH has evolved organically with the growth of the code. For instance, the first version had no clear design document, the second version had a loosely implied design guidance, and the third version documented the whole design process. The third version also published the developer's guide, which is a straight adaptation from the design document. Because of multiple developers with different production targets, versioning repository was introduced early in the code life cycle. The repository used has been SVN since 2003, although its branching system has been used in unorthodox ways to meet the particular needs of the Flash Center. Unlike most software projects where branches are kept for somewhat isolated development purposes, FLASH uses branches also to manage multiple ongoing projects. This particular need arose when four different streams of physics capabilities were being added to the code. All projects needed some code from the trunk, but the code being added was mostly exclusive to the individual project. It was important that the branches stay more or less in sync with the trunk and that the new code be tested regularly. This objective was accomplished by turning the trunk into essentially a merge area, with a schedule of merge from individual branches, and an intermediate branch for forward merge. The path was tagged-trunk => forward-branch => projects => merge into trunk => tag trunk when stabilized. The forward branch was never allowed a backward merge in order to avoid the possible inadvertent breaking of code for one project by another one. For the same reason the project branches never did a forward merge directly from the trunk.

One of the biggest challenges in managing a code like FLASH occurs during major version changes, when the infrastructure of the code undergoes deep changes. FLASH has undergone two such changes. The first transition took the approach of keeping the development branch synchronized with the main branch at all times. An effort was made to keep new version backward compatible with the old version. During and after the process the team realized many shortcomings of this approach. One was that the code needed to have deeper structural changes than were possible under this approach. Also, the attempt to keep the development and production versions in sync placed undue demands on the developers of the new version, leading to inefficient use of their time. The adoption of the new version was delayed because keeping up with the ongoing modifications to the older version (needed by the scientists to do their work) turned the completion of the transition into a moving target.

Because of these lessons learned, the second transition took a completely different approach and was much more successful. The infrastructural backbone/framework for the new version was built in isolation from the old version in a new repository. The framework design leveraged the knowledge gained by the developers about the idiosyncracies of the solvers in earlier versions and focused on the needs of the future version. There was no attempt at backward compatibility with the framework of the previous version. Once the framework was thoroughly tested, physics modules were transitioned. Here the emphasis was on transitioning all the capabilities needed for one project at the same time, starting with the most stable modules. Once a module was moved to the new version, it was effectively frozen in the old version (the reason for selecting the most stable and mature code sections). Any modification after that point had to be made simultaneously in the new version as well. Although it sounds like a lot of duplicate effort, in reality such instances were rare. This version transition was adopted by the scientists quickly.

FLASH's documentation takes a comprehensive approach with a user's guide, a developer's guide, robodoc API, inline documentation, and online resources. Each type of documentation serves a different purpose and is indispensable to the developers and users of the code. Scripts are in place that look for violations of coding standards and documentation requirements. The user's guide documents the mathematical formulation, algorithms used, and instructions on using various code components. It also includes examples of relevant applications explaining the use of each code module. The developer's guide specifies the design principles and coding standards with an extensive example of the module architecture. Each function in the API is required to have a robodoc header explaining the input/output, function, and special features of the function. Except for the third-party software, every nontrivial function in the code is required to have sufficient inline documentation so that a nonexpert can understand and maintain the code.

FLASH effectively has two versions of release: internal, which is close to the agile model, and general, which is no more than twice a year. The internal release amounts to tagging a stable version in the repository for the internal users of the code. This signals to the users that a forward merge into their production branch is safe. General releases have a more rigorous process that makes them more expensive and therefore infrequent. For a general release the code undergoes pruning, checking for compliance with coding and documentation standards, and more stringent than usual testing. The dual model ensures that the quality of code and documentation is maintained without unduly straining the team resources, while near-continuous code improvement is still possible for ongoing projects.

1.5.1.4 Policies

In any project, policies regarding attributions, contributions and licensing matter. In scientific domains, intellectual property rights and interdisciplinary interactions are additional policy areas that are equally important. Some of these policy requirements are a direct consequence of the strong gatekeeping regimes that majority of publicly distributed scientific software follow. Many arguments are forwarded for dominance of this model in the domain; the most compelling one relates to maintaining the quality of software. Recollect that the developers in this domain are typically not trained in software engineering and that software quality control varies greatly between individuals and/or groups of developers. Because of tight, and sometimes lateral, coupling between functionalities of code modules, a lower-quality component introduced into the code base can have a disproportionate impact on the overall reliability of output produced by the code. Strong gatekeeping is desirable, and that implies having policies in place for accepting contributions. FLASH again differentiates between internal and external contributors in this regard. The internal contributors are required to meet the quality requirements such as coding standards, documentation, and code verification in all their development. Internal audit processes minimize the possibility of poorly written and tested code from getting into a release. The internal audit also goes through a periodic pruning to ensure that bad or redundant code gets eliminated.

The external contributors are required to work with a member of the internal team to include their code in the released version. The minimum set required from them is (1) code that meets coding standards and has been used or will be used for results reported in peer-reviewed publication; (2) at least one test that can be included in the test-suite for nightly testing; (3) documentation for the user's guide, robodoc documentation for any API functions and inline documentation explaining the flow of the control; and (4) a commitment to answer questions on a user's mailing list. The contributors can negotiate the terms of release; a code section can be excluded from the release for a mutually agreed period of time in order to enable contributors to complete their research and publish their work before the code becomes public. This policy permits potential contributors to be freed from the necessity of maintaining their code independently while still retaining control over their software until an agreed-upon release time. As a useful side effect their code remains in sync with the developments in the main branch between releases.

Another model of external contribution to FLASH involves no intervention from the core gate-keeping team. In this model anyone can host any FLASH-compatible code on their site. The code has no endorsement from the distributing entity, the Flash Center, which does not take responsibility for its quality. The Flash Center maintains a list of externally hosted "as-is" code sites; the support for these code sections is entirely the responsibility of hosting site.

The attribution practices in computational science and engineering are somewhat ad hoc. For many developers, the only metric of importance is scientific publications that result from using the software. When a team is dominated by such developers, proper attribution for code development is not given enough importance or thought. Other teams also employ computing professionals whose career growth depends on their software artifacts, and publications describing their algorithms and artifacts. FLASH falls into the latter category. All contributors' names are included in the author list for the user's guide; and the release notes explicitly mention new external contributions and their contributors, if any, for that release. Internal contributors rely on software related publications for their attribution. This policy usually works well, although one exception has been citations skewed in favor of early developers: users of FLASH typically cite Fryxell et al. [33], published in 2000, which does not include any of the later code contributors in its author list, so the later authors are deprived of legitimate citations for their work. Many major long-running software projects have this problem, which is peculiar to the academic world where these codes reside and are used.

1.5.2 Amanzi/ATS

Amanzi and its sister code the Advanced Terrestrial Simulator (ATS), provide a good contrasting example to FLASH. Developed starting in 2012 as the simulation capability for the U.S. Department of Energy's Environmental Management program, Amanzi solves equations for flow and reactive transport in porous media, with intended applications of environmental remediation for contaminated sites [42]. Built on Amanzi's infrastructure, ATS adds physics capability to solve equations for ecosystem hydrology, including surface/subsurface hydrology, energy and freeze/thaw cycles, surface energy balance and snow, and vegetation modeling [15, 47]. Amanzi was initially supported by a development team of several people with dedicated development money. ATS was largely developed by one person, postdocs, and a growing set of collaborators from the broader community and was supported by projects whose deliverables are ecosystem hydrology papers.

Amanzi/ATS's history makes it a good contrast to FLASH. Developed from the ground up in C++ using relatively modern software engineering practices, it has few legacy code issues. Unlike FLASH, Amanzi/ATS makes extensive use of third-party libraries, with associated advantages and disadvantages (currently Amanzi/ATS uses nearly 10k lines of cmake to build it and its libraries). However, they also share a lot of commonalities. Like FLASH, version control has played a critical role in the development process, especially because developers are spread across multiple physical locations and networks. Like FLASH, Amanzi/ATS makes extensive use of module-level and regression-level testing to ensure correctness and enable refactoring. And like FLASH, Amanzi/ATS has found the open source strategy to be incredibly useful; in particular, the open source nature of the code has eliminated some of the natural competition between research groups at different DOE national laboratories and helped establish a growing community of users and developers.

1.5.2.1 Multiphysics Management through Arcos

Recognizing early the wide variety of multiphysics applications that would be targeted with Amanzi/ATS, a formal multiphysics framework was designed, implemented, and adopted. This framework, later named Arcos [24], consists of three main components: a *process tree*, a *dependency graph*, and a *state/data manager*.

The process tree describes the hierarchical coupling between equations and systems of equations to be solved. Each leaf node of the tree is a single (partial) differential equation, such as conservation of mass. Each interior node of the tree couples the children below it into a system of equations. Every node presents a common interface to the nodes above it. Much of the coupling of internal nodes can be automated by using this interface – sequential couplers can be fully automated, while globally implicit coupled schemes can be nearly automated (with off-diagonal blocks of preconditioners and globalization of nonlinear solvers the lone exceptions). This representation of multiphysics models is natural to the coupled physical system and implicitly exists in most codes; Arcos makes this explicit, while providing hooks for customization to the specific system.

A second view of the system of equations is stored in the dependency graph, much like that of Notz et al. [44]. The dependency graph is a directed, acyclic graph (DAG) where each node is a variable (either primary, secondary, or independent) and each edge indicates a dependency. The graph is built up from the leaves of the DAG, which are primary variables (those variables to be solved for) and independent variables (data provided to the model). Roots of the DAG are, for instance, corrections to the primary variable formed through a nonlinear solve, or time derivatives of primary variables used in time integrators. Between these, each interior node is a secondary variable and consists of both data and an *evaluator*, or small, stateless (functional) unit of code that stores the physics or numerics of how to evaluate the variable given its dependencies.

A state object is a glorified container used to manage data. Through the state's interface, *const* access is allowed to all evaluators, and non-*const* access is strictly limited to the evaluator of that variable.

This framework, while at times seeming heavy-handed, results in several important implications from a software engineering perspective. Here we focus on the dependency graph as used in Amanzi/ATS and how it encourages and enables good software engineering practices.

1.5.2.2   Code Reuse and Extensibility

The first observation of this framework is that it results in extremely fine-grained modularity for physical equations. Most computational physics codes are modular at the level of equations; Amanzi/ATS is modular at the level of terms in the equation.

An example illustrates the usefulness of this in multiphysics applications. In a thermal hydrology code, the liquid saturation is a variable describing the volume fraction of pore space that is water. This is a secondary variable and is a function of either liquid pressure (in isothermal cases) or of liquid pressure and temperature (in non-isothermal cases). By explicitly forming a dependency graph, terms that depend upon the liquid saturation need not know whether the model is isothermal or not. Furthermore, there is no concern of "order of equation evaluation" that is common in other multiphysics codes. As both the energy and mass conservation equations need liquid saturation, this model should be evaluated when it is first needed, but it is likely not necessarily evaluated in both equations, because its dependencies have not changed. Optimization of evaluating a model only when its dependencies have changed results in tightly coupled, monolithic physics implementations. Often codes will have "modes" that reimplement the same mass conservation equation twice, once to support the isothermal case and once to support the nonisothermal case as coupled to an energy conservation equation.

By storing these dependencies in an explicit graph, the framework can keep track of when dependencies have changed and can lazily evaluate models exactly when needed. In tightly coupled multiphysics, a dependency graph eliminates the need for an omnipotent programmer to carefully orchestrate when and where each equation term is evaluated. As a result, a dependency graph eliminates code duplication and discourages monolithic physics code.

Furthermore, this strategy greatly improves code extensibility. Many variations in model structure are easily implemented by writing a new evaluator and using it in an existing conservation equation. Once past an initial developer learning curve, Amanzi/ATS developers are able to quickly adapt the code to new models.

1.5.2.3   Testing

Testing is an extremely sensitive subject in computational software engineering – so much so that it merits its own chapter: 4. Few scientific codes are sufficiently tested by conventional software engineering (SE) standards, and many scientific code developers are aware of the shortcoming. As discussed above, frequently scientific codes are limited to component-level tests, because it can be difficult to write sufficiently fine-grained unit tests. SE techniques such as mocking objects are almost never practiced, because mocked objects would require nearly all of the same functionality of the real object in order to properly test the physics component. The claim is that most physics code cannot be tested without including discretizations, solvers, meshes, and other components.

This viewpoint, however, is somewhat narrow. Physics at the level of a differential equation cannot be tested at the granularity of a unit test. Physics at the level of a term within an equation, however, is much easier to test. By forcing componentization at the level of an evaluator, Amanzi/ATS allows a large portion of its physics implementation to be unit tested. Evaluators (and their derivatives) are stateless and therefore can be tested without additional components. Pushing the majority of the physics implementations into evaluators and out of monolithic, equation-level classes greatly improves the code coverage of fine-grained unit tests. Amanzi/ATS still makes extensive use of medium-grained component tests for discretizations, solvers, etc, but a significantly large portion of physics testing is done at the unit-test granularity.

Amanzi/ATS additionally maintains a large list of coarse-grained system-level tests. These test the full capability and serve additionally as documentation and example problems for new users. This strategy, of providing large suites of sample problems for both testing and documentation, has become common in the scientific community, and is widely considered a scientific best practice. By greatly lowering the bar for new users, this collection of dual-purpose examples encourages community; in ATS, each new physics contribution must be accompanied by a new system-level test for inclusion in these test suites.

In Amanzi/ATS, unit and component granularity tests are automated using ctest and run sufficiently fast to be run prior to every commit. While Amanzi/ATS does not practice true continuous integration, all developers are expected to run this testsuite prior to committing to the main repository.

1.5.2.4   Performance Portability

Amanzi/ATS was designed from the ground up with awareness of ongoing, disruptive architecture changes. Performance portability in the face of these changes is an issue that will continue to confront all codes. Amanzi/ATS takes several strides to buffer itself from such potentially disruptive change.

First, by leveraging popular, supported, open source libraries with significant community, Amanzi/ATS is able to immediately leverage advances in these codes. For instance, a significant portion of time is spent in inverting a preconditioner using approximate linear solvers. By using a common interface and a wide variety of existing solver libraries through Trilinos, Amanzi/ATS is able to immediately leverage advances in any one of these libraries.

Second, by encouraging overdecomposition of physics into smaller, more heterogeneous units, Amanzi/ATS is set up to leverage task-based programming models with novel runtime systems. While not currently implemented, using one of the several emerging "coarse task" runtime environments [17, 37, 39] is an exciting research area for the community.

Third, Arcos's evaluators are a functional programming concept and are stateless functors with no side effects. As a result, they abstract "what is evaluated" from "on what data and chip is it evaluated." This design decision allows the implementation of multiple versions of the latter (i.e., GPU, many-core) without touching any of the former code.

Key Insights

- Both FLASH and Amanzi took a long term view and are designed for extensibility.

- Both codes have found open development beneficial for many reasons, including robustness of results and community penetration.

- FLASH takes a broader view of unit testing; similar tests are described as component tests by Amanzi.

- Both codes use different levels of granularity in testing to obtain coverage.

- FLASH adopted and evolved software engineering practices over time; Amanzi started with many more practices in place.

- Because of its age and code accumulation over time, refactoring FLASH is a large undertaking. It has a big challenge in adapting for future heterogeneous platforms

1.6 Generalization

Not all the solutions described in the earlier sections for computational science specific challenges are generalizable to all scientific software, but the vast majority of them are. Indeed at a workshop on community codes in 2012 [30], all represented codes had nearly identical stories to tell about their motivation for adopting software engineering practices and the ones that they adopted. This was true irrespective of the science domains these codes served, the algorithms and discretization methods they used, and communities they represented. Even their driving design principles were similar at the fundamental level, although the details differed. The codes represented the state of the art in their respective communities in terms of both the model and algorithmic research incorporated and the software engineering practices. Note that these are the codes that have stood the test of time and are respected in their communities. They are widely used and supported and have more credibility for producing reproducible reliable results than do smaller individualistic efforts. At a minimum they provide a snapshot of the state of large scale computing and its dependence on software engineering in the era of relatively uniform computing platforms.

One practice that is universally adopted by all community codes and other large-scale codes is versioning repositories. That is worthy of mention here because even this practice has not penetrated the whole computational science community; many small projects still do not use versioning, though their number is steadily decreasing. Other common practice is licensing for public use and making many of the codes freely available to download along with their source. Testing is also universal, although the extent and methodologies for testing vary greatly. A general verification and validation regime is still relatively rare, although regression testing is more common. Unit tests are less common than integration tests and bounded-change tests. Almost all codes have user-level documentation and user support practices in place. They also have well-defined code contribution policies.

Another feature that stands out is similarity in high-level design of all the multiphysics codes. Every code exercises separation of concerns between mathematical and structural parts and between sequential and parallel parts. In almost all cases this separation is dictated by the need to reduce complexity for efforts needing specific expertise. Also, all the codes have basic backbone frameworks that orchestrate the data movement and ownership. This feature is usually driven by the need for maintenance and flexibility. And where it is realized well, it provides extensibility; the ability to add more physics and therefore greater capabilities and fidelity in the models being computed. Majority of frameworks are component based with composability of some sort. The reason is that different models need different capability combinations. Most codes use self-describing I/O libraries for their output in order to facilitate the use of generally available analysis and visualization tools.

The degree to which teams from vastly different scientific domains producing community codes have arrived at essentially similar solutions points to a possibility that seemingly diverse problems can have a uniform solution if they are trying to achieve similar objectives. For the codes highlighted in this section, the objectives were capabilities, extensibility, composability, reliability, portability, and maintainability. They were achieved through design choices conscious of trade-offs, most often with raw performance that individual components or specific platforms were capable of. The lesson here is that similar objectives can yield a general solution even if there is great diversity in the details of the individual problem. It is not beyond the realm of possibility that similar generalized solution will emerge for the next generation software faced with heterogeneous computing described in the next section.

Key Insights

- High-level framework design of multiphysics codes follows componentization and composability, and is cognizant of trade-offs with raw performance.

- Extensibility in the code is critical for long-term adoption of scientific codes because as scientific understanding grows, it places new demands on the code.

- Open development is beneficial.

- In order to balance continuous development with ongoing production, good contribution and distribution policies are important.

1.7 Additional Future Considerations

An aspect of software design that is a unique requirement of the scientific domain is fast becoming a great challenge; performance portability. In the past, machine architectures were fairly uniform across the board for large stretches of time. The first set of effective HPC machines in routine use for scientific computing were all vectors machines. They later gave way to parallel machines with RISC processor as their main processing element. A code written for one machine of its time, if portable, had reasonable performance on most of its contemporary machines. The abstract machine model to which the codes of the era were programming was essentially the same for all machines of that era. Arguably wholesale changes had to occur in codes for transitioning from vector to RISC-parallel machines, but the transition was from one long-term stable paradigm to another long-term stable paradigm. In addition, the codes were not as large as the multiphysics codes of today. Thus although the transitions took time, the codes that adapted well to the prevailing machine model thrived for several years.

The computing landscape is undergoing significant changes. Now there are machines in the pipeline that have deep enough architectural differences among them that one machine model cannot necessarily describe their behavior. A look at the top supercomputers in the world shows a variety of architectures, from accelerator models to many-core systems. Even though many different vendors are moving to architectures with lighter and smaller cores, the different cache and memory hierarchies on these systems make portability across architectures difficult. In addition, the lack of a high performing, common programming model across architectures poses an even greater challenge for application developers. And, because the codes are significantly larger than they were during the last architecture paradigm shift, the transition will be even more challenging. More important, some aspects of the challenges are not unique to the large multiphysics codes. Because the deep architectural changes are occurring at the level of nodes that will go into all platforms, the change is ubiquitous and will affect everyone. Portability in general, and performance portability in particular, is an issue for everyone. At this writing the impact of this paradigm shift is not fully understood. Means of combating this challenge are understood even less. The general consensus is that more programming abstractions are necessary, not just for the extreme scale, but also for small-scale computing. The unknown is which abstraction or combination of abstractions will deliver the solution. Many solutions have been proposed, for example [54] (also see [10] for a more comprehensive and updated list). Of these, some have undergone more testing and exercise under realistic application instances than others. Currently, no approach has been shown to provide a general solution that can be broadly applicable in the ways that optimizing compilers and MPI were in the past. This is an urgent and serious challenge facing the scientific communities today. Future viability of scientific codes depends on significant help from software engineering expertise and motivation within the community.

Acknowledgments

This work was supported by the U.S. Department of Energy, Office of Science, under contract number DE-AC02-06CH11357; National Energy Research Scientific Computing Center, a DOE Office of Science User Facility under Contract No. DE-AC02-05CH11231; Department of Energy at Los Alamos National Laboratory under contract DE-AC52-06NA25396 and the DOE Office of Science Biological and Environmental Research (BER) program in Subsurface Biogeochemical Research. Support was also provided through the IDEAS scientific software productivity project (www.ideas-productivity.org), funded by the U.S. Department of Energy Office of Science, Advanced Scientific Computing Research and Biological and Environmental Research programs. One software described in this work was in part developed by the DOE-supported ASC / Alliance Center for Astrophysical Thermonuclear Flashes at the University of Chicago under grant B523820.

Chapter 2

A Rational Document Driven Design Process for Scientific Software

W. Spencer Smith

2.1 Introduction

This chapter motivates, justifies, describes and evaluates a rational document driven design process for scientific software. The documentation is adapted from the waterfall model [71, 114], progressing from requirements, to design, to implementation and testing. Many researchers have stated that a document driven process is not used by, nor suitable for, scientific software. These researchers argue that scientific developers naturally use an agile philosophy [55, 59, 67, 101], or an amethododical process [79], or a knowledge acquisition driven process [80]. Just because a rational process is not currently used does not prove that it is inappropriate, only that past efforts have been unsuccessful. The problem could be inadequate customization to the needs of the scientific community and incomplete training of practitioners. To date, the "from the textbook" Software Engineering (SE) approach may have failed, but that does not mean it should be abandoned. With some modification to suit scientific needs, the benefits of traditional SE can be realized. For instance, a rational design process can provide quality improvements, and Quality Assurance (QA), as shown in Table 2.1. Moreover, documentation, written before and during development, can provide many benefits [96]: easier reuse of old designs, better communication about requirements, more useful design reviews, easier integration of separately written modules, more effective code inspection, more effective testing, and more efficient corrections and improvements.

One argument against a document driven process is that scientists do not view rigid, process-heavy approaches, favorably [59]. As an example from a scientific software developer, Roache [99, p. 373] considers reports for each stage of software development as counterproductive. However, the reports are only counterproductive if the process used by the scientists has to follow the same waterfall as the documentation. This does not have to be the case. Given the exploratory nature of science, developers do not typically follow a waterfall process, but, as Parnas and Clements [95] point out, the most logical way to present the documentation is still to "fake" a rational design process. "Software manufacturers can define their own internal process as long as they can effectively map their products onto the ones that the much simpler, faked process requires" [88]. Reusability and maintainability are important qualities for scientific software. Documentation that follows a faked rationale design process is easier to maintain and reuse because the documentation is understandable and standardized. Understandability is improved because the faked documentation only includes the "best" version of any artifacts, with no need to incorporate confusing details around the history of their discovery [95]. Standardization on any process, with a rational process being a logical choice as a standard, facilitates design reviews, change management and the transfer (and modification) of ideas and software between projects [95].

Another argument against a rational process, where software is derived from precise requirements, centers around the opinion that, in science, requirements are impossible to determine up-front, because the details can only emerge as the work progresses [59,102]. Is science really so different from other software domains? No, requirements are challenging for every domain. The differences between science and other domains might actually make producing a first draft of the requirements easier. For instance, scientific requirements, in terms of physical models, have a high potential for reuse [108]. The laws of physics are stable; they are almost universally accepted, well understood, and slow to change. At the appropriate abstraction level, many problems have significant commonality, since a large class of physical models are instances of a relatively small number of conservation equations (conservation of energy, mass and momentum). Moreover, scientific software does not typically have

Table 2.1: Improving Scientific Software Qualities via Rational Design

Verifiability involves "solving the equations right" [99, p. 23]; it benefits from rational documentation that systematically shows, with explicit traceability, how the governing equations are transformed into code.

Validatability means "solving the right equations" [99, p. 23]. Validatability is improved by a rational process via clear documentation of the theory and assumptions, along with an explicit statement of the systematic steps required for experimental validation.

Usability can be a problem. Different users, solving the same physical problem, using the same software, can come up with different answers, due to differences in parameter selection [99, p. 370]. To reduce misuse, a rational process must state expected user characteristics, modelling assumptions, definitions and the range of applicability of the code.

Maintainability is necessary in scientific software, since change, through iteration, experimentation and exploration, is inevitable. Models of physical phenomena and numerical techniques necessarily evolve over time [59, 102]. Proper documentation, designed with change in mind, can greatly assist with change management.

Reusability provides support for the quality of reliability, since reliability is improved by reusing trusted components [66]. (Care must still be taken with reusing trusted components, since blind reuse in a new context can lead to errors, as dramatically shown in the Ariane 5 disaster [91, p. 37–38].) The odds of reuse are improved when it is considered right from the start.

Understandability is necessary, since reviewers can only certify something they understand. Scientific software developers have the view "that the science a developer embeds in the code must be apparent to another scientist, even ten years later" [79]. Understandability applies to the documentation and code, while usability refers to the executable software. Documentation that follows a rational process is the easiest to follow.

Reproducibility is a required component of the scientific method [63]. Although QA has, "a bad name among creative scientists and engineers" [99, p. 352], the community need to recognize that participating in QA management also improves reproducibility. Reproducibility, like QA, benefits from a consistent and repeatable computing environment, version control and separating code from configuration/parameters [63].

to deal with concurrency (except for the case of parallel processing), real-time constraints, or complex user interactions. The typical scientific software design pattern is simply: Input $\Rightarrow$ Calculate $\Rightarrow$ Output. All domains struggle with up-front requirements, but scientists should remember that their requirements do not have to be fully determined a priori. As mentioned in the previous paragraph, iteration is inevitable and a rational process can be faked.

Although current practice tends to neglect requirements documentation, it does not have to be this way. To start with, when researchers say that requirements emerge through iteration and experimentation, they are only referring to one category of scientific software. As observed previously [80,106], scientific software can be divided into two categories: specific physical models and general purpose tools. When scientific software is general purpose, like a solver for a system of linear equations, the requirements should be clear from the start. General purpose tools are based on well understood mathematics for the functional requirements, as shown in scientific computing textbooks [73]. Even the nonfunctional requirements, like accuracy, can be quantified and described through error analysis and in some cases validated computing, such as interval arithmetic.

Even specialized software, like weather prediction or structural analysis, can be documented a priori, as long as the author's viewpoint takes into account separation of concerns, a broad program family approach and consideration for future change management. With respect to separation of concerns, the physical models should be clearly separated from the numerical methods. Knowing the most appropriate numerical technique is difficult at the outset, but this is a decision for the design, not the requirements, stage. In addition, rather than aim for a narrow specification of the model to be implemented, the target should be a broad specification of the potential family of models. A program family approach, where commonalities are reused and variabilities are identified and systematically handled, is natural for scientific software [110]. As pointed out previously, at an abstract level, the modeller will know which governing conservation equations will need to be satisfied. The challenge is to know which simplifying assumptions are appropriate. This is where the "experimentation" by scientists comes in. If the assumptions are documented clearly, and explicit traceability is given to show what part of the model they influence, then changes can be made later, as understanding of the problem improves. Using knowledge from the field of SE, the documentation can be built with maintainability and reusability in mind.

This chapter shows how SE templates, rules and guidelines, which have been successful in other domains, can be adapted to handle rapid change and complexity. The document driven approach is first described (Section 2.2) and then illustrated via the example of software to model a solar water heating tank (Section 2.3). Justification (Section 2.4) for the document driven process is shown through a case study where legacy nuclear safety analysis code is re-documented, leading to the discovery of 27 issues in the original documentation. Further justification is given through a survey of statistical software for psychology, which shows that quality is highest for projects that most closely follow a document driven approach.

2.2   A Document Driven Method

Table 2.2 shows the recommended documentation for a scientific software project. The documents are typical of what is suggested for scientific software certification, where certification consists of official recognition by an authority, or regulatory body, that the software is fit for its intended use. For instance, the Canadian Standards Association (CSA) requires a similar set of documents for quality assurance of scientific programs for nuclear power plants [62].

To achieve the qualities listed in Table 2.1, the documentation in Table 2.2 should have the following qualities: *complete, correct, consistent, modifiable, traceable, unambiguous*, and *verifiable*. All of these qualities are listed in the IEEE recommended practice for software requirements [76]. The IEEE guidelines are for requirements, but most qualities are relevant for all documentation artifacts. Another relevant quality, which is not on the IEEE list, is *abstract*. Requirements should state what is to be achieved, but be silent on how it is to be achieved. Abstraction is an important software development principle for dealing with complexity [71, p. 40]. Smith and Koothoor present further details on the qualities of documentation for scientific software [103].

The recommended rational process (Figure 2.1) is a variation on the waterfall model that is similar to the V-model. The steps proceed as for the waterfall model up to the requirements specification, but then detour to create the V&V plan, before renewing the waterfall. In the full V-model, each

Table 2.2: Recommended Documentation

Problem Statement	Description of problem to be solved
Development Plan	Overview of development process/infrastructure
Requirements	Desired functions and qualities of the software
V&V Plan	Verification that all documentation artifacts, including the code, are internally correct. Validation, from an external viewpoint, that the right problem, or model, is being solved.
Design Specification	Documentation of how the requirements are to be realized, through both a software architecture and detailed design of modules and their interfaces
Code	Implementation of the design in code
V&V Report	Summary of the V&V efforts, including testing
User Manual	Instructions on installation, usage; worked examples

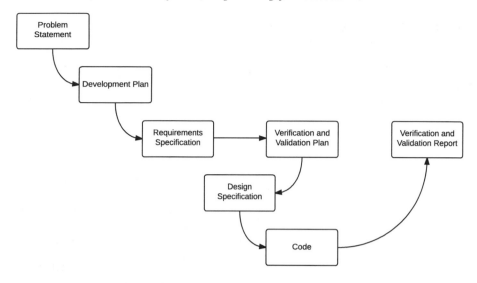

Figure 2.1: Overview of recommended process for documentation.

development phase has a corresponding test plan and report. The proposed process does not go this far; one document summarizes the V&V plan at the crucial initial stage of development and provides an overview for the V&V of the other phases. In the traditional waterfall, test plans are in a later stage, but thinking about system tests early has the benefit that test cases are often more understandable than abstract requirements. System test cases should be considered at the same time as requirements; the tests themselves form an alternative, but incomplete, view of the requirements. Iteratively working between requirements and system tests builds confidence that the project is moving in the correct direction before making significant, and expensive, decisions.

2.2.1   Problem Statement

A problem statement is a high level description of what the software hopes to achieve. Like a mission statement in a strategic plan [92, p. 22], the problem statement summarizes the primary purpose of the software, what it does, who the users are and what benefits the software provides. A problem statement should be abstract. That is, it should state what the mission is, but not how to achieve it. The length of a problem statement should usually be about half a page, or less. The seismology software Mineos [60] provides a good example of a problem statement, starting with "Mineos computes synthetic seismograms in a spherically symmetric non-rotating Earth by summing normal modes."

The problem statement's main impact on software quality is through improving reuse, since a clear statement positions the current work relative to similar software products. If the problem statement shows too much overlap with existing products, the decision may be made to go in another direction. Moreover, the information in the problem statement might be enough to encourage future users and developers to adopt this product, rather than develop something new. The problem statement also improves quality, since it provides focus for subsequent work and documents.

2.2.2   Development Plan

The recommendations in this section imply a set of documents (Table 2.2), but the specific contents of these documents and the process that underlies them is not prescribed. As mentioned in Section 2.1, the external documentation follows a "faked" rational process, but the internal process can be anything that the developers desire. The development plan is where this internal process is specified. The specific parts of the plan should include the following:

- What documents will be created?

- What template, including rules and guidelines, will be followed?

- What internal process will be employed?

- What technology infrastructure (development support tools) will be used (see Section 2.2.8)?

- What are the coding standards?

- In the case of open source software, how does one contribute?

GRASS (Geographic Resources Analysis Support System) [72] provides a good example of community developed software that has a clear software development process and development support tool infrastructure [85]. The seismology software Earthworm [77] provides another solid example. The development plan for Earthworm distinguishes between three different categories of software: core, contributed and encapsulated. In addition, details are provided on the expected coding standards and on how to contribute to the project. Unfortunately, the requirements for contributing to Earthworm are sparse and the support tools seem to be limited to issue tracking.

The presence of a development plan immediately improves the qualities of visibility and transparency, since the development process is now defined. The plan also improves reproducibility, since it records the development and testing details. Depending on the choices made, the development support tools, such as version control and issue tracking, can have a direct impact on the quality of maintainability.

2.2.3 Software Requirements Specification (SRS)

The Software Requirements Specification (SRS) records the functionalities, expected performance, goals, context, design constraints, external interfaces and other quality attributes of the software [76]. Writing an SRS generally starts with a template, which provides guidelines and rules for documenting the requirements. Several existing templates contain suggestions on how to avoid complications and how to achieve qualities such as verifiability, maintainability and reusability [69, 76, 89]. However, no template is universally accepted. For the current purpose, a good starting point is a template specifically designed for scientific software [108, 109], as illustrated in Figure 2.2. The recommended template is suitable for science, because of its hierarchical structure, which decomposes abstract goals to concrete instance models, with the support of data definitions, assumptions and terminology. The document's structure facilitates its maintenance and reuse [108], by using separation of concerns, abstraction and traceability, as discussed in Section 2.1.

Figure 2.2: SRS table of contents.

An SRS improves the software qualities listed in Table 2.1. For instance, usability is improved via an explicit statement of the expected user characteristics. Verifiability is improved because the SRS provides a standard against which correctness can be judged. The recommended template [108, 109] facilitates verification of the theory by systematically breaking the information into structured units, and using cross-referencing for traceability. An SRS also improves communication with stakeholders. To facilitate collaboration and team integration, the SRS captures the necessary knowledge in a self-contained document. If a standard template is adopted for scientific software, this would help with comparing between different projects and with reusing knowledge.

2.2.4   Verification and Validation (V&V) Plan and Report

Verification is not just important for the code. As shown by the IEEE Standard for Software Verification and Validation Plans [114, p. 412], V&V activities are recommended for each phase of the software development lifecycle. For instance, experts should verify that the requirements specification is reasonable with respect to the theoretical model, equations, assumptions etc. This verification activity is assisted by the use of a requirements template tailored to scientific software, as discussed in Section 2.2.3. Verification of the design and the code can potentially be improved by the use of Literate Programming, as discussed in Section 2.2.6. An important part of the verification plan is checking the traceability between documents to ensure that every requirement is addressed by the design, every module is tested, etc.

Developing test cases is particularly challenging for scientific software, since scientific problems typically lack a test oracle [81]. In the absence of a test oracle, the following techniques can be used to build system tests:

- Test cases can be selected that are a subset of the real problem for which a closed-form solution exists. When using this approach, confidence in the actual production code can only be built if it is the same code used for testing; that is, nothing is gained if a separate, simpler, program is written for testing the special cases.

- Verification test cases can be created by assuming a solution and using this to calculate the inputs. For instance, for a linear solver, if A and x are assumed, b can be calculated as $b = Ax$. Following this, $Ax^* = b$ can be solved and then x and x^*, which should theoretically be equal, can be compared. In the case of solving Partial Differential Equations (PDEs), this approach is called the Method of Manufactured Solutions [99].

- Most scientific software uses floating point arithmetic, but for testing purposes, the slower, but guaranteed correct, interval arithmetic [74] can be employed. The faster floating point algorithm can then be verified by ensuring that the calculated answers lie within the guaranteed bounds.

- Verification tests should include plans for convergence studies. The discretization used in the numerical algorithm should be decreased (usually halved) and the change in the solution assessed.

- Confidence can be built in a numerical algorithm by comparing the results to another program that overlaps in functionality. If the test results do not agree, then one, possibly both of the programs is incorrect.

- The verification plan should also include test plans for nonfunctional requirements, like accuracy, performance and portability, if these are important implementation goals. Performance tests can be planned to describe how the software responds to changing inputs, such as problem size, condition number etc. Verification plans can include relative comparisons between the new implementation and competing products [106].

In addition to system test cases, the verification plan should outline other testing techniques that will be used to build confidence. For instance, the plan should describe how unit test cases will be selected, although the creation of the unit test cases will have to wait until the design is complete. The test plan should also identify what, if any, code coverage metrics will be used and what approach will be employed for automated testing. If other testing techniques, such as mutation testing, or fault testing [114], are to be employed, this should be included in the plan. In addition to testing, the verification plan should mention the plans for other techniques for verification, such as code walkthroughs, code inspections, correctness proofs etc. [71, 114].

Validation is also included in the V&V plan. For validation, the document should identify the experimental results for comparison to the simulated results. If the purpose of the code is a general purpose mathematical library there is no need for a separate validation phase.

Figure 2.3 shows the proposed template for capturing the V&V plan. The first two sections cover general and administrative information, including the composition of the testing team and important deadlines. The "Evaluation" section fleshes out the methods, tools and techniques while the "System Test Description" provides an example of a system test. In an actual V&V report, there would be multiple instances of this section, each corresponding to a different system test. In cases where validation tests are appropriate, each validation test would also follow this template.

The corresponding document for the V&V plan is the V&V report. Once the implementation and other documentation is complete, the V&V activities take place. The results are summarized in the report, with enough detail to convince a reader that all the planned activities were accomplished. The report should emphasize those changes that were made in a response to issues uncovered during verification and validation.

Figure 2.3: Proposed V&V plan table of contents.

2.2.5   Design Specification

As for other documents, the design document serves three purposes: design, implementation and maintenance [75, p. 16]. The initial document is verified to ensure it provides a good start, then it is used for software creation, and later, when changes are needed, it is a reference for maintainers. The recommended approach to handle complexity in design is abstraction [114, p. 296]. For science, the inspiration for abstraction is the underlying mathematics.

The documentation should include a high level view of the software architecture, which divides the system into modules, and a low level view, which specifies the interfaces for the modules. A module is defined as a "work assignment given to a programmer or group of programmers" [94]. Wilson et al. advise modular design for scientific software [117], but are silent on the decomposition criterion. A good criterion is the principle of information hiding [93]. This principle supports design for change through the "secrets" of each module. As implied in Section 2.1, design for change is valuable for scientific software, where a certain amount of exploration is necessary.

The modular decomposition can be recorded in a Module Guide (MG) [94], which organizes the modules in a hierarchy by their secrets. Given his interest in embedded real time systems, the top-level decomposition from Parnas [94] includes a hardware hiding module. For scientific software on standard hardware, with serial algorithms, simplification is usually possible, since the virtualization of the hardware will typically not have to be directly implemented by the programmer, being generally available via libraries, such as `stdio.io` in C. Further simplifications are available in scientific software, by taking advantage of the Input $\Rightarrow$ Calculate $\Rightarrow$ Output design pattern mentioned in Section 2.1. This pattern implies the presence of an input format hiding module, an input parameter data structure hiding module and an output format hiding module [75]. The bulk of the difference between designs comes through the modules dealing with calculations. Typical calculation modules hide data structures, algorithms and the governing physics. The application of the Parnas approach to scientific software has been illustrated by applying it to the example of a mesh generator [111].

Figure 2.4 shows the proposed template for the MG document. The document begins with an explicit statement of the anticipated, or likely, changes. These anticipated changes guide the design. If a likely change is required, then ideally only one module will need to be re-implemented. The "Module Decomposition" section lists the modules, organized by a hierarchy of related secrets. The top level decomposition of the hierarchy consists of hardware hiding, behavior hiding and software decision hiding modules [94]. For each module the secret it encapsulates and the service it provides are listed. Care is taken that each module lists only one secret and that secrets are in the form of nouns, not verbs. The example modules listed in the section of Figure 2.4 are typical of scientific software. The "Traceability Matrix" section shows how the anticipated changes map to modules, and how the requirements from the SRS map to modules. Section 2.3.2 describes an example MG, along with the uses hierarchy between modules.

The modular decomposition advocated here has much in common with Object Oriented (OO) design, which also emphasizes encapsulation. However, care must be taken with overusing OO languages, since a significant performance penalty is possible using dynamic dispatch, especially in an inner loop. Operator overloading should also be used with care, since the operator semantics may change depending on the type of its operands.

The MG alone does not provide enough information. Each module's interface needs to be designed and documented by showing the syntax and semantics of its access routines. This can be done in the Module Interface Specification (MIS) [75]. The MIS is less abstract than the architectural design. However, an MIS is still abstract, since it describes what the module will do, but not how to do it. The interfaces can be documented formally [68,111] or informally. An informal presentation would use natural language, together

Figure 2.4: Proposed MG table of contents.

with equations. The specification needs to clearly define all parameters, since an unclear description of the parameters is one cause of reusability issues for libraries [65]. To assist with interface design, one can take inspiration from the common design idioms for the structures of set, sequence and tuple [75, p. 82–83]. In addition, the designer should keep in mind the following interface quality criteria: consistent, essential, general, minimal and opaque [75, p. 83].

2.2.6   Code

Comments can improve understandability, since comments "aid the understanding of a program by briefly pointing out salient details or by providing a larger-scale view of the proceedings" [82]. Comments should not describe details of how an algorithm is implemented, but instead focus on what the algorithm does and the strategy behind it. Writing comments is one of the best practices identified for scientific software by Wilson et al. [117]. As said by Wilson et al., scientific software developers should aim to "write programs for people, not computers" and "[t]he best way to create and maintain reference documentation is to embed the documentation for a piece of software in that software" [117]. Literate Programming (LP) [84] is an approach that takes these ideas to their logical conclusion.

B.6.2   Computing h_c, h_g and T_S

Using this clad conductivity (k_c), we compute the heat transfer coefficient (h_c) and the gap conductance (h_g) as DD18 and DD19 of the SRS, respectively. That is,

$$h_c = \frac{2k_c h_b}{2k_c + \tau_c h_b},$$ (B.23)

$$h_g = \frac{2k_c h_p}{2k_c + \tau_c h_p}$$ (B.24)

21   ⟨ Calculation of heat transfer coefficient (h_c) and the gap conductance (h_g) 21 ⟩ ≡
      /* calculation of heat transfer coefficient */
    *h_c = (2 * (*k_c) * (*h_b))/((2 * (*k_c)) + (*tau_c * (*h_b)));
      /* calculation of gap conductance */
    *h_g = (2 * (*k_c) * (*h_p))/((2 * (*k_c)) + (*tau_c * (*h_p)));
    This code is used in chunks 15 and 60

Figure 2.5: Example literate code documentation.

LP was introduced by Knuth [84]. The central idea is that "...instead of imagining that our main task is to instruct a computer what to do, let us concentrate rather on explaining to human beings what we want a computer to do" [84, pg. 99]. When using LP, an algorithm is refined into smaller, simpler parts. Each of the parts is documented in an order that is natural for human comprehension, as opposed to the order used for compilation. In a literate program, documentation and code are maintained in one source. The program is written as an interconnected "web" of "chunks" [84]. LP can be used as a strategy for improving verifiability, understandability and reproducibility for scientific software. One example of a commonly used LP tool is Sweave [86]. (This tool is discussed further in Section 2.4.1.) Other examples of LP in scientific software include a validated ODE solver [90] and a photorealistic renderer [97].

Figure 2.5 shows a sample of literate code documentation drawn from a program to analyze heat transfer in a nuclear reactor fuel pin [103]. The example shows how documentation and code can be interleaved. The excerpt begins with the mathematical formulae for the heat transfer coefficients and ends with the actual C code used for their calculation. By having the theory and the code side by side in this manner, a human reviewer will have an easier time verifying the code implements the theory. The excerpt also illustrates how LP automatically manages chunk numbering and referencing.

2.2.7   User Manual

The presence of a user manual will have a direct impact on quality. The quality of usability in particular benefits from a user manual, especially if the manual includes a getting started tutorial and fully explained examples. A user manual also benefits installability, as long as it includes linear installation instructions. Advice for writing user manuals and technical instructions can be found in technical writing texts [115]. The seismology software Mineos [60] provides a good example of a user manual for scientific software.

2.2.8   Tool Support

Scientific software developers should use tools for issue tracking and version control. Issue tracking is considered a central quality assurance process [56]. Commercial issue trackers, such as Jira, are available, along with free tools such as, iTracker, Roundup, GitHub and Bugzilla [78]. For version control, frequently recommended tools are Subversion [98] and Git [87]. Version control tools can support reproducibility, since they are able to record development information as the project progresses. Davison [63], recommends more flexible and powerful automated reproducibility tools, such as Sumatra [64] and Madagascar [70]. Issue tracking and version control tools should be employed for all of the documents mentioned in the preceding sections.

Tool use for code documentation falls on a continuum between no tool use, all the way up to full LP (discussed in Section 2.2.6). In between these extremes there are code documentation assistants like Javadoc, Doxygen, Sphinx and publish for MATLAB. These tools can be thought of as code first, then documentation. LP flips this around with documentation first, then code. Tools for LP include cweb, noweb, FunnelWeb and Sweave.

Tools also exist to make the testing phase easier. For functional testing, unit testing frameworks are popular. A unit testing framework has been developed for most programming languages. Examples include JUnit (for Java), Cppunit (for C++), CUnit (for C), FUnit (for FORTRAN), and PyUnit (for Python). For nonfunctional testing related to performance, one can use a profiler to identify the real bottlenecks in performance [117]. A powerful tool for dynamic analysis of code is Valgrind. The specific choices of tools for a given project should be documented in the V&V plan (Section 2.2.4).

2.3   Example: Solar Water Heating Tank

This section provides highlights of the documentation produced via a rational document driven process for a software program called SWHS. This program simulates a Solar Water Heating System (SWHS) incorporating Phase Change Material (PCM) [100]. Tanks are sometimes designed with PCM to reduce the tank size over a water only tank. Incorporating PCM reduces tank size since PCM stores thermal energy as latent heat, which allows higher thermal energy storage capacity per unit weight. Figure 2.6

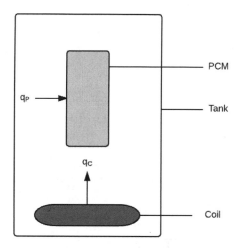

Figure 2.6: Solar water heating tank, with heat flux q_c from coil and q_P to the PCM.

provides a conceptual view of the heat flux (q) in the tank. The full set of documents, code and test cases, for the SWHS example can be found at: https://github.com/smiths/swhs.git.

2.3.1 Software Requirements Specification (SRS)

Figure 2.2 shows the table of contents for the SRS for SWHS. Although the SRS document is long (25 pages), this is in keeping with the knowledge capture goal. Someone like a new undergraduate or graduate student with a physics and mathematics background (as given in SRS Section 3.1, User Characteristics) will have all that they need to understand the software. The documentation is not written only for experts on heat transfer, but also for people that are trying to become experts. The documentation alone will not make someone an expert, but the intention is that it will provide enough detail, and enough pointers to additional information, that it can serve as a valuable learning, and later a reference, resource.

The table of contents shows how the problem is systematically decomposed into more concrete models. Specifically, the presentation starts with the high level problem goals (Figure 2.7), then the SRS provides the appropriate theoretical models to achieve the goals. The theoretical models are then refined into what are termed instance models, which provide the equations needed to solve the original problem. During this refinement from goals to theory to mathematical models, the scientist applies different assumptions, builds

---

4.1.3   Goal Statements

Given the temperature of the coil, initial conditions for the temperature of the water and the PCM, and material properties, the goal statements are:

GS1: predict the water temperature over time

GS2: predict the PCM temperature over time

GS3: predict the change in the energy of the water over time

GS4: predict the change in the energy of the PCM over time

Figure 2.7: Goal statements for SWHS.

general definitions and creates data definitions. The template aids in documenting all the necessary information, since each section has to be considered. This facilitates achieving completeness by essentially providing a checklist. Besides requiring that section headings be filled in, the template also requires that every equation either has a supporting external reference, or a derivation. Furthermore, for the SRS to be complete and consistent every symbol, general definition, data definition, and assumption needs to be used at least once.

The goal statements for SWHS, given in Figure 2.7, specify the target of the system. In keeping with the principle of abstraction, the goals are stated such that they describe many potential instances of the final program. As a consequence, the goals will be stable and reusable.

As mentioned in Section 2.1, scientists often need to experiment with their assumptions. For this reason, traceability information needs to be part of the assumptions, as shown in Figure 2.8. As the assumptions inevitably change, the analyst will know which portions of the documentation will potentially also need to change.

The abstract theoretical model for the conservation of thermal energy is presented in Figure 2.9. As discussed in Section 2.1, this conservation equation applies for many physical problems. For instance, this same model is used in the thermal analysis of a nuclear reactor fuel pin [103]. This is possible since the equation is written without reference to a specific coordinate system.

T1 (Figure 2.9) can be simplified from an abstract theoretical model to a more problem specific General Definition (GD). Figure 2.10 shows one potential refinement (GD2), which can be derived using Assumptions A3–A6 (Figure 2.8). The specific details of the derivation are given in the full SRS on-line, but not reproduced here for space reasons. This restating of the conservation of energy is still abstract, since it applies for any control volume that satisfies the required assumptions. GD2 can in turn be further refined to specific (concrete) instanced models for predicting the temperature of the water and the PCM over time.

4.2.1 Assumptions

This section simplifies the original problem and helps in developing the theoretical model by filling in the missing information for the physical system. The numbers given in the square brackets refer to the theoretical model [T], general definition [GD], data definition [DD], instance model [IM], or likely change [LC], in which the respective assumption is used.

A1: The only form of energy that is relevant for this problem is thermal energy. All other forms of energy, such as mechanical energy, are assumed to be negligible [T1].

A2: All heat transfer coefficients are constant over time [GD1].

A3: The water in the tank is fully mixed, so the temperature is the same throughout the entire tank [GD2, DD2].

A4: The PCM has the same temperature throughout [GD2, DD2, LC1].

A5: Density of the water and PCM have not spatial variation; that is, they are each constant over their entire volume [GD2].

A6: Specific heat capacity of the water and PCM have no spatial variation; that is, they are each constant over their entire volume [GD2].

Figure 2.8: Sample assumptions for SWHS.

IM1 and IM2 provide the system of ODEs that needs to be solved to determine T_w and T_P. If a reader would prefer a bottom up approach, as opposed to the default top down organization of the original SRS, they can start reading with the instance models and trace back to find any additional information that they require. IM2 is shown in Figure 2.11. Hyperlinks are included in the original documentation for easy navigation to the associated data definitions, assumptions and instance models.

To achieve a separation of concerns between the requirements and the design, the SRS is abstract, as discussed in Section 2.2. The governing ODEs are given, but not a solution algorithm. The focus is on "what" the software does, not "how" to do it. The numerical methods are left to the design document. This approach facilitates change, since a new numerical algorithm requires no changes to the SRS.

If an expert reviewer is asked to "sign off" on the documentation, he or she should find an explanation/justification for every symbol/equation/definition. This is why IM2 not only shows the equation for energy balance to find T_P, but also the derivation of the equation. (The derivation is not reproduced here for space reasons, but it can be found at `https://github.com/smiths/swhs.git`.)

Table 2.3 shows an excerpt for the table summarizing the input variables for SWHS. With the goal of knowledge capture in mind, this table includes constraints on the input values, along with data on typical values. When new users are learning software, they often do not have a feel for the range and magnitude of the inputs. This table is intended to help them. It also provides a starting point for later testing of the software. The uncertainty information

Number	T1
Label	**Conservation of thermal energy**
Equation	$-\nabla \cdot \mathbf{q} + g = \rho C \frac{\partial T}{\partial t}$
Description	The above equation gives the conservation of energy for time varying heat transfer in a material of specific heat capacity C and density ρ, where $\mathbf{q}$ is the thermal flux vector, g is the volumetric heat generation, T is the temperature, t is time, and ∇ is the gradient operator. For this equation to apply, other forms of energy, such as mechanical energy, are assumed to be negligible in the system (A1).
Source	http://www.efunda.com/formulae/heat_transfer/conduction/overview_cond.cfm
Ref. By	GD2

Figure 2.9: Sample theoretical model.

is included to capture expert knowledge and to facilitate later uncertainty quantification analysis.

Table 2.3: Excerpt from Table of Input Variables for SWHS

Var	Physical Constraints	Software Constraints	Typical Value	Uncertainty
L	$L > 0$	$L_{\min} \leq L \leq L_{\max}$	1.5 m	10%
D	$D > 0$	$\frac{D}{L}_{\min} \leq \frac{D}{L} \leq \frac{D}{L}_{\max}$	0.412 m	10%
V_P	$V_P > 0$ (*)	$V_P \geq \text{minfract} \cdot V_{\text{tank}}(D, L)$	0.05 m^3	10%
	$V_P < V_{\text{tank}}(D, L)$			
A_P	$A_P > 0$ (*)	$V_P \leq A_P \leq \frac{2}{h_{\min}} V_P$ (#)	1.2 m^2	10%
ρ_P	$\rho_P > 0$	$\rho_P^{\min} < \rho_P < \rho_P^{\max}$	1007 kg/m^3	10%
T_{melt}^P	$0 < T_{\text{melt}}^P < T_C$		44.2 °C	10%

2.3.2 Design Specification

The modular decomposition for SWHS is recorded in a Module Guide (MG), as discussed in Section 2.2.5. The table of contents of the MG for SWHS is similar to that shown in Figure 2.4, but with a few different modules. The specific modules for SWHS are shown in Figure 2.12, which summarizes the uses relation between the modules, where module A uses module B if a correct execution of B may be necessary for A to complete the task described in its specification. The relation is hierarchical, which means that subsets of the design can be independently implemented and tested. Some specific points about the MG are as follows:

Number	GD2
Label	**Simplified rate of change of temperature**
Equation	$mC\frac{dT}{dt} = q_{in}A_{in} - q_{out}A_{out} + gV$
Description	The basic equation governing the rate of change of temperature, for a given volume V, with time.
	m is the mass (kg).
	C is the specific heat capacity ($\mathrm{J\,kg^{-1}\,°C^{-1}}$).
	T is the temperature (°C) and t is the time (s).
	q_{in} and q_{out} are the in and out heat transfer rates, respectively ($\mathrm{W\,m^{-2}}$).
	A_{in} and A_{out} are the surface areas over which the heat is being transferred in and out, respectively ($\mathrm{m^2}$).
	g is the volumetric heat generated ($\mathrm{W\,m^{-3}}$).
	V is the volume ($\mathrm{m^3}$).
Ref. By	IM1, IM2

Figure 2.10: Sample general definition.

- Likely changes for SWHS include "the format of the initial input data" and the "algorithm used for the ODE solver." The likely changes are the basis on which the modules are defined.

- One straightforward module is the Input Format Module (M2). This module hides the format of the input, as discussed generically in Section 2.2.5. It knows the structure of the input file, so that no other module needs to know this information. The service that the Input Format Module provides is to read the input data and then modify the state of the Input Parameters Module (M3) so that it holds all of the required information.

- Several of the modules that are documented, such as the Sequence Data Structure Module (M8) and the ODE Solver Module (M9), are already available in MATLAB, which is the selected implementation environment for SWHS. These modules are still explicitly included in the design, with a notation that indicates that they will be implemented by MATLAB. They are included so that if the implementation environment is later changed, the developer will know that they need to provide these modules.

- The MG shows the traceability matrix between the modules and the SRS requirements. This traceability increases confidence that the design is complete because each requirement maps to a module, and each module maps to at least one requirement.

Number	IM2
Label	**Energy balance on PCM to find T_P**
Input	m_P, C_P^S, C_P^L, h_P, A_P, t_{final}, T_{init}, T_{melt}^P, $T_W(t)$ from IM1
	The input is constrained so that $T_{\text{init}} < T_{\text{melt}}^P$ (A13)
Output	$T_P(t)$, $0 \leq t \leq t_{\text{final}}$, with initial conditions, $T_W(0) = T_P(0) = T_{\text{init}}$ (A12), and $T_W(t)$ from IM1, such that the following governing ODE is satisfied. The specific ODE depends on T_P as follows: $$\frac{dT_P}{dt} = \begin{cases} \frac{dT_P}{dt} = \frac{1}{\tau_P^S}(T_W(t) - T_P(t)) & \text{if } T_P < T_{\text{melt}}^P \\ \frac{dT_P}{dt} = \frac{1}{\tau_P^L}(T_W(t) - T_P(t)) & \text{if } T_P > T_{\text{melt}}^P \\ 0 & \text{if } T_P = T_{\text{melt}}^P \text{ and } 0 < \phi < 1 \end{cases}$$ The temperature remains constant at T_{melt}^P, even with the heating (or cooling), until the phase change has occurred for all of the material; that is as long as $0 < \phi < 1$. ϕ (from DD4) is determined as part of the heat energy in the PCM, as given in IM4 $t_{\text{melt}}^{\text{init}}$, the temperature at which melting begins. $t_{\text{melt}}^{\text{final}}$, the temperature at which melting ends.
Description	T_W is water temperature (°C). T_P is the PCM temperature (°C). $\tau_P^S = \frac{m_P C_P^S}{h_P A_P}$ is a constant (s). $\tau_P^L = \frac{m_P C_P^L}{h_P A_P}$ is a constant (s).
Sources	[4]
Ref. By	IM1, IM4

Figure 2.11: Sample instance model.

2.4   Justification

Part of the justification for the document driven approach presented in this chapter is an appeal to the value of a systematic, rigorous, engineering approach. This approach has been successful in other domains, so it stands to reason that it should be successful for scientific software. The example of the solar water heating tank provides partial support for this, since the documentation and code were positively reviewed by a mechanical engineer. Although only providing anecdotal evidence in support of the documentation, the reviewer liked the explicit assumptions; the careful description of names, nomenclature and units; and, the explicit planning for change in the design. The reviewer thought that the documentation captured knowledge that would facilitate new project members quickly getting up to speed. The

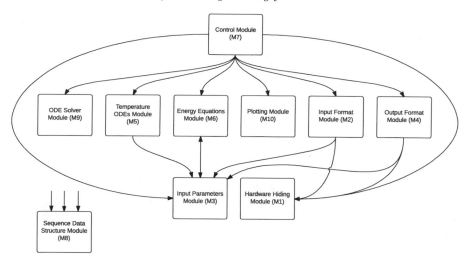

Figure 2.12: Uses hierarchy among modules.

reviewer's main concern was the large amount of documentation for such a relatively simple, and non-safety critical, problem. This concern can be mitigated by the following observations: i) the solar water heating example was intentionally treated more seriously than the problem perhaps deserves, so that a relatively small, but still non-trivial example, could be used to illustrate the methods proposed in this paper; and, ii) if the community recognizes the value of rational documentation, then tool support will follow to reduce the documentation burden. This last point is explored further in the Concluding Remarks (Section 2.5).

Justification by appeals to success in other domains, and by positive comments from a review of SWHS, are not entirely satisfying. Maybe there really is something about science that makes it different from other domains? The research work presented below further justifies that this is not the case.

2.4.1   Comparison between CRAN and Other Communities

The value of documentation and a structured process is illustrated by a survey of statistical software for psychology [104, 105]. The survey compares the quality of statistical software when it is developed using an ad hoc process versus employing the CRAN (Comprehensive R Archive Network [61]) process.

Thirty software tools were reviewed and ranked with respect to their adherence to software engineering best practices. For the surveyed software, R packages clearly performed better than the other categories for qualities related to development, such as maintainability, reusability, understandability and visibility. Commercial software, for which the development process was unknown, provided better usability, but did not show as much evidence of verifiability. With respect to usability, a good CRAN example is mokken [113].

The overall high ranking of R packages stems largely from their use of Rd, Sweave, R CMD check and the CRAN Repository Policy. The policy and support tools mean that even a single developer project can be sufficiently well documented and developed to be used by others. A small research project usually does not have the resources for an extensive development infrastructure and process. By enforcing rules for structured development and documentation, CRAN is able to improve the quality of scientific software.

2.4.2 Nuclear Safety Analysis Software Case Study

To study the impact of a document driven process on scientific software, a case study was performed on legacy software used for thermal analysis of a fuel pin in a nuclear reactor [103, 107]. The legacy code and theory manual were compared to a redeveloped version of the code and documentation using the rational process described in this paper. The redeveloped documentation focused on a single module, the thermal analysis module, and emphasized the SRS and the use of LP. The case study is considered representative of many other scientific programs.

Highly qualified domain experts produced the theory manual for the original software. Their goal was to fully explain the theory for the purpose of QA. The documentation followed the usual format for scientific journals or technical report. Even with an understanding of the importance of the original documentation, the redeveloped version uncovered 27 issues in the previous documentation, ranging from trivial to substantive. Although no errors were uncovered in the code itself, the original documentation had problems with incompleteness, ambiguity, inconsistency, verifiability, modifiability, traceability and abstraction.

The redeveloped code used LP for documenting the numerical algorithms and the code, in what was termed the Literate Programmer's Manual (LPM). An excerpt from the LPM is shown in Figure 2.5. This excerpt shows that the LPM was developed with explicit traceability to the SRS. The traceability between the theory, numerical algorithms and implementation, facilitates achieving completeness and consistency, and simplifies the process of verification and the associated certification. The case study shows that it is not enough to say that a document should be complete, consistent, correct and traceable; practitioners need guidance on how to achieve these qualities.

The case study highlights how a document driven process can improve verifiability. To begin with, verification is only possible with an explicit statement of the requirements, or, in the terminology of Table 2.1, a list of the "right equations." The case study found that, due to inconsistent use of symbols for heat transfer coefficients, two equations for thermal resistance in the original theory manual were actually the "wrong equations." A more systematic process and explicit traceability between theory and code, would have caught these mistakes. The use of LP was also shown to improve the quality of verifiability, since all the information for the implementation is given, including the details of the numerical algorithms, solution techniques, assumptions and the program flow. The understandability of LP is a great benefit for code reading, which is a key activity for scientists verifying their code [79].

Although some of the problems in the original documentation for the case study would likely have been found with any effort to redo the documentation, the rational process builds confidence that the methodology itself improves quality. The proposed SRS template assisted in systematically developing the requirements. The template helped in achieving completeness by acting as a checklist. Since the template was developed following the principle of separation of concerns, each section could be dealt with individually, and the details for the document could be developed by refining from goals to instanced models. The proposed template provides guidelines for documenting the requirements by suggesting an order for filling in the details. This reduces the chances of missing information. Verification of the documentation involves checking that every symbol is defined; that every symbol is used at least once; that every equation either has a derivation, or a citation to its source; that every general definition, data definition and assumption is used by at least one other component of the document; and, that every line of code either traces back to a description of the numerical algorithm (in the LPM), or to a data definition, or to an instance model, or to an assumption, or to a value from the auxiliary constants table in the SRS.

In all software projects, there is a danger of the code and documentation getting out of sync, which seems to have been a problem in the legacy software. LP, together with a rigorous change management policy, mitigates this danger. LPM develops the code and design in the same document, while maintaining traceability between them, and back to the SRS. As changes are proposed, their impact can be determined and assessed.

2.5 Concluding Remarks

This chapter has shown the feasibility of a rational document driven process for scientific software. In the past, scientific software has likely suffered from the vicious cycle where documentation quality is continually eroded [96]. Since software documentation is disliked by almost everyone, the documentation that is typically produced is of poor quality. The reduced quality leads to reduced usage, and the reduced usage in turn leads to a reduction in both resources and motivation. The reduced resources and motivation means further degradation in quality, and the vicious cycle repeats. Following a document driven process, like that described here, can potentially end this vicious cycle.

The approach recommended in this paper is to produce the full suite of software artifacts described in Section 2.2. However, this may be a daunting task to start out with, especially for projects that begin with a small scope. A practical starting point is to adopt tools wherever possible to simplify and improve the development process. In particular, a version control system is an important building block [116]. Ideally developers should adopt a full web solution, like GitHub, or SourceForge, which provide documentation and code management, along with issue tracking. This approach provides the advantage that the product website can be designed for maximum visibility [85]. Moreover, the project can gradually grow into the use of the available tools as the need arises. For code documentation, developers should initially use a tool like Doxygen, since this enforces consistency and produces documentation so that other developers can more easily navigate the source code.

Although requirements are important, a more natural starting point for many developers seems to be test cases, likely because test cases are less abstract than requirements. To ease into a rational process, a project might begin the development process by writing test cases, which in a sense form the initial requirements for the project. If an infrastructure for automated testing is created early in a project, this can help improve verification and validation efforts going forward.

One potential shortcoming of the proposed approach is its reliance on human beings. Following the documentation templates in Section 2.2, and keeping all software artifacts in sync, should produce high quality software, but this places a burden on the developers and reviewers to pay attention to many details. Future work is planned to reduce this burden. Additional tool support, such as the Drasil framework [112], can be incorporated into the process. The fundamental task for Drasil is knowledge capture, so that this knowledge can be used to generate the SRS, V&V plan, MG, code, etc. In Drasil, each individual piece of knowledge is a named chunk, as in LP. Chunks are assembled using a recipe and a generator then interprets recipes to produce the desired document. With Drasil, the task of reusing knowledge, managing change and maintaining traceability sits with the computer, which is much better suited to these tasks than the typical human being.

Just as a compiler can check that all variables have been initialized, the new tools can check the SRS for completeness and consistency and verify that rules, like the one that all symbols are defined, are enforced. Code generation techniques for scientific software [57,58,83] can be used to generalize the idea of LP from the code to cover all software artifacts. A Domain Specific Language (DSL) can be designed for capturing mathematical knowledge for families of scientific software. For instance, any repetition between documents can automatically be generated, rather than relying on a manual process. Ideally, code generation can be used to transform portions of the requirements directly into code. Furthermore, generation techniques may be used to generate documentation to suit the needs of a particular user. For instance, the details on the proof or derivation of equations can be removed for viewers using the software for maintenance purposes, but added back in for reviewers verifying the mathematical model. The user can specify the "recipe" for their required documentation using the developed DSL.

Tool support will make the process easier, but practitioners should not wait. The document driven methods as presented here are feasible today and should be employed now to facilitate high quality scientific software. If an approach such as that described in this paper becomes standard, then the work load will be reduced over time as documentation is reused and as practitioners become familiar with the templates, rules, and guidelines.

Chapter 3

Making Scientific Software Easier to Understand, Test, and Communicate through Software Engineering

Matthew Patrick

3.1 Introduction

When a piece of insulation foam broke off and hit the left wing of the Space Shuttle Columbia, NASA (The National Aeronautics and Space Administration) consulted a computational model to determine the extent of the damage [150]. Although the model predicted debris had penetrated the left wing, NASA decided to ignore this conclusion because their previous experiences led them to believe the model was over-conservative. On the 1st of February 2003, the Space Shuttle Columbia disintegrated as it made its descent, resulting in the deaths of all seven of its crew members. It is of course vitally important scientific software is correct. However, in this example the model gave the right prediction. It is therefore equally important that scientists understand and have faith in the software they are using and developing. This chapter focuses on the application of software engineering techniques to make scientific software easier to understand, test and communicate.

Scientific researchers are increasingly turning to computational resources to help them with their research. For example, computational models are used to inform key decisions on a wide variety of topics, ranging from finance [120] and health-care [133] through epidemiology [141] and conflict [126], as well as many other important areas. The application and development of scientific software is increasing and more than half of scientists say they develop more software now than they did 10 years ago [129]. In a recent survey [135], 70% of biological, mathematical and physical science researchers said they develop software as part of their job and 80% claimed it would not be possible to conduct their work without such software. Since scientific software is used and developed to answer important research questions, it is crucial that it performs correctly and the people using it understand how it works.

Scientific software can be challenging to understand because of its high levels of *essential complexity* and *accidental complexity* [144]. Essential complexity arises due to the need to represent biological, chemical, or physical real-world systems. For example, in epidemiology, computational models are used to describe the stochastic behavior of biological systems over a range of spatiotemporal scales. These models frequently involve complex interactions between species, with nonlinear dynamics. With these models, scientists expect to perform Bayesian and other forms of complex statistical inferences.

Accidental complexity arises because of the disconnect between the sophistication and transparency of the models and the computational methods used to implement them. Programming language syntax can be restrictive and performance optimizations are introduced to handle the large volumes of data and mathematical calculations. The scientists using and developing this software are typically trained in their own field of research rather than in software engineering, so it is not surprising they sometimes have difficulty understanding the way the software behaves.

Software testing techniques are used to find faults. They help testers understand how the software operates and why it behaves the way it does, so they can check it is working correctly. More than half of scientists admit they do not have a good understanding of software testing techniques [142] and one group retracted five papers from top level journals, such as *Science*, because they later discovered their software had a fault which inverted the protein crystal structures they were investigating [142]. Similarly, nine packages for seismic data processing were found to produce significantly different results due to problems such as off-by-one errors [134]. The predictions made from the packages would have led people using them to come to different conclusions, potentially leading to $20 million oil wells being drilled in the wrong place. We need more effective and easy to apply testing techniques for scientific software.

Another area in which scientific software development needs to improve is communication. Researchers often report difficulties in using code someone else has written, partly because the software is necessarily complex, but also because of the way it is written. Scientific software typically includes undocumented assumptions and it is unclear why these were made or how they impact the results. This increases the risk of undetected errors that could compromise the inferences made from the models. The lack of transparency also makes it difficult to reproduce results and constrains the use of models by other researchers. Communication should be made an essential part of the development process because testing and understanding are easier for other people when the motivations behind these assumptions are explained.

Scientific software presents many unique software engineering challenges, both technical and sociological. The errors that scientific software produces are not always the result of programming mistakes. There may be additional problems, for example due to the way in which experimental data is collected and the choice of modeling approximation used [129]. However, there is a considerable divide between the techniques known by the software engineering community and the ways in which scientists actually test their software [138]. Scientists typically determine whether or not their code is working by looking at the output and checking it matches what they expect. However, this approach is likely to miss important errors, since the output may appear reasonable and still be incorrect. A more rigorous approach is required.

This chapter investigates the challenges involved in making scientific software easier to understand, test, and communicate by exploring three case studies of scientific software development in different research groups. We look at the things these researchers are doing well and the things they are struggling with, so we can understand how to help. We then present two new techniques: Iterative hypothesis testing helps scientists to understand how and why their software behaves the way it does; and search-based pseudo-oracles make it possible to identify differences between highly complex stochastic implementations. These techniques enable scientists to communicate their software, by separating the model and hypotheses from the program code, as well as representing the reasoning behind each implementation assumption.

3.2 Case Studies

We investigate the practices of three research groups in the Department of Plant Sciences at the University of Cambridge. The Epidemiology and Modelling Group, under Professor Chris Gilligan, develops and applies models for the optimization of disease control. This is the group the authors of this paper belong to. The Theoretical and Computational Epidemiology Group, under Dr. Nik Cunniffe, also works with large-scale stochastic simulations, but its members tend to have a more theoretical focus on the spread and control of plant diseases. Finally, the Bioinformatics Group, under Dr. Krys Kelly, works to process and analyze high-throughput data for RNA (ribonucleic acid) and DNA (deoxyribonucleic acid) sequences.

Members of these groups use mathematical, statistical, and computational techniques in their research. For example, computational simulations are used to understand how various factors affect the spread of an epidemic. Group members are typically trained in mathematics, biology and physics rather than software engineering. They also make extensive use of big data. For example, the Bioinformatics group uses genome data to understand the role of small RNAs in silencing mechanisms and regulatory networks. The Epidemiology and Modelling group use large scale meteorological information to predict the effect of weather and climate conditions on the dispersal of pathogens.

The work conducted within these groups has a wider impact beyond the groups themselves. For example, members of the Bioinformatics group work closely with wet-lab biologists to design, implement and analyze genome scale studies and laboratory experiments. They have developed a sequence analysis pipeline for small RNA, ChIP (chromatin immunoprecipitation) and genome data used by researchers across the department. The Epidemiology and Modelling Group and Theoretical and Computational Epidemiology Group produce computational modeling results that are used to inform key policy decisions in government organizations, such as DEFRA (Department for Environment, Food and Rural Affairs) and the USDA (United States Department of Agriculture). This means work done on improving the way members of these groups test their software could be highly worthwhile.

3.3 Challenges Faced by the Case Studies

It can be difficult to understand, test, and communicate the scientific software developed and used by the groups in our case studies because it is written to simulate, model, and analyze the behavior of complex biological systems. In particular, there are issues related to big data, stochastic processes and

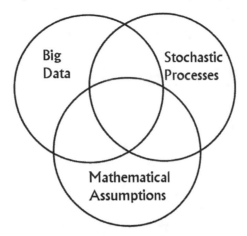

Figure 3.1: Some challenges in testing the software.

mathematical assumptions (see Figure 3.1). These three factors interact in such a way that if an error occurs in the results of the software, it is difficult to know whether it is due to one of these factors, or if it is caused by a fault in the program code.

Big data causes difficulties for testing and understanding the results of scientific software because it must often be optimized for speed and memory usage rather than readability. Consider for example the high throughput sequencing data processed and analyzed by the bioinformation group. Their software needs to be able to process whole genomes, consisting of multiple terabytes of data, within a reasonable time-frame. Similarly, epidemiological models that are used to investigate real-world diseases need to process large quantities of spatial and temporal information in the form of habitat, disease, and meteorological data, over a range of spatiotemporal scales.

Big data poses an additional problem in that the larger the dataset, the more likely it is to contain errors. Subtle faults may only be triggered under highly specific input conditions. For example, the time at which hosts move from one compartment to another in an epidemiological model depends on their proximity to infected hosts. The relative spatiotemporal arrangement of hosts is often more important than their precise locations. Similarly, bioin-formaticians are often interested in the correlations between different regions of sequence data. We need to evaluate these correlations and spatiotemporal relationships if we are to test the software thoroughly.

When the biological system the software is being used to study has a stochastic component, or stochasticity is introduced to deal with unknown sources of error, there is no one correct output for any given input. Instead, each time the software is run, it is likely to give a different result. Stochastic interactions occur between multiple species and epidemiological models frequently involve highly nonlinear dynamics. Additionally, suitable model parameters are identified by statistical inference of historical disease incidence data. It is difficult to test whether the software is correct because it is valid for the outputs to have a number of different values for the same set of inputs.

One way to address this problem is to fix the random seed during testing. This makes the test cases deterministic, but it does not test the stochastic properties (such as mean or variance) of the software. We therefore need to calculate the probability of the output being correct. This requires the use of appropriate statistical techniques to compare the observed outputs with an expected probability distribution. Test cases need to be run multiple times before we can make a decision as to the likelihood that the outputs are correct. The problem is that, depending upon the random seed, we may conclude the software is correct when it is faulty (a false negative) or that it is faulty when it is correct (a false positive). Also, since it requires a considerable amount of effort to determine whether the outputs for a single set of inputs are correct, this could limit the number of inputs that can feasibly be tested and makes it difficult to test stochastic software rigorously.

Finally, scientific software approximates the behavior of real-world systems through a series of mathematical and computational abstractions. Each layer of abstraction has the potential to introduce new errors into the model. Assumptions are required to formulate and simplify the behavior of the system, so that mathematical representations can be produced. These mathematical assumptions can have a significant effect on the results of the software. For example, a decision must be made when modeling the spread of an epidemic, as to whether to model individuals or to take a mean-field approach. Although these techniques might be expected to give similar results, the details will differ depending on the biological system. Software testing is challenging as we do not know what effect assumptions will have on the results.

Inaccuracies from big data, approximations, and stochasticity make it difficult to understand the behavior of the software and communicate it in an appropriate way. They can also mask the presence of faults, so that it is hard to know if an error indicates a fault in the code or is due to one of these factors. We need to separate the unavoidable error in data, stochasticity, and mathematical assumptions from any programming mistakes. This is made more difficult in scientific software because it is typically developed to answer new research questions, to which scientists do not yet know the answers. If the answers to these questions were already known, there would be no need to create the software. As a result of these challenging problems, scientific software is often difficult to understand, test, and communicate.

The aim of this study is to understand the ways in which scientists currently work to make sure they are developing correct software. It is hoped this will allow us to locate areas in which improvements can be made, e.g. through additional training or new techniques. To this end, we asked 12 researchers in the Epidemiology & Modelling and Theoretical & Computational Epidemiology groups to tell us about the practices they employ in their software development work. The participants were given a survey to find out if they use and/or have heard of 10 commonly used software engineering techniques.

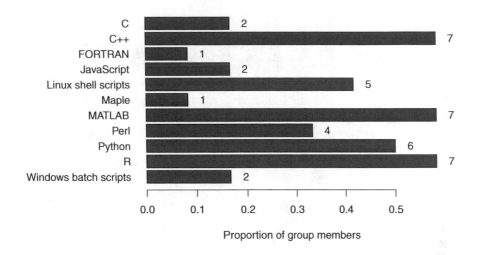

Figure 3.2: Program languages used in the Department of Plant Sciences.

Since some of the techniques involve specific terminology, we also gave the researchers additional explanations of the techniques in non-technical terms.

In analyzing the results of this study, it is important to take into account the languages in which the scientists are writing software. For example, the challenges in testing scripts and compiled software are often considerably different. Other research attempts have been conducted to investigate software engineering practices in scientific research [129] [135], but our study is unique in considering the impact of the programming languages used within the groups (see Figure 3.2). Although half of the members program in C++, scripting languages such as MATLAB (Matrix Laboratory) and R are used by the same number of researchers. C++ is popular for back-end programs because of its efficiency, but scripting languages are used for more everyday usage, since they are easy to program and have useful libraries for mathematical modelling. In the Bioinformatics group, scripting languages such as R, Python and Perl are used for everyday tasks, whereas the back-end is written in C. The large number of languages used within these groups, the wide variety of tasks they are applied to and the diverse range of programming abilities all pose challenges to ensuring software is correct.

Figure 3.3 shows the software engineering techniques researchers from the Epidemiology & Modelling and Theoretical & Computational Epidemiology groups have heard of and use. Some of the techniques were used by all the researchers (e.g. manual testing) and some were used by none (e.g. coverage metrics). The techniques cover topics in black box testing, white box testing and code clarity. We interviewed group members individually after the survey to learn more about the reasons as to why they used particular techniques.

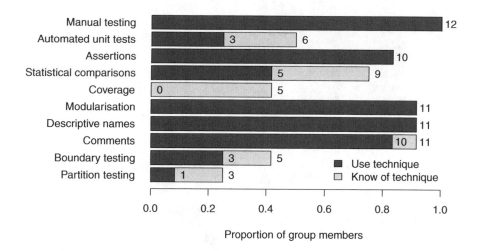

Figure 3.3: Software engineering techniques used in the department.

Researchers typically test the software they develop by running its code with certain inputs (that are carefully chosen by hand) and then visually checking that the outputs appear to be correct. This process is reflected in our study by the popularity of manual testing. All 12 participants use manual testing in their work. The outputs are checked manually in an ad-hoc way, either by taking advantage of the researchers' own intuitive understanding of the expected values of the results, or by comparing the outputs to previous results by other researchers (e.g. from published research).

The respondents have found manual testing to be useful in their work, but it is not ideal and they were interested in using more sophisticated testing techniques. However, the researchers were worried these techniques might be time consuming to learn. More sophisticated techniques such as automated unit tests, coverage metrics and boundary/partition testing are seldom used by the researchers in these groups. Many respondents claim to be using assertions, but interviews later revealed that they were using if-statements to check the values of their variables. Systematic techniques may be less popular than manual testing because they require software engineering knowledge group members do not have, but they are also more difficult to use because they need a more formal representation of the particular software testing problem.

3.3.1 Intuitive Testing

Few of the researchers we surveyed had made use of the more advanced techniques for software testing (such as coverage metrics, boundary testing or partition testing). They instead tended to prefer the use of simpler techniques (such as manual testing, modularization and commenting) as they do not require the researchers to learn new software engineering concepts. Fewer than half of the researchers had heard of boundary or partition testing and less than a quarter have actually used them. In addition, no-one had used coverage metrics to evaluate the quality of their test cases. These results reflect the results of other studies, that there is a lack of training in software testing and development, within the scientific research community [129].

It was interesting that, although the respondents did not employ advanced software engineering techniques, half of the researchers use advanced statistical techniques (applied manually) to test their software and almost all of the researchers knew of such techniques, even if they did not use them. This suggests that if we could somehow align software testing techniques with the skills that scientists already have, they would be able to test software more rigorously and in a more sophisticated way. During our interviews, we found that the respondents sometimes used their own intuition to identify techniques similar to those used in software engineering. For example, researchers often use some form of partial or pseudo oracle to test their software. This is an approach recommended in software engineering [154] for programs that are difficult to test, as the correct outputs are not known in advance.

Our interviews revealed two ways in which partial and pseudo oracles are used by the researchers: toy data sets and existing literature. Toy data sets simplify the problem of knowing what the outputs should be, as they can be produced using straightforward and well understood methodologies. Spatial simulations of epidemiological models can, for example, be tested against the results of a non-spatial simulation. Comparisons can be made by running the spatial simulator on a landscape with a single location, such that we remove the spatial elements of the simulation. Similarly, the mean or median result of a stochastic simulation can be compared with the analytical solution of a deterministic version of the model. The other approach, using existing literature, is to find an example of a similar model with results that have been published by other people. The researchers start by building that same model and comparing its output against the results provided in the publication, before moving on to extend the model for the functionality they desire. Of course this process would be easier if the scientists who developed the existing model made their source code available, but unfortunately examples of this can sometimes be hard to find, due to issues related to intellectual property.

There are cases where suitable psuedo-oracles are not available. Our interviews revealed in these situations, scientists use a technique known in software engineering as metamorphic testing [122]. Although the respondents did not use this terminology, it was clear they had applied their intuition to come up with a similar approach. The scientists used their understanding of the biological system to predict how the software should behave when the inputs are changed. In epidemiology, when the distance that disease particles (e.g. fungal spores) are allowed to travel is increased, the resulting epidemic (as predicted by the computational simulation) should be dispersed over a wider area.

Boundary testing and partition testing [136] are widely used techniques within the field of software engineering. They help testers to produce test suites that thoroughly cover the input domain, whilst at the same time they decrease the number of tests that need to be executed. Very few of the researchers we surveyed used these techniques, or were even aware of their existence. Upon explaining the techniques to one researcher, the respondent remarked that they could not see how these techniques could be used in their work. However, upon digging deeper, we found that the scientists are already using techniques similar to boundary and partition testing - they are just not aware of the software engineering terminology.

Group members typically look for strange or unexpected results in the output of their software (boundary testing), such as values that are too high or frequencies that do not add up to one. This is generally performed in an ad-hoc way and could potentially gain from being transformed into a more standardized process. Members of the Epidemiology & Modelling group and Theoretical & Computational Epidemiology group also make use of a concept known as the basic reproduction number (R0) [124]. If R0 is greater than one, the disease can be expected to spread, otherwise the disease can be expected to die out. Members typically of these groups take advantage of this information when manually testing their software, considering both cases in their tests. This is essentially a form of partition testing and it might be made more rigorous by using results from software engineering research in this area.

In addition to testing the software, it is also important to make sure the data is correct. The Epidemiology & Modelling and Theoretical & Computational Epidemiology groups clean the data before they use it by checking the quantities and distributions of host are correct and making sure there are no hosts in unexpected locations. Members of the bioinformatics group use data cleaning techniques too, but they also work more closely with their data providers (wet-lab scientists) to design and conduct experiments. This provides an opportunity to ensure data correctness at multiple stages of research. They can assist in preparing appropriate block designs and use statistical analyses to check the data that is produced. It is advantageous (where possible) for computational scientists to be involved in the data generation process.

3.3.2 Automating Tests

Test automation is a technique intended to reduce the amount of effort involved in software testing and it makes it easier to test software more rigorously. In comparison with manual testing, automated tests can significantly decrease the human effort involved in testing [121]. It is surprising therefore that, among the researchers we interviewed, the main reason for not using automated tests is that they require too much work. Less than a quarter of the researchers we surveyed use automated tests on their software. The primary reasons why the respondents felt automated tests require significant effort is because it is necessary to learn a new approach in order to use them and the researchers did not know where to start in creating the automated tests.

The biggest challenge scientific researchers face in creating automating tests is in describing how the software should behave in a formalized way. Although scientists may know what to expect when they manually check the outputs of their software, transforming this into a set of test cases is often non-trivial. They are able to identify potentially incorrect results intuitively, but can struggle to describe what the outputs should be before the software is run. It is inevitable that manual testing will remain an important part of scientific software engineering, as scientific research is inherently an exploratory process. Yet, any techniques that allow us to represent the scientists' intuition as automated unit tests would be valuable, as they could help scientific sets to test their software more rigorously and systematically.

Since it is difficult for scientific researchers to know what the test cases should be before they start to execute their software, it is important to make the process of test suite generation iterative. As more information becomes available through scientific research, the test suite can be incrementally expanded to make it more rigorous. Initially, unit tests can be created of the basic functionality of the software, but later tests can be made more sophisticated to test the overall behavior of the software. This approach has some similarities with regression testing [121] which compares the output of software with previous results, except instead of checking whether the software behavior has changed, the aim would be to determine whether the test suite needs to be improved (more details of this approach are provided in Section 3.4).

One way to formalize the intuition of scientific researchers is with assertions, which can be used to check the state of the software at various points during its execution. Some group members already use assertions in conjunction with an automated test framework, but the majority check for errors by inserting 'if' statements into their code and printing an error message on the screen if an unexpected value occurs. This approach is not ideal, since it is possible for these warnings to be missed amongst the other text that is produced by the program. This approach is also difficult to automate and the error information is typically not recorded in a structured way. A better approach is to integrate the assertions into unit tests, so that a clear record is produced of any errors that gave occurred and the test cases that were used to find them. This makes it easier to find the locations of faults in the software and the information can be used to inform the future refinement of test cases.

Even if automated tests are used, there is still the issue of knowing whether the software has been tested sufficiently. To address this problem, structural coverage metrics [121] have been developed to assess the quality of the test suite and its ability to identify potential failures. So far, no-one in the group has used coverage metrics to evaluate their test cases. One researcher pointed out a limitation of coverage metrics in that, even if each part of the code is covered by the test suite, the tests might still not be able to identify any faults. Test suites are only as useful as the oracle used to check the outputs. However, coverage metrics can still help to encourage more rigorous tests.

Beyond simple control coverage, we might consider whether more sophisticated metrics, such as data flow or mutation analysis are useful [121]. It may also be possible to devise new metrics for scientific research, that consider how thoroughly we have tested our answers to the research questions. However, since not even the structural coverage metrics are used often, any new metrics should be introduced gradually. There is likely to be a trade-off between the sophistication of the technique and the number of people who are willing to learn how to use it. Nevertheless, by creating techniques that fit well with the groups' (scientific) ways of working, it may be possible to devise new metrics that are both easy for the users to apply and effective.

3.3.3 Legacy Code

Members of the Epidemiology & Modelling and Theoretical & Computational Epidemiology groups expressed they have had problems with legacy code. It is difficult to continue the research of people who have left the group because it is unclear why particular constants were chosen in the code and many functions/variables are undocumented. It can therefore take considerable time to reproduce the results of previous research before the software can be extended for further research. We believe it is important to improve the clarity of the code, as this allows software to be reused in the future.

There is also an argument for code clarity from a testing point of view. It is difficult to make sure a program is working correctly if you do not know how it is supposed to work. The person testing the software is likely to address errors by removing the symptoms without understanding their cause. This means the fault still exists within the software, it is just now even more difficult to find. So that faults can be correctly identified and fixed, we need to ensure that the programming code and other soft artifacts (requirements specification, design document, verification/validation report etc.) are clear and easy to read.

Things are slightly different in the bioinformatics group because the journals they publish their work in encourage (and sometimes require) authors make their code publicly available. This also includes the scripts that have been used to produce each of the figures. In addition, the code that is written in this group is uploaded to Bioconductor, a large bioinformatics software project that is curated and managed by moderators. These rigorous procedures help to encourage scientists to improve the clarity of their programming. More generally, it is important to recognize and give credit for the publishing of code. Since research scientists are typically motivated by publications, this would encourage them to spend more time developing quality software.

One of the biggest factors that has an effect on the clarity of the program code is the way in which it is divided into modules (e.g. information hiding [145]). The results of our interviews suggest group members tend to start with a single large module, then put parts of the code into functions that represent a self-contained feature or are frequently executed. Although this can be helpful, it may still result in large and complex modules if the developers do not divide the code into modules early enough. One of the researchers we interviewed used to create packages for code written in R, but has stopped doing this as it is too time-consuming. Code is often copied and pasted rather than extracted into a function, as this is faster and easier to do. However, actions that take less time now may cause maintenance problems in the future.

Another factor that may cause some confusion is that group members do not always use a consistent naming system. They sometimes apply CamelCase and underscores within the same program. Although the particular naming system used is not so important, clarity may be improved if the system is used consistently [139]. It is also important for the names to be meaningful. The names of variables and functions should be carefully chosen to reveal their intention (i.e. reason for existing and how they should be used) [139]. If suitable names are used, there is no need to describe the purpose of a variable or function further in a comment.

Rather than describing the purpose of each variable, the most helpful use of comments is to provide information about implementation decisions and describe the underlying concepts of the code [139]. The researchers we interviewed seemed to have a good understanding of how comments should be used. For example, group members described using comments to clarify the equations or models used in their code and to identify any edge cases. Furthermore, researchers explained the importance of keeping the comments short and concise, deliberately excluding redundant information that is obvious from the code. However, upon examining the group's version control repository, we found that the group members do not always follow these principles. Large sections of the code had no comments and some comments were used to disable old code rather than to provide useful information.

Even though the researchers we interviewed know how to write clear and easily readable code, they often do not do this in practice because it is too time consuming. Researchers are rewarded for writing publications rather than developing software, so they tend to distribute their time accordingly. This makes it difficult to encourage researchers to write code that is easy to understand, test and communicate. It could help to perform code reviews, pair programming [139] or to make the code open source. Yet it is understandable that researchers often do not want to take time out of their research. Another approach is to focus on the benefits to individuals of being able to use their own code again. If large sections of the code are copied and pasted, there is a danger errors may be introduced, since subsequent changes are not propagated throughout the program. By contrast, the quality of software may be increased by improving the clarity of its code.

3.3.4 Summary

Most of the researchers we surveyed test their software manually by checking if the output matches their expectation. Part of the reason why automated testing is underused is because traditional techniques are not well suited for scientific software. They do not take into account other sources of error (e.g. data or modelling assumptions) and they are often too technical or abstract for scientists to apply. Another reason is because these techniques do not fit well with the paradigm of many researchers. Scientists are typically more interested in conducting research than thinking about software engineering. Yet, although scientists are often not aware of advanced software testing techniques, they sometimes use their own intuition to find solutions similar to those in software engineering. This seems like a good place to start.

1. Scientists typically use manual testing rather than advanced techniques.

2. The advanced techniques are not well suited for scientific research.

3. We will reinterpret existing techniques to make them more intuitive.

3.4 Iterative Hypothesis Testing

To help scientists move towards more rigorous forms of software testing, it makes sense to utilize the strategies that scientists are already familiar with from their research. In this section, we introduce a software testing approach that is based upon iterative hypothesis testing, a core component of the scientific research method. Scientists typically start their a research project with some initial hypotheses about how the system they are studying is expected to behave. Then, as these hypotheses are tested and explored, new information is gathered that can be used to add to and refine them [129].

Similarly, scientists might have some initial understanding as to what the outputs of the software they are developing should be, but they do not (at least at first) have sufficient information to create a rigorous set of test cases. Instead, iterative hypothesis testing can be used to find situations in which these hypotheses do not hold, so that the scientist is aware of how their hypotheses need to be refined. They can then use this information to iteratively improve their hypotheses and test cases. Ultimately, this approach helps scientists to build stronger test suites. However, since it is designed to operate in a form that scientists are already familiar with, it should be straightforward for them to adopt this technique in testing their scientific software.

In addition to the scientists' intuition, initial hypothesis tests may be created with the Method of Manufactured Solutions [148]. The idea behind this approach is to solve a partial differential equation backwards, i.e. start with the solution and then invert the equation to determine what inputs were necessary to create it. Other approaches suggested by Salari and Knupp [148], include trend tests (varying the input parameters and checking the overall pattern), symmetry tests (e.g. changing the order of inputs and checking that the results are the same) and comparison tests (using pseudo-oracles).

Our iterative hypothesis testing technique repeatedly refines a set of hypotheses using random testing to search for discrepancies in the output. Random testing is a straightforward and inexpensive software testing technique [125]. It can generate a large number of input values in a short amount of time, then verify the results using automatic tests of our hypotheses. Despite its simplicity, random testing is often an efficient technique [118] and it can sometimes be more effective than advanced tools for software testing [149]. Our iterative hypothesis testing technique is therefore straightforward to use and it has the ability to reveal useful properties that help us to improve our tests. We evaluate our technique by applying it to an epidemiological *SEIR* model.

3.4.1   The Basic SEIR Model

While there are many different approaches to the modelling of disease, it is common for models to track the hosts of a pathogen through several exclusive compartments. The model we are investigating in this chapter is an *SEIR* model (see Figure 3.4). This means it includes the following compartments: *Susceptible* (not infected), *Exposed* (infected but neither infectious nor showing symptoms), *Infectious* (infectious and showing symptoms) and *Removed* (no longer infectious, because they are dead or recovered). Hosts may start off susceptible (S), but when they are exposed (E) to infectious hosts, they enter into a latent period before being infectious (I) themselves; later the infectious hosts are removed (R) from the population and cannot infect any other host.

Equation 3.1 presents the differential equations for each compartment in the *SEIR* model. The rates at which host move between compartments depends upon the choice of parameters (β, γ and μ) and the amount of host already in each compartment. The *SEIR* model we are testing in this section

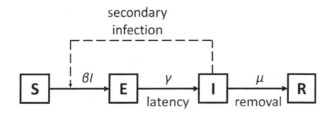

Figure 3.4: SEIR model schematic.

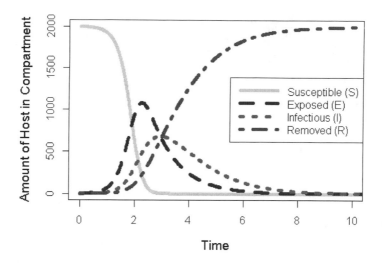

Figure 3.5: Typical SEIR graph.

is a continuous-time continuous-host non-spatial deterministic model. A typical example of the grah for a single run of the *SEIR* model is shown in Figure 3.5. This is one of the simplest models used in epidemiology, but as we will see, implementations of this model are still challenging to test.

$$\frac{dS}{dt} = -\beta IS, \qquad \frac{dE}{dt} = \beta IS - \gamma E, \qquad \frac{dI}{dt} = \gamma E - \mu I, \qquad \frac{dR}{dt} = \mu I. \quad (3.1)$$

3.4.2   Experimental Methodology

For each hypothesis, we ran 100 random tests. A random test consists of a single run of the model with a particular set of parameters, after which the outputs are compared with an automated unit test representing a particular hypothesis. Each run of the model spans 50 time units and the state of the model is recorded every 0.01 units. The total amount of host is fixed at 2000 and a random amount of infectious host (I) is selected for each test (up to half the total amount); the remaining host is placed into the susceptible (S) compartment (the amount in E and R is set to zero). This arrangement was chosen to represent the conditions under which new infectious material enters the population. Values for γ and μ were selected at random within the range 0 to 1, whereas β values were selected up to the reciprocal of the total amount of host (i.e. between 0 and $1/N$). β needs to be sampled over a different range because it is multiplied by both S and I (see Equation 3.1). If we cannot find any discrepancies at first, we then increase the number of test cases that are applied and we also consider boundary conditions (such as setting β to 0).

The hypotheses in this section were implemented in R using QuickCheck [147]. QuickCheck allows hypotheses to be written as assertions, which are then tested with automatically generated random test cases. The process of transforming hypotheses into QuickCheck assertions is straightforward and the code required is minimal. This means it is easy for scientists to use and we can have confidence that our tests do not themselves contain faults.

3.4.3   Initial Hypotheses

The initial hypotheses can be divided into three broad categories: *sanity checks* represent output results our intuition tells us should never happen; *metamorphic relations* describe what we expect to happen if parameter values are modified; and finally, *mathematical derivations* use analytically calculable results for part of the model. These hypotheses were constructed in consultation with epidemiological modellers. However, they should not be considered the final set of tests these modellers would develop if given enough time, rather they represent some first thoughts on how the model should behave.

3.4.3.1   Sanity Checks

Tests of Instantaneous State:-

H1: None of the compartments should ever contain a negative amount of host
It is biologically impossible for a compartment to contain a negative amount of host. Yet, there is no mathematical or computational reason why values in the equations have to be positive. We therefore need to check the amount of host in the Susceptible (S), Exposed (E), Infectious (I) and Removed (R) compartments is at least zero in every time step.

H2: The total amount of host should not differ at each time step
Our model assumes a closed population, i.e. there are no births, deaths or migration. Although host may move from one compartment to another, it should never leave the model, nor should any new host enter it. We therefore need to check that the amount of host in the compartments (S, E, I and R) adds up to the same total at every time step.

Tests of the Time Series:-

H3: The amount of susceptible host (S) should never increase
In the *SEIR* model, host leaves the S compartment upon exposure to host from the I compartment. However, there is no way once host has become infected for it to return to being susceptible. The S curve should therefore be monotonically decreasing and under no circumstances should the amount of susceptible host ever increase.

H4: The amount of removed host (R) should never decrease
Once host in the *SEIR* model enter the R compartment, it never leaves. It is not possible for removed host to recover and become susceptible again. The R curve should therefore be monotonically increasing and the amount of removed host ever decrease.

H5: The exposed host (E) peak should not occur after the infectious host (I) peak
Host in the *SEIR* model enters the E compartment before it reaches the I compartment. Since exposed host is not infectious, it simply acts as a buffer for the I compartment. We should therefore expect the E compartment will reach its peak before the I one.

3.4.3.2 Metamorphic Relations

H6: Increasing the infection rate (β) should increase the peak of E
The infection rate parameter (β) determines how quickly host move from the S to the E compartment. If the rate at which host leaves the E compartment (γ) is kept the same, increasing β should lead to a greater build up on host and hence a higher peak in E.

H7: Increasing the latent rate (γ) should reduce the time until the peak of I
The latent rate parameter (γ) determines how quickly host move from E to I. Assuming all other parameters remain the same, increasing γ should reduce the time taken by host to move from S through E to I, hence allowing the peak of I to occur more quickly.

H8: Increasing μ should increase the final amount of host in S
The removal rate parameter (μ) determines how quickly host move from I to R. This in turn influences the rate at which host leaves S, as there are fewer host in I to infect them. We can therefore expect that more host will remain susceptible if μ is increased.

H9: Increasing β should decrease the final amount of host in S
The other parameter determining the amount of host that remains susceptible is β. Since it controls the rate at which host leave S, it makes more host infectious and increases the infection pressure on S. Together, β/μ is known as the basic reproduction number (R_0).

H10: Increasing the number of susceptible host (S_0) should increase the peak of I
Apart from the parameters described previously (β, γ and μ), it is also possible to affect the progress of the I curve by altering the starting conditions. Increasing S_0 provides a greater number of host to become infected, so we can expect the peak of I to be higher.

3.4.3.3   Mathematical Derivations

H11: **I should be increasing when $\gamma E > \mu I$, otherwise it should be decreasing**
From the rate equation for the I compartment ($dI = \gamma E - \mu I$), it is clear that I should increase if $\gamma E - \mu I > 0$. We should therefore check that when $\gamma E > \mu I$, the amount of host is higher in the next time step than the current one, otherwise it should be lower.

H12: **If $I = E = 0$, the state of the model should not change**
Every term in the rate equations contains the value I or E. If both of these values are zero, the amount of host in none of the compartments can change. This is the same as saying that once all the infections have died out, the model has reached its equilibrium.

H13: **Exact analytical solutions are available when $\gamma = 0$**
Setting $\gamma = 0$ reduces the Infectious rate equation to $dI = -\mu I$. Solving this gives $I_t = I_0 e^{(-\mu t)}$. We can substitute it into the dS equation and solve to give $S_t = S_0 e^{\frac{\beta I_0 (e^{-\mu t} - 1)}{\mu}}$. We should expect the I and S curves to be the same as these solutions at every time step.

H14: **Exact analytical solutions are available when $\beta = 0$**
Setting $\beta = 0$ gives us $dE = -\gamma E$, which can be solved as $E_t = E_0 e^{(-\gamma t)}$. We can substitute this into the dI equation and solve to give $I_t = \frac{e^{-\gamma t}(E_0 \gamma (e^{t(\gamma - \mu)} - 1) + I_0(\gamma - \mu)e^{t(\gamma - \mu)})}{\gamma - \mu}$. We should expect the E and I curves to be the same as these solutions at every time step.

H15: **A final size equation can determine the value of S when $t = \infty$**
The Susceptible rate equation $dS = -\beta IS$ may be solved and rearranged at $t = \infty$[1] to give a final size equation for the S compartment in the $SEIR$ model: $\ln(\frac{S_0}{S_\infty}) = \frac{\beta}{\mu}(N - S_\infty)$. We can use this equation to check the equilibrium value for S at the end of the simulation.

3.4.4   Exploring and Refining the Hypotheses

The hypotheses described above serve as a starting point for testing implementations of a deterministic non-spatial $SEIR$ model. However, they should not yet be used to construct a final set of test cases, since there are implementation details still to be taken into account. We now apply our iterative

---

[1] We divide both sides of the Susceptible rate equation by S to give $\int_0^\infty \frac{1}{S} dS = \int_0^\infty \beta I dt$. Adding up the rate equations for S, E and I gives $(S + E + I)' = -\mu I$. At $t = \infty$, there should be no infectious or exposed host, so the total change for these three compartments is the difference between N and the final value of S, i.e. $\int_0^\infty I dt = -\frac{1}{\mu} \int_0^\infty (S + E + I)' dt = -\frac{N - S_\infty}{\mu}$. Substituting this into the previous equation and performing the integration gives $\ln(S_\infty) - \ln(S_0) = -\frac{\beta}{\mu}(N - S_\infty)$, which can then be rearranged to $\ln(\frac{S_0}{S_\infty}) = \frac{\beta}{\mu}(N - S_\infty)$.

approach to explore and refine these hypotheses so they can be used to construct a test suite. We use random testing, coupled with boundary analysis, and scrutinize the results to determine how the hypothesis should be changed.

3.4.4.1   Complexities of the Model

Even though our deterministic *SEIR* model is simpler than many other epidemiological models, there are still some situations not taken into account by the hypotheses. In **H5** we reasoned that since host pass through the E compartment on their way to the I compartment, the peak of E would be before that of I. We constructed a unit test from this hypothesis and applied random testing to find a situation in which this did not hold ($I_0 = 477$, $\beta = 4.95 \times 10^{-4}$, $\gamma = 0.285$, $\mu = 0.986$). Figure 3.6a shows that with these input parameters, E contains a peak, even though I is monotonically decreasing.

This happens because host enters E faster than it leaves, but leaves I faster than it enters, thus creating a buildup of host in E causing a peak. A similar problem occurs with **H7**. We have found using random testing it is possible for the I curve to be monotonically decreasing under the original set of input parameters (i.e. the maximum of I occurs at $t = 0$). Yet, when γ is increased, this introduces a peak, thus violating the hypothesis. An epidemiological modeller could have identified these eventualities by studying the equations, but it is much easier to do this using the results of random testing.

Another example in which random testing was able to find a problem with one of the hypotheses is **H10**. When I is monotonically decreasing ($I_0 = 816$, $\beta = 3.80 \times 10^{-4}$, $\gamma = 0.018$, $\mu = 0.146$), modifying S_0 has no effect on its peak (see Figure 3.6b). In this situation, it would be more useful to compare the areas under the curves (AUC) rather than their peaks. However, this is not a general solution because, when I is not monotonically decreasing two

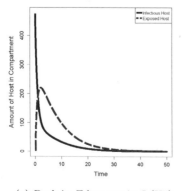

(a) Peak in E but not in I (H5)

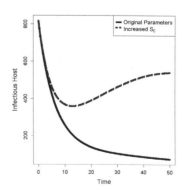

(b) AUC is more appropriate (H10)

Figure 3.6: Unexpected complexities of the model.

curves can have the same AUC but yet have different shapes. We therefore need to use both metrics (AUC and peak host) to characterize the difference.

Random testing is not effective at finding situations under which hypotheses only fail for a specific set of input values. We therefore augmented our random testing with boundary analysis by setting the input parameters to zero one at a time. For example in **H6**, we found that when $S = 0$, increasing β has no effect on the peak of E, because there is no host to move into E from S. Similarly in **H8**, increasing μ has no effect on the final amount of host in S when $\beta = 0$ because host will never leave S regardless. Our approach to boundary analysis could miss some important cases because it does not take the differential equations into account. It might also be possible to apply a more advanced symbolic approach to analyze the equations directly.

3.4.4.2 Complexities of the Implementation

In addition to complexities of the model, we must also consider complexities of the implementation. Even if our hypotheses perfectly characterize the mathematical behavior of the model, there may still be some unexpected discrepancies when the model is implemented on a computer. For example, we applied our technique to identify situations in which **H11** did not hold because the points at which I transitions between increasing and decreasing are incorrectly identified (see Figure 3.7a). For the point at the maximum, $\gamma E > \mu I$, but the amount of infectious host in the next time step is still lower. This is because the solver operates at a finer resolution than the time steps we have asked it to produce, and the size of each time step is varied for optimal efficiency I can therefore reach its peak and then start to decrease during a single time step. Likewise, the minimum of I may be passed over when the curve is transitioning from decreasing to increasing.

Another way to determine when I should be increasing or decreasing (at least for SIR models) is with the effective reproduction number (R_t), which is calculated using $\frac{\beta S}{\mu N}$. R_t is essentially the same as the basic reproduction number, but corrected for the proportion of host that is susceptible at time t. In the SIR model, the amount of infectious host should be increasing as long as $R_t > 1$. However, this approach cannot be used for $SEIR$ models because of the effect of the E compartment. Figure 3.7a is a good example of this problem ($I_0 = 137$, $\beta = 8.64 \times 10^{-5}$, $\gamma = 0.589$, $\mu = 0.123$). The I curve initially decreases because the starting conditions include some amount of host in I but none in E, so that it takes some time for the dynamics to stabilize. This is why in this case the graph does not have a single peak.

It is not possible to measure the state of a model at an asymptote, since the rate at which this value is approached gets smaller the closer we get to it (see Figure 3.7b). **H15** suggests using the amount of host at the end of the simulation, but we have found through random testing that this does not work because the asymptote has yet to be reached. One way to determine the amount of host there should be in the S compartment when $t = \infty$ is

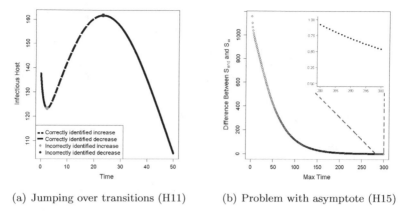

(a) Jumping over transitions (H11)   (b) Problem with asymptote (H15)

Figure 3.7: Unexpected complexities of the implementation.

with Lambert's W, a special function which finds solutions to equations of the form $xe^x = z$. We can rearrange the equation in **H15** to use Lambert's W as follows: $S_\infty = -\frac{1}{R_0}W(-R_0 S_0 e^{-R_0 N})$, where $R_0 = \beta/\mu$.

Although this allows us to determine the asymptote of the model mathematically, we are still not able to run the simulation long enough to reach this value. For example Figure 3.7b ($I_0 = 164$, $\beta = 3.56 \times 10^{-4}$, $\gamma = 0.055$, $\mu = 0.443$) shows that the amount of host in S is still decreasing after 300 time periods. We could check the gradient and the gradient of the gradient of the S curve, so as to predict where the asymptote will take place. However, this approach will never be completely accurate. We therefore need to consider ways to evaluate whether the value we have observed (or estimated) from the simulation is sufficiently close to the value we expect from the equation.

3.4.4.3 Issues Related to Numerical Precision

We need some way to account for output values from the simulation not being exactly the same as those we would expect from the model. Floating point numbers are represented on a computer using a binary encoded exponent and mantissa. The size of the exponent determines the range of numbers that can be represented and the size of the mantissa determines their precision. Many hypotheses fail because the limitations of numerical precision make it impossible to evaluate the outputs exactly. One way to address this is to introduce a tolerance threshold. Rather than checking if a value is the same as expected, we can check if it is within some range of tolerance.

Figure 3.8 shows the effect of changing the tolerance threshold on two hypotheses (**H1** and **H2**). When the threshold is set to zero (i.e. only exact comparisons are allowed), the hypotheses fail for almost every run (95/100 for **H1** and 100/100 for **H2**). However, as the threshold is increased, the hypotheses hold more and more frequently, until at some point they almost never fail. For **H1** (none of the compartments contain a negative amount of

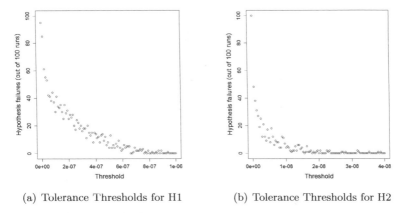

(a) Tolerance Thresholds for H1   (b) Tolerance Thresholds for H2

Figure 3.8: The effect of tolerance thresholds.

host), this occurs when the threshold is around 1×10^{-6} (see Figure 3.8a); for **H2** (the sum of hosts does not differ from the initial total), it occurs when the threshold is around 2×10^{-8} (see Figure 3.8b).

It can be difficult to set the threshold appropriately in advance, since the optimum value depends upon the hypothesis being tested. However, we discovered numerical error in **H1** is dominated by a stopping condition in the solver (by default, at no more than 1×10^{-6} from the correct value). The optimum threshold for **H2** appears to be smaller than **H1**, because adding up the compartments cancels out some of the error. Yet, in the worst case, these errors accumulate instead of cancelling out. Error in the mathematical derivations is dominated by the use of numerical operations whose results cannot be represented precisely by the data type. Experimentation is required to choose an appropriate tolerance threshold for the various interacting sources of error, but a better understanding of these errors helps us test our hypotheses.

There are also some issues due to the way in which the equation for I_t in **H14** is written. When γ and t are big, and μ is small, the term $e^{t(\gamma-\mu)}$ will evaluate to infinity (as it is outside the range of representable numbers). Subsequently, when multiplied by $e^{-\gamma t}$ (which evaluates to zero due to the limits of precision), the result is NaN (not a number) for many time steps. This problem can be avoided by separating out the $e^{-\mu t}$ and $e^{-\gamma t}$ terms such that they go to zero rather than infinity when the exponents become large: $I_t = \frac{E_0 \gamma (e^{-\mu t} - e^{-\gamma t}) + I_0 (\gamma - \mu) e^{-\mu t}}{\gamma - \mu}$. A special case must also be constructed for $\gamma = \mu$, to avoid problems due to division by zero.

3.4.5   Summary

Iterative hypothesis testing is easy for scientists to use because it is modelled on the scientific method. It found discrepancies in all but one of the hypotheses we tested (**H4**) and the information generated can be used to refine them (see below). In addition to testing the software, iterative hypothesis testing allows scientists to understand their software more thoroughly and the resulting tests are helpful for communicating the way in which it works. However, the refined hypotheses are not guaranteed to be perfect. It may be possible under some specific input condition that they will still fail.

1. Scientists are familiar with the idea behind iterative hypothesis testing

2. We reinterpret testing this way to make it more accessible to scientists

3. It constructs rigorous tests, even starting with imperfect information

Refined Hypotheses:-

H1: **None of the compartments should ever contain a negative amount of host** (allowing for a suitable tolerance threshold)

H2: **The total amount of host should not differ at each time step** (allowing for a suitable tolerance threshold)

H3: **The amount of susceptible host (S) should never increase** (allowing for a suitable tolerance threshold)

H4: **The amount of removed host (R) should never decrease**

H5: **The exposed host (E) peak should not occur after the infectious host (I) peak** (unless I is monotonically decreasing)

H6: **Increasing the infection rate (β) should increase the peak of E** (unless S is equal to zero, allowing for a suitable tolerance threshold)

H7: **Increasing the latent rate (γ) should reduce the time until the peak of I** (unless I is monotonically decreasing)

H8: **Increasing μ should increase the final amount of host in S** (unless β is equal to zero, allowing for a suitable tolerance threshold)

H9: **Increasing β should decrease the final amount of host in S** (unless S or I is equal to zero, allowing for a suitable tolerance threshold)

H10: **Increasing the number of susceptible host (S_0) should increase the peak of I** (unless I is equal to zero and also check AUC)

H11: I **should be increasing when $\gamma E > \mu I$, otherwise it should be decreasing** (except for points at which the direction of I transitions)

H12: **If $I = E = 0$, the state of the model should not change** (allowing for a suitable tolerance threshold)

H13: **Exact analytical solutions are available when $\gamma = 0$** (allowing for a suitable tolerance threshold)

H14: **Exact analytical solutions are available when $\beta = 0$** (rearrange analytical solution and allow suitable tolerance threshold)

H15: A final size equation can determine the value of S when $t = \infty$
(use Lambert's W to calculate the asymptote and the gradient of the gradient from the actual run, allowing for a suitable tolerance threshold)

3.5   Testing Stochastic Software Using Pseudo-Oracles

In addition to the challenges faced when testing deterministic scientific software, there are further difficulties involved with software that is stochastic. Since the output changes according to the random seed, we need to check the distribution of outputs produced over multiple executions with different seeds. It is likely that the distribution of outputs for a faulty program will overlap with those for the correct program, so we need some way of distinguishing between these distributions. This section introduces a technique to test stochastic scientific software using search-based optimization to maximize the differences in output between a pseudo-oracle and the software under test.

Pseudo-oracles are used to test software for which no oracle is available, either because it is too difficult to determine what the correct output should be, or because an oracle is impossible to produce [154]. Although pseudo-oracles can also be used to test deterministic software, they are particularly well suited to the problems of stochastic software: their complexity makes predicting what the output should be extremely arduous and it is not possible to identify any one correct result (there is a distribution of potentially correct results). Pseudo-oracles address these problems by circumventing the need to specify the correct output [154]. Instead, they look for discrepancies in the outputs of multiple independent implementations of the software. Although this does not immediately indicate which (if any) implementations are incorrect, it provides a suitable starting point to begin looking for faults in the code.

The motivation behind pseudo-oracles originates from a common-sense policy towards fault tolerance. If we are worried what would happen in the event that the information we are using is incorrect, we should compare it against other sources of information, preferably derived using different techniques. For example, the HMS Beagle carried 22 chronometers [151], produced by different manufacturers, to ensure accurate longitudinal positioning of the lands they were surveying, even if some of the chronometers failed or were damaged on the journey. Pseudo-oracles also compare information from different sources, but rather than doing this for fault tolerance reasons, they use the information to find faults. Pseudo-oracles therefore apply an old and well-established strategy to the more recent problem of testing complex software.

The implementations do not need to have been developed for exactly the same purpose and it is not a problem for there to be some differences between them, as long as they can be parametrized and/or restricted to behave in

Software Engineering for Science

the same way. As we have seen earlier, computational modellers often start by building software that has already been developed, before extending it for their new research. This provides an opportunity in that there are often multiple implementations of a basic model available. By widening the differences between these implementations using search, we can identify the worst case disagreements, use statistical analyses to assess whether they are significant and find software faults more easily amongst the other sources of error.

3.5.1 The Huánglóngbìng SECI Model

We compare two implementations of a stochastic model for the spread of Huánglóngbìng (HLB), a plant disease also known as citrus greening [119]. Stochastic models are often used to help researchers understand epidemics (e.g. estimate which source of infection is likely to be contributing the most new cases) and to make predictions (e.g. estimate the total number of cases that will result from an epidemic, or the possible impact of vaccination). Stochastic models have been widely applied to many other diseases (such as foot-and-mouth disease [137] and Ebola [127]). However, in this case we have decided to apply our technique to HLB because both the Epidemiology & Modelling Group and the Theoretical & Computational Epidemiology group have produced implementations of a stochastic model for this disease.

HLB is caused by bacteria of the genus *Candidatus Liberibacter* and is spread by Asian and African citrus psyllids. It is characterized by yellow shoots, stunted tree growth and misshaped fruit that stays green on the underside. HLB is considered to be the most destructive disease of citrus in the world, leading to reductions in yield between 30% and 100% [128]. It is therefore highly important to both research and industry that implementations of HLB models are correct. However, even if the implementations themselves contain no faults, we need to make sure they are used correctly. We will therefore illustrate how our technique can be used to help someone, using these implementations for the first time, understand the assumptions and outputs of each implementation so that they can interpret the results correctly.

As with the previous *SEIR* model, the model for HLB tracks the number of hosts (i.e. trees) through several exclusive compartments. It is an *SECI* model (see Figure 3.9). This means it includes the following compartments: *Susceptible* (not infected), *Exposed* (infected but neither infectious nor showing symptoms), *Cryptic* (infectious but not showing symptoms) and *Infectious* (infectious and showing symptoms). There is also an implicit *Removed (R)* compartment, into which trees enter when they die, but since we are modelling the disease over a sufficiently short period of time and all the hosts start in the Susceptible compartment, this is not included.

Within the basic structure of an *SECI* model, there are many different options to choose from: the model may be continuous or discrete (in time and/or the numbers of hosts in each compartment); it may incorporate explicit spatial heterogeneity or assume the law of mass action can be applied.

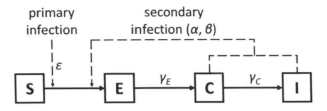

Figure 3.9: Model schematic for HLB.

The rates at which hosts move between compartments in the model depend upon the choice of parameters (α, β, ϵ, γ_E and γ_C) and the number of hosts already in each compartment (notably, the number of cryptic and infectious hosts). The HLB model used in this chapter is a continuous-time discrete-host spatially-explicit stochastic model. The values of γ_E and γ_C are fixed, but α, β, ϵ can be adjusted by our search-based optimization technique.

When there are no cryptic or infectious trees, the amount of time before a given susceptible tree moves to the exposed compartment is exponentially distributed with rate parameter ϵ. This process reflects infectious material coming from outside the citrus grove, and is termed 'primary infection'. The time spent in the exposed and cryptic compartments are also exponentially distributed, with rate parameters γ_E and γ_C respectively. The number of cryptic and infectious trees increases the rate at which susceptible trees become infected ('secondary infection'). The rate at which a susceptible host i becomes infected at time t when there are some number of cryptic and/or infectious trees is given in Equation 3.2.

$$\phi_i(t) = \epsilon + \frac{\beta}{\alpha^2} \sum_j k\left(\frac{r_{ji}}{\alpha}\right), \tag{3.2}$$

The summation in the above equation is restricted to trees j that are cryptic or infectious. Therefore, when there are no cryptic or infectious trees, this equation reduces to the primary infection term ϵ. The value of r_{ji} is the distance between a cryptic or infectious tree j and a susceptible tree i. The 'dispersal kernel' k determines the probability that HLB will spread over a certain distance; it is given by the equation $k(u) = exp(-u)$. β is the rate of secondary infection and α is a scaling parameter.

We compare two implementations of the HLB disease model: one developed by Parry et al. [146] (which we label M1) and one developed by Cunniffe et al. [123] (M2). M1's parameters were estimated using data from a commercial citrus plantation in Florida, USA, which had been surveyed for disease between 2005 and 2007. M2 is presented in a more general study of optimal culling strategies to combat plant disease[2]. M1 is implemented in C++, and

---

[2]M2 [123] also contains a case study of HLB, but with different parameters. To ensure the models are the same, we use the parameters given in M1 [146].

M2 in C. Program codes were obtained from their authors. We made minor changes to M1 to make it theoretically identical to M2[3].

3.5.2 Searching for Differences

Pseudo-oracles provide a mechanism for determining whether there are differences between various implementations of a model, given a suitable set of test cases. In the previous section, we used random testing to generate the test cases we used. However, we also saw that this can be inefficient when discrepancies only appear for a specific range or set of input values. Since we are now working with stochastic models, it is possible to calculate the probability that the difference is significant (i.e. it is no longer all or nothing). It might be possible to learn from this information so as to maximize the differences between the implementations. In this section, we investigate a new technique to maximize these differences using search-based optimization.

To maximize the differences between the implementations, we need suitable metrics to characterize the size of each difference. Stochastic models have to be run a number of times to combat their uncertainty. Maximizing the difference of the means of these runs might be the simplest approach, but it ignores the potentially large error due to stochasticity. It is also not feasible to compare every possible pair of outputs, as this would require too many comparisons. We therefore collect statistics to characterize the outputs of each implementation individually, then we maximize the differences between these statistics.

The HLB model outputs a time series for each of its compartments (S, E, C and I). For series that are monotonically increasing or decreasing, we can characterize each run by the area under the curve (AUC). However, depending upon the parameters chosen, the number of hosts in each compartment might initially increase and then decrease. One way to account for this is to fit a parametrized distribution to the data [143]. However, it is difficult to assume a particular distribution, as the time series will vary significantly when the model parameters are adjusted. We therefore record for each compartment the peak number of hosts and the time at which this peak is reached.

Now we have statistics (AUC, peak time, peak hosts) to characterize each run, we can perform a statistical analysis to determine whether the output of each implementation is the same. We do this using the Kolmogorov–Smirnov test [140], a nonparametric test for the equality of two probability distributions. The p-value for each test is included in our objective function (see Equation 3.3). We also test that the total number of hosts (over all the time steps for every compartment) is the same between each implementation.

We use the minimum of the p-values as an objective function to minimize, because we want to maximize at least one of the differences between the outputs. p-values represent the probability of obtaining a result equal to or

---

[3]There are several options in M1 for the amount of time a host spends in the Exposed compartment; for consistency with M2, we set the amount of time to be distributed according to an exponential distribution.

"more extreme" than what was actually observed. Since we are comparing the outputs of two different implementations, the smaller the p-value for a particular statistic, the more confident we can be that the values of that statistic differ from one implementation to the other. By taking the minimum of the p-values for multiple statistics, we aim to make at least one of the p-values as small as possible. This allows our optimizer to make at least one of the differences in outputs between implementations as large as possible.

$$
f = min \left(min_{c \in \{S,E,C\}} \left(\begin{array}{c} p(\text{peak\_hosts}_{c,i}, \text{peak\_hosts}_{c,j}) \\ p(\text{peak\_time}_{c,i}, \text{peak\_time}_{c,j}) \\ p(\text{AUC}_{c,i}, \text{AUC}_{c,j}) \\ p(\text{total\_hosts}_{c,i}, \text{total\_hosts}_{c,j}) \end{array} \right) \right) \quad (3.3)
$$

(c is the model compartment, i and j are the implementations, $p(x, y)$ is the p-value of the Kolmogorov–Smirnov test for x and y)

It is important the optimization technique we use is sufficiently robust to cope with stochastic noise. Covariance Matrix Adaptation Evolution Strategy (CMA-ES) [130] is a population-based technique, so does not get stuck in a local optimum as often as other techniques (e.g., 1+1-ES). CMA-ES adapts the search distribution at the same time as the candidate solutions, to locate the global optimum more efficiently. It can solve difficult optimization problems (including non-linear fitness landscapes) without manual parameter tuning. In a recent black-box comparison study with 25 benchmark functions, CMA-ES outperformed other optimization algorithms in terms of the number of function evaluations before the global optimum value was reached [132].

Evolution strategies differ from some genetic algorithms in that they optimize numerical values rather than bit strings and focus on mutation over recombination [153]. Evolution strategies optimize numerical values through Gaussian adaptation. Gaussian adaptation is a suitable mechanism for generating new candidate solutions because it favors values close to the old ones, but still allows exploration of values further away. CMA-ES represents the search neighborhood using a multivariate Gaussian distribution [130]. Compared with the univariate approach, multiple dimensions of variance allow the search to adapt more precisely to the underlying fitness landscape. A covariance matrix is used to represent the shape of the distribution and a scaling factor to represent its size. CMA-ES adjusts the size and shape of the distribution according to pairwise dependencies in the covariance matrix [130].

Algorithm 1 describes how model parameters α, β and ϵ are optimized, starting with an initial mean $\bar{\alpha}, \bar{\beta}, \bar{\epsilon}$ and standard deviation σ. As per the advice of Hansen [131], we scale parameters to the range $[0, 10]$, with initial mean 5 and $\sigma = 2$. We also specify the number of new parameter sets to generate at each iteration λ and how many times to run each set on each implementation n. The covariance matrix cov is initially set to the identity matrix, as we do not presume any prior relationships. However, this is automatically updated (along with the means and standard deviation), to maximize the likelihood of previously successful search steps and candidate solutions. We generate time series t_1 and t_2 from model implementations $M1$ and $M2$, then characterize them using the peak hosts ph, peak time pt and area under the curve auc statistics, along with the total number of hosts th.

3.5.3　Experimental Methodology

We identified differences between the two implementations of the *SECI* HLB model by applying search-based optimization to minimize the p-values for the Kolmogorov–Smirnov tests of various statistics (AUC, peak time, peak hosts and total hosts). In other words, we maximized the differences between the distribution of time series for each implementation. We performed experiments on a landscape of 2000 hosts, spatially distributed to represent part of a commercial plantation in Florida (the dataset used by M1 [146]). This therefore represents a real-world test of our optimization technique.

We allowed our search-based optimization technique 40 iterations in each trial and we ran 50 trials in total. This number of iterations was chosen because we found that on average this meant that each trial took approximately one hour on the desktop computer we used to perform the experiments (Intel Core i7, 8GB of memory). We consider this a reasonable amount of time for a computational modeller to wait for the results. Each test case (set of input parameters) is run 100 times to address stochasticity. Test cases are generated within the range [0,20] for α, [0,100] for β and [0,0.1] for ϵ, in line with those used by [146]. We then used the results of our tests to identify statistically differences in the time series output by the two implementations (M1 and M2). This information was used as a guide to help us inspect the code for the reasons behind these differences in output behavior.

Although the differences identified by our technique cannot be considered a measure of test coverage, they serve as case studies for the ways in which our technique can be used. If conditions are the same (i.e. same programs, same coverage metric), test coverage could be used to compare techniques. However, since the programs under test in this chapter are highly specialized, and there are unlikely to be any other publications on testing them, we felt it would be more helpful to the reader to present them as case studies.

3.5.4　Differences Discovered

We ran our search-based technique 50 times and investigated the reasons for the significant differences we observed in the output of M1 and M2. Each time we found the cause of a difference, we modified the code to make M1 and M2 give the same result. In many cases, we believe the differences we found were linked to the same cause because when we changed the code these differences disappeared. Details are provided of four unique differences we identified between M1 and M2, which we believe to have been the cause of

---

Algorithm 1 Optimizing model parameters (α, β, ϵ)

Input: $\bar{\alpha}, \bar{\beta}, \bar{\epsilon}, \sigma, \lambda, n$

1: **repeat**
2:     $cov \leftarrow$ identity matrix
3:     $f \leftarrow \{\}$
4:     **for** $i \in \{1 \ldots \lambda\}$ **do**
5:        $(\alpha_i, \beta_i, \epsilon_i) \leftarrow \mathcal{N}((\bar{\alpha}, \bar{\beta}, \bar{\epsilon}), \sigma^2 cov)$
6:        $\{s_{\{S,E,C\} \times \{ph,pt,auc\},th}\} \leftarrow \{\}$
7:        **for** $j \in \{1 \ldots n\}$ **do**
8:           $t_1 \leftarrow M1(\alpha_i, \beta_i, \epsilon_i)$
9:           $t_2 \leftarrow M2(\alpha_i, \beta_i, \epsilon_i)$
10:          **for** $k \in \{S, E, C\}$ **do**
11:             $s_{k,ph}.append(max(t_{1,k}), max(t_{2,k}))$
12:             $s_{k,pt}.append(argmax(t_{1,k}), argmax(t_{2,k}))$
13:             $s_{k,auc}.append(sum(t_{1,k}), sum(t_{2,k}))$
14:          **end for**
15:          $s_{th}.append(\sum_{k \in \{S,E,C,I\}} sum(t_{1,k}),$
                          $\sum_{k \in \{S,E,C,I\}} sum(t_{2,k}))$
16:        **end for**
17:        $f.append(min(ks\_test(\{s_{\{S,E,C\} \times \{ph,pt,auc\},th}\})))$
18:     **end for**
19:     **sort** $\{\alpha_i, \beta_i, \epsilon_i\}$ with respect to $\{f_i\}$
20:     **update** $\bar{\alpha}, \bar{\beta}, \bar{\epsilon}, \sigma$ and cov
21. **until** stopping condition met

---

the differences in output we observed. The parameter values used to find these differences are shown in Table 3.1 and the p-values of the Kolmogorov–Smirnov test on 100 time series for each difference are shown in Table 3.2.

While M1 and M2 should behave identically in theory, running the same simulations on both was in practice complicated by each model having different additional features, parameterization, and input/output formats. We emphasize the differences described below do not invalidate the results or conclusions of [146] or [123]. Rather, they highlight that two theoretically

Table 3.1: Model Parameters Used to Find Differences

Parameter	Difference			
	1	*2*	*3*	*4*
α	11.801	18.087	7.270	2.139
β	31.744	998.182	449.415	179.576
ϵ	0.013	0.090	0.086	5.124×10^{-6}

Table 3.2: p-Values Used to Find Differences

Statistic	Difference			
	1	*2*	*3*	*4*
AUC_S	0.013	5.112×10^{-33}	0.961	1.888×10^{-5}
AUC_E	0.677	5.774×10^{-37}	0.193	0.675
AUC_C	0.556	1.212×10^{-7}	0.443	1.000
PT_S	1.000	1.000	1.000	1.000
PT_E	0.047	5.113×10^{-33}	0.894	0.675
PT_C	0.961	1.317×10^{-38}	0.677	1.000
PH_S	1.000	1.000	1.551×10^{-45}	1.000
PH_E	0.140	3.963×10^{-16}	0.961	0.675
PH_C	0.099	5.335×10^{-42}	0.677	1.000
TH_{All}	1.000	1.000	1.000	0.006

identical models can be implemented in slightly different ways, and show the challenges involved in using two different implementations to simulate the same system.

1) *Start time/age category.* Among the features of M1 not in M2 were the starting time and age categories. The rate at which trees move from the Exposed compartment to the Cryptic compartment depends on their age (i.e. γ_E is different). The time at which the epidemic starts is given by t_0; before t_0, ϵ is effectively 0, so none of the trees become infected. We presumed the starting time was not relevant for our purposes, so we set $t_0 = 0$. However, we discovered that as well as controlling the starting time, t_0 also affects the age category, thus impacting the rate at which HLB spreads.

Age categories do not exist in M2, so M1 and M2 had different values for γ_E until trees were old enough to change category. The differences can be seen in Figure 3.10a and 3.10b. Notably, the Exposed curve reaches its peak earlier for M1 than M2. This is because younger trees move from Exposed to Cryptic more quickly. It also affects the time the cryptic curve reaches its peak and feeds back through secondary infection to the Susceptible compartment. The difference was picked up[4] by the Kolmogorov–Smirnov test (see Table 3.2) in the time of the exposed peak (PT_E) and area under the susceptible curve (AUC_S). We resolved this issue by setting $t_0 = 1$.

2) *Distribution of time spent in Cryptic compartment.* In M2, the time spent in the cryptic compartment is exponentially distributed (as is common for disease models), but we discovered it is gamma distributed in M1. Even when M1 and M2 had identical means, the distributions were different, so the time series were not the same (see Figure 3.10c and 3.10d). The most obvious difference is that in M1, the cryptic curve rises further ahead of the Infectious

---

[4]Significance is determined at the 95% confidence interval.

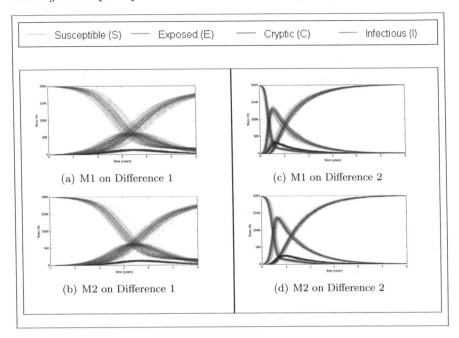

Figure 3.10: Two differences identified between M1 and M2.

curve than in M2. Our technique made this difference more prominent by maximizing β (see Table 3.1).

This was the largest difference we observed between M1 and M2. The Kolmogorov–Smirnov test (see Table 3.2) identified a significant[4] difference in all of the statistics, apart from the susceptible peak and the total hosts, which should not change under any circumstances. We removed this difference by modifying the code of M1 to use an exponential distribution.

3) *Initial number of Susceptibles.* We started all the simulations with 2000 Susceptible hosts, so the peak of the susceptible curve should not change. However, the Kolmogorov–Smirnov test (see Table 3.2) showed this value was significantly[4] different between M1 and M2. Upon closer inspection, we found the initial number of Susceptible hosts in M1 was 1999. This was caused by a mistake in the mechanism we created to make the output formats of M1 and M2 the same. The state *after* the first transition from susceptible to exposed was being copied back, instead of the state *before* being used.

4) *Modified output/truncation.* For extremely low values of ϵ (see Table 3.1), there are sometimes simulations in which no infections occur. In the modified output for M1, these resulted in a single-line output comprising only the initial state (with all hosts susceptible). It was expected to contain the state at subsequent times as well, but these were not produced. This difference was found by the Kolmogorov–Smirnov test (see Table 3.2) in the area under the susceptible curve when ϵ was equal to 5.124×10^{-6}.

Table 3.3: Comparison of Areas under p-Value Progress Curves for the Search-Based Technique and Random Testing (significant results are in **bold**)

Statistic	K-S Distance	p-Value	Effect Size
AUC for Susceptible (AUC_S)	0.22	0.1786	0.130
AUC Exposed (AUC_E)	0.16	0.5487	0.017
AUC for Cryptic (AUC_C)	**0.36**	**0.002835**	**0.391**
Peak Hosts for Susceptible (PH_S)	0	1	NA
Peak Hosts for Exposed (PH_E)	**0.26**	**0.06779**	**0.211**
Peak Hosts for Cryptic (PH_C)	0.22	0.1786	0.130
Peak Time for Susceptible (PT_S)	0	1	NA
Peak Time for Exposed (PT_E)	**0.34**	**0.005842**	**0.357**
Peak Time for Cryptic (PT_C)	**0.32**	**0.01151**	**0.321**
Total Hosts for All (TH_{All})	**0.36**	**0.003068**	**0.388**

3.5.5   Comparison with Random Testing

We evaluate the effectiveness of our search-based technique by comparing its progress with that of random testing, using the same number of test cases to make the comparisons fair. Table 3.3 and 3.4 indicate the search-based technique to be slightly faster at achieving low p-values for most statistics, with the obvious exception of total hosts. We think this is because the p-value for total hosts is never lowest, so our technique does not try to minimize it. Minimizing other p-values may increase the p-value of total hosts, but this is unimportant as its p-value is never small enough to be significant[4].

To statistically compare the two techniques, we applied a Kolmogorov–Smirnov test to the area under each of the p-value progress curves (see Table 3.3). The differences were significant[4] for the Cryptic (AUC and peak time)

Table 3.4: Comparison of p-Values Achieved after 1 Hour for the Search-Based Technique and Random Testing (significant results are in **bold**)

Statistic	Median		Standard Deviation		Wilcoxon Test	
	Optimized	Random	Optimized	Random	p-Value	Effect Size
AUC_S	0.0030	0.0030	0.0041	0.0079	0.2176	0.1755
AUC_E	0.0014	0.0024	0.0037	0.0051	0.5603	0.0834
AUC_C	0.0030	0.0050	0.0045	0.0046	0.1354	0.2120
PH_S	1	1	0	0	NA	NA
PH_E	0.0082	0.0082	0.0101	0.0103	0.1437	0.2077
PH_C	**0.0050**	**0.0082**	**0.0073**	**0.00854**	**0.01275**	**0.3491**
PT_S	1	1	0	0	NA	NA
PT_E	0.0030	0.0050	0.0043	0.0037	0.2592	0.1607
PT_C	0.0050	0.0050	0.0057	0.0087	0.07965	0.2482
TH_{All}	**0.7942**	**0.5560**	**0.2919**	**0.2551**	**0.002483**	**0.4201**

and Exposed (peak hosts and peak time) compartments, in addition to the total hosts statistic. The effect sizes[5] are considered to be small to medium, since they are mostly between 0.2 and 0.5 [152]. We also applied a Wilcoxon signed rank test (see Table 3.4) to the final p-values achieved by each technique. Only the peak hosts in the cryptic compartment and the total hosts are significantly different[4]; the effect sizes[5] for these tests are also not large.

3.5.6   Summary

Stochastic software is difficult to test because the distribution of output values may overlap even when the programs are different. We can use search-based optimization and statistical (Kolmogorov–Smirnov) tests to find input parameters for which the outputs of the implementations differ the most. Using this technique, we were able to identify and remove four previously unknown differences related to the way in which the implementations were used by a third party that could have a significant impact on the results. The technique presented in this section makes the causes of the differences more readily identified, increases the speed at which software may be tested and allows differences to be observed that might otherwise have been overlooked.

1. Our technique tests stochastic software with pseudo-oracles

2. Pseudo-oracles may be used when the correct outputs are unclear

3. It helped a scientist understand the implementation decisions of a model

3.6   Conclusions

In this chapter, we explored three case studies of scientific software development in different research groups in the Department of Plant Sciences in the University of Cambridge (the Epidemiology and Modelling group, the Theoretical and Computational Epidemiology group and the Bioinformatics group). We then presented two new techniques (iterative hypothesis testing and search-based pseudo-oracles) that help to make it easier for these researchers to understand, test and communicate their scientific software.

Scientific software is difficult to test because it is not always clear what the correct outputs should be; scientists' perceptions change as they are exploring the results. There are also challenges from big data, stochastic processes and mathematical assumptions. Yet the results are important, as (for the groups we investigated) they are used to inform government policy decisions and act

---

[5] Two-sample Cohen's d effect sizes calculated using $d = Z\sqrt{\frac{1}{n_1} + \frac{1}{n_2}}$.

as a starting point for future research. We need to make sure, not only that the software is correct, but that the researchers fully understand how it works and communicate this information to other people who will use the software.

The group members we surveyed were not trained in software engineering techniques and they tended not to test their programs methodically. Part of the reason is because they could not see how traditional software engineering techniques applied to their work and they were worried it would take too much time away from their research. However, some group members were using their intuition to discover for themselves techniques which are similar to those recommended in software engineering. It therefore makes sense to engage these researchers from their perspective. This is why we introduced two techniques that correspond well with the scientific research method.

Iterative hypothesis testing allows researchers to understand the behavior of their software in more detail. It does this by automatically finding situations that challenge their initial perceptions. It found discrepancies in all but one of our initial hypotheses and the information generated was used to produce a refined set that reflects a new understanding of the software. Our search-based pseudo-oracle technique allows researchers to identify differences between highly complex implementations, that are difficult to tell apart due to their stochastic nature. This makes it possible to understand intricate details that might otherwise be overlooked. Using this technique, we identified and removed four differences related to the way in which the implementations were used by a third party that could significantly affect the results.

An increasing number of researchers are using and developing scientific software because of its benefits in scale, speed and economy. The majority of this software will be developed by scientists rather than software engineers, so it is important they are equipped with tools suitable for them. The techniques described in this chapter are applicable to a wide range of scientific software and computational models. They work in a way scientists understand.

3.7 Acknowledgments

This work was supported by the University of Cambridge/ Wellcome Trust Junior Interdisciplinary Fellowship "Making scientific software easier to understand, test and communicate through modern advances in software engineering." We thank Andrew Craig, Richard Stutt, James Elderfield, Nik Cunniffe, Matthew Parry, Andrew Rice and Chris Gilligan for their helpful advice and useful discussions.

This work is based on an earlier work: Software Testing in a Scientific Research Group, in Proc. ACM Symposium on Applied Computing, 2016 [in press]

Chapter 4

Testing of Scientific Software: Impacts on Research Credibility, Development Productivity, Maturation, and Sustainability

Roscoe A. Bartlett, Anshu Dubey, Xiaoye Sherry Li, J. David Moulton, James M. Willenbring, and Ulrike Meier Yang

4.1   Introduction

High quality scientific software has always required extensive testing to be a reliable tool for scientists. Good testing practices have become even more important today, since software projects are facing significant refactoring efforts due to increased demands for multiphysics and multiscale coupling, as well as significant computer architecture changes, especially with a view towards exascale computing. Regular, extensive testing of software is very important for many reasons, because it:

- Promotes high-quality software that delivers correct results and improves confidence in the software;

- Increases the quality and speed of development, thereby reducing development and maintenance costs;

- Maintains portability to a wide variety of (ever changing) systems and compilers; and

- Facilitates refactoring and the addition of new features into library code without unknowingly introducing new errors, or reintroducing old errors

The focus of software for computational science and engineering (CSE) is often on the immediate need for new scientific results, which may be in the form of new algorithms, improved implementations, or domain-science knowledge and understanding. A common tendency is to assume that the code will have a short life-cycle. In reality, even software in a research environment often has a long life-cycle because successive rounds of users take over the code and build upon existing capabilities. For software that continues to be maintained and extended, it has been shown that the creation and development of strong automated tests, particularly at an early stage, is far superior, i.e., faster and cheaper, than using few or no automated tests, manual testing, reliance on user bug reports, etc [177]. Automated testing leads to overall better quality software. So, in the long term or even shorter term, a project cannot afford to **not** create and maintain strong automated tests!

Despite the cost savings that can be achieved by creating and maintaining strong automated tests, there are various reasons that prevent projects from creating such test suites. They often don't have enough resources to gain the knowledge and skills needed to develop strong automated tests, since funding is generally geared towards science and less towards the writing of high quality software. However, even for short-lived research codes, such tests are needed to ensure correct science research results, since scientific software with unrecognized faults can generate wrong research results misleading whole research communities; see Section 4.3.1 and [178]. This chapter not only investigates the multitude of reasons why software testing is so important but also provides some information on how to perform it (and provides references to more detailed sources of information). While much of the information can also be applied to general scientific software, there is particular focus on software challenges pertaining to mathematical and physical models, which are part of many scientific and engineering codes. The chapter does not address all software challenges for all CSE domains. A large amount of its content is based on the authors' experiences.

Often research teams are not aware of tools that facilitate better testing or do not have the software skills to use them accurately or efficiently, and gaining the knowledge and skills requires a non-trivial investment. In some cases they might not even have access to computing resources that would allow them to perform regular automated testing. Consequently, code testing requirements and practices vary greatly among projects, going from none to excellent. To some extent they depend upon the size and visibility of the software. Among the worst offenders are codes developed by individuals or very small teams in science domains where the only users are internal. The best managed and tested codes are the ones that have regular public releases and are therefore subject to external scrutiny. Even within well tested codes there is some variability in the types (see Section 4.2) and extent of testing. Many scientific codes are under constant development. Some of the development relates to new features or capabilities, and some relates to bug-fixing. Specific to scientific codes, a lot of development also relates to improvements in algorithms and features because of new research findings. A desirable testing cycle for large multiphysics projects, which have the most stringent requirements, would have the elements described in this section. Testing for many other projects will be some proper subset of these practices. Ongoing maintenance of CSE codes relics upon regular, preferably daily, automated building and testing. Here, the test suites aim to provide comprehensive coverage for existing features. The developers monitor the outcome and strive to fix any failures promptly. The same testing regime is applicable to minor feature additions or modifications, and bug fixes. With a bug report after release, it may be necessary to modify some of the tests. Larger feature additions or modifications may involve the addition of new tests, or tweaking already existing tests (see Section 4.6.1). Prior to a public release codes should undergo comprehensive testing which includes regression tests and possibly acceptance tests required by the users.

New capability development in CSE codes has its own testing requirements. This is where the research component of software becomes the dominant determinant of the kind of tests. Some of these tests do not fall under any of the general categories applicable to other software. For example numerical algorithms have to be verified for validity of range, stability and numerical accuracy. They also have to be tested for the order of convergence. All of these tests are applied along with the general verification tests as the algorithm is developed. Once the algorithm is verified to perform as expected, a similar set of tests may need to be applied during the integration phase. This is because interaction between different numerical components or physical regimes in the application may give rise to defects of stability or order which is not demonstrated by the components individually. Additionally, if the software is targeted for high performance computing (HPC) platforms, it may need to include scalability and portability tests.

In the following sections, we look at the concepts mentioned above in more detail. In Section 4.2, we define the testing terminology used here, since the understanding of certain terms can vary. Section 4.3 describes who the stakeholders are, the team roles of a successful CSE software project and what pitfalls to avoid to be successful. Section 4.4 discusses the importance of automated testing in research, development productivity and software maturity and sustainability, including the dangers to insufficient testing. Section 4.5 focuses on CSE specific challenges in testing, including floating point computations, scalability testing and model testing. Testing practices based on the authors' experiences are discussed in Section 4.6 including details on how to add tests to CSE codes, how to maintain a test suite, an example of a test suite, the benefit of test harnesses, and some policies that have been shown to be useful. Section 4.7 concludes the chapter.

4.2 Testing Terminology

Commonly, CSE software projects use varying terminology to describe the tests for their project. They may also consider only type or granularity, but not both. Tests can be categorized by their granularity and type. Granularity captures the scope of code being tested, and type categorizes the metrics for evaluating correctness. This section provides a common set of definitions and terminology that serve as a baseline for communicating important testing concepts and principles later in this chapter; see also [10].

4.2.1 Granularity of Tests

Having tests at different levels of granularity is valuable for detecting and resolving software defects efficiently. For example, a test failing at the smallest level of granularity points to a small section of code that may contain a defect. Finding the same defect based on a failing test that exercises the entire software system typically will require more effort to pinpoint the issue. Similarly, passing tests at the smallest granularity are valuable information when debugging a failing test at a higher granularity level.

Unit tests are tests at the smallest level of granularity and are focused on testing individual software units such as individual functions or individual classes. They are usually written by code developers before or during code development to detect faults quickly and prevent faults from beinig introduced. By definition, unit tests must build fast, run fast, and localize errors. An example of a unit-level test in a CSE code would be a test for a quadrature rule over a few basic element geometries. This test would pass in points from various known functions and verify whether the results are correct, e.g., a 3rd order quadrature rule should exactly integrate a cubic polynomial.

Integration tests are focused on testing the interaction of larger pieces of software but not at the full system level. Integration tests typically test several objects from different types of classes together and typically do not build and run as fast, or localize errors as well as unit tests. An example of an integration-level test in CSE software would be an element calculation for a specific set of physics over a single element or a small number of elements.

System-level tests are focused on testing the full software system at the user interaction level. For example, a system-level test of a CFD code would involve passing in complete input files and running the full simulation code, and then checking the output and final solutions by some criteria. System-level tests on their own are typically not considered a sufficient foundation to effectively and efficiently drive code development and code refactoring efforts. There are different hierarchies of system-level tests, for example, they could be testing complete single-physics, possibly varying constitutive or sub-scale models, which would be on a lower level than various combinations and scenarios of the complete coupled physics code.

4.2.2 Types of Tests

Distinct from the granularity of a test is the test type. The type reflects the purpose of the test. For example, a test might measure performance, verify that an algorithm is implemented correctly, or ensure that code of particular interest to a specific customer meets the customer's requirements.

Verification tests are inwardly focused tests that verify that the code implements the intended algorithms correctly. These tests check for specific mathematical properties or other clear specifications. For example, a verification test for a linear conjugate gradient solver might check that a small diagonal system with N distinct eigenvalues fully solves the system in exactly N iterations. By just looking at the test specification and the pass/fail criteria, it is clear that the code is meeting a specific requirement or behavior. Verification tests can be written at the unit, integration, or system level.

Acceptance tests are outwardly focused tests that assert acceptable functioning for a specific customer or set of customers. For example, an acceptance test for a linear solver might check the linear solver convergence rates for a particular customer's linear systems. In the CSE domain, **validation tests** are a special class of acceptance tests where formal uncertainty qualification(UQ)-based methods are applied to validate a code against a set of problems for a range of conditions (typically using data from experiments). Acceptance/validation tests are usually applied at the system level.

Acceptance tests are contrasted from the other types of tests defined here in that their focus is on user-level requirements for specific customers of the software. All other types of tests are owned by the software package itself.

No–change tests or **characterization tests** simply compare current observable output from the code to some "gold standard" output, typically produced by a previous version of the software. For CSE numerical codes, examples include comparing the number of iterations and/or the final solution (e.g., on a mesh) to previous outputs for a set of generic test problems. When floating-point computations are involved (see Section 4.5.1), a no–change test necessarily becomes a **bounded–change test** which compares the test output v_1 to a previous gold standard result v_2 but allows for a bounded difference $\text{error}(v_1, v_2) \leq \text{tol}$ using some error norm and a tolerance. Note that the term no–change test may be used to imply a bounded–change test with a non-zero tolerance when floating point computations are involved. If such a test requires a zero error tolerance (i.e., binary compatibility), then it will be noted as such.

The key difference between a no–change test and a verification test is that it is not clear if the code is correct by just looking at the output of a no–change test. One has to independently "verify" the gold standard output.

Performance tests focus on the runtime and resource utilization of the software in question. Examples of performance tests include CPU time, CPU cycles, scalability to larger problem sizes, or more MPI processors, etc. This category of test is largely orthogonal to the previously discussed types, i.e., all verification, validation, and no-change tests can pass but the code can run 10 times slower.

Performance tests described here are specifically designed to measure the performance of a particular piece of code or subsystem as opposed to putting a timer around an existing generic test, or running some analysis tool for memory usage error detection or code coverage. Performance tests can be written at the unit, integration, or system level.

4.2.3   Organization of Tests

Beyond having a set of tests that provides adequate confidence in the code base, it is also highly recommended that a software project adopt policies and tools that organize test subsets logically and assist in test execution and result analysis.

A **regression test suite** is a set of tests that helps to check that a code is not losing capabilities and behaviors that it had in previous versions of the code (i.e., the code is not "regressing"). Any of the above types of tests (i.e., verification, acceptance, no–change, performance) and granularity of tests (i.e., unit, integration, system-level) as well as different types of test analysis/tools can be included in a regression test suite.

A **non-regression test suite** is a set of new tests that are developed to test new functionality, including verification tests and acceptance tests.

A **test harness** is an automated testing framework. It is used to organize and execute tests, and can include all types of tests. It can also aid the analysis of test results. A **unit test harness** provides these capabilities for unit tests only. For more information on test harnesses see Section 4.6.4.

4.2.4 Test Analysis Tools

There are various diagnostic tools that are run on a code using an already defined test suite.

Memory checkers are tools that are used to verify that the software uses memory correctly. They are typically run on software written in unsafe languages like C, C++, and Fortran and check for uninitialized variables, array bound checks, memory leaks, and other memory usage errors. Some memory checkers like Valgrind [183] can be applied after the executables are built, whereas others need to be included at compile time, e.g., Insure++ [173]. It is good testing practice to test all new code for memory issues, and include memory checking with regression testing to catch memory issues early.

Code coverage investigates which lines of code are executed, what logical branches are run, etc. A coverage test tool is run on a given test suite for the software of interest and then the results are displayed for analysis. Its use helps to decide whether additional tests are needed to ensure that a sufficiently large portion of the code is actually tested.

4.3 Stakeholders and Team Roles for CSE Software Testing

This section discusses who the stakeholders are for CSE software testing and what is at stake for them. It introduces the key team roles for effective testing in general and how they apply to CSE codes. It spells out how to have a successful testing strategy and which pitfalls to avoid.

4.3.1 Stakeholders

High quality CSE software testing is crucial for many parties. First of all, domain scientists need correctly operating simulation and analysis tools that can be used to produce reliable scientific results. These results will in turn affect other scientists who use them as a foundation for their research. If software produces wrong results unknown to the scientists and software developers due to insufficient testing, whole research communities can be negatively affected.

An example of such an incident is a case where an array indexing problem that inverted two columns in a protein folding code resulted in incorrect protein structures being published in several papers [178]. When the defect was finally discovered (after several other researchers found inconsistent results), the author retracted five papers containing incorrect results. But the five retracted papers and the damage to the reputation of this particular researcher was not the only negative impact of this defect. Since this researcher was a highly recognized expert in his field, several papers and proposals from competing researchers whose results conflicted with his results had been rejected. Consequently the reputations and careers of other researchers had been damaged as well.

Besides testing for correctness, performance testing is also important, particularly for scientists who want to generate timely solutions to their research problems as well as facility operators who want to optimize productive machine use. Other stakeholders for both correct and efficient CSE software are the agencies who fund these research programs and expect to see correct research results in a timely fashion for the money they are spending. Since CSE software is used in a variety of fields, including biology, medical science, climate science and more, for simulations such as blood flow in the heart, climate change of the planet, etc., software faults leading to incorrect simulation results can have serious consequences.

4.3.2   Key Roles in Effective Testing

Tests come in various granularities as defined in Section 4.2, and the testing needs of different software teams vary. However, all teams - small or large - benefit from adopting appropriate levels of testing. The rational unified process (RUP) for software development [184] defines four testing roles that are generally applicable to many development efforts, however small. Designers define the testing approach and configurations, analysts identify targets of - and ideas behind - the tests, testers implement tests and test suites, and managers are responsible for the mission, motivations and overall quality of testing. The roles are not necessarily assigned individually; a team member can assume different roles at different times or even multiple roles at the same time. This might be especially necessary in a small team of only a few developers, whereas in a large team there might be several people occupying a particular role. Irrespective of the size of the team, a good understanding of these roles helps to clarify the testing needs and scope of the software.

This is particularly true in CSE environments where often individuals simultaneously occupy more than one of these roles. Some of the overlap is out of necessity - there are seldom enough resources available in CSE teams to assign distinct roles to individuals. But a large part of the overlap stems from the nature of the software itself. There are highly specialized code components that need domain and mathematical expertise that is usually not duplicated in the team. The individuals developing a code component are best suited for scoping the target and the design of the test, and are often the best choice for implementing the test. The implementer of the test suite can be distinct from the implementer of tests, with primary responsibility being compilation of tests into the test suite. An effective testing process still needs a manager with an overall vision of the testing goals and motivations. This is especially true where interoperability of components and composability of the software are important. A test suite implementer can often be an effective manager of the testing process for the larger teams with some resources to devote to the software process.

In the context of CSE software, an orthogonal categorization of roles is necessary to fully understand the process: verification and validation tester, performance tester, maintenance tester, and finally, manager. This classification offers a closer reflection of expertise division within the team. Thus verification and validation testers are experts in modeling and numerics with a responsibility for developing and testing the mathematical aspects of the software. A performance tester has the knowledge of the target platform and general high performance computing. A maintenance tester is responsible for the test suite, including running, optimization of resource use, monitoring the state and general health of the test suite. A manager has the overall responsibility for testing which includes coverage, policies, quality of verification and validation, targeted testing for production campaigns etc.

For a successful testing regime it is important for all team members to understand their CSE specific roles defined earlier. Every verification and validation tester will fulfill the roles of designer and analyst with a partial role of tester thrown in. This is because of the research aspects of the software where expertise is tied to the model and the algorithm. Design, scoping and analysis of verification, test results (which include convergence, stability and accuracy tests), all demand expertise in the physical model being implemented. A performance tester covers the roles of analyst and tester where the goal is to define the performance targets and ensure that they are met. The remainder of the tester role is fulfilled by the maintenance tester. This role is of interest to everyone associated with the software development effort, all code developers and users, including external ones, if there are any. The manager's role is similar in both definitions, that of ensuring the quality of testing and coverage, and determining policy and process. This role is important for all developers and users of the code to ensure quality software.

4.3.3   Caveats and Pitfalls

As with any process, each project has to institute its own testing regime based upon its needs and resources. Too strict an adherence to a specific formal process may result in overreach, and too little formalization may leave gaps in testing. Either scenario can ultimately lead to failure in reaching testing goals. The pitfall of undertesting is more likely to plague a small and resource limited team, because the developers are already wearing too many hats. It may seem like a small team should prioritize giving the roles of designer and analyst to its members, but in fact one member taking on the role of the manager is likely to be much more critical to success. This is because in the absence of overall testing strategy and goals, it is easy to overlook some components. With someone taking the managerial responsibility, it is much more likely that testing itself does not get shortchanged in face of other pressures.

In CSE software teams, because interdisciplinary interactions are common, the distribution of roles is much more challenging. The human tendency to blame the "other" side can be particularly difficult to overcome when there are code components that come from different disciplines. It is an entirely feasible scenario that each component has undergone its own testing to the satisfaction of the corresponding team, but the test design does not cover some interactions that come into play only when combined with another component. In such a situation, if there is no trust between the designers and analysts, the results could be unhealthy blame apportioning.

4.4 Roles of Automated Software Testing in CSE Software

In this section, when we use the term "test" we typically mean an automated test, not a manual test. The purpose of testing is twofold. First and foremost, automated tests should execute important use cases and scenarios and check that code produces correct results and behaves correctly. Likewise, automated tests help to reduce defects in a few different ways. First, the process of writing automated verification tests requires thought about how the software component under test should behave and that helps to analyze the implementation and find defects before a test is even run. Second, any type of automated test run as part of a regression test suite helps to avoid the introduction of new defects as further changes are made to the software.

Typically tests that strive to achieve high line, branch and data flow coverage fall under the area of structural testing [177]. This type of testing is usually best done while trying to test for correct behavior (i.e., verification and acceptance tests) instead of just trying to blindly cover the code (i.e., characterization or no–change tests).

In the following sections, the specific roles of testing in research, development productivity, and maturity and sustainability are discussed.

4.4.1 Role of Testing in Research

The goal of research software is to demonstrate effectiveness or numerical properties of a proposed algorithm or numerical method, or to otherwise generate results of scientific interest. Generally, the results or insights that the software provides are more valuable than the software itself. Some research software is written from scratch for a specific scientific study and then no longer used. Therefore, one often is less concerned about the long-term maintainability of short-lived research software compared to longer-lived software. Tests are very important even in software that is only used by researchers. Defects in research software can be just as damaging as in production software. While a defect in production software used in a business environment may cost a company money and result in damage to the company's reputation, a defect in research software can damage and retard scientific advancements in major ways. Several examples of this can be found in the literature. One example is the case of the protein folding code [178] already mentioned in Section 4.3. Another example is the claim of the successful simulation of Cold Fusion [182]. Therefore, the most important role that automated testing plays in research software is the reduction of defects that damage the integrity of the research and science itself.

Another important usage of automated tests for research software is the demonstration of numerical properties that are claimed in research publications. For example, if some new numerical method claims to be second-order convergent, then the research code should have tests that demonstrate second-order convergence on a few manufactured problems. Such tests help to reduce defects as well as test the numerical analysis presented in the paper. If the researcher's proof of second order convergence is false and the method is actually only first-order convergent, it will be nearly impossible to construct exhaustive tests that show second-order convergence. This should cause the researcher to go back to the proof and discover the mistake. Note that such tests can also be focused on finer-grained sub-algorithms whose numerical properties can be demonstrated and checked as well.

Another role of testing in research software is to help provide a foundation for other researchers to continue the work. By having tests in place that demonstrate and protect the major behaviors and results of the research code, other researchers can tinker with the implemented algorithms and methods and have confidence that they have not damaged the existing algorithms. Thus, other researchers can build on existing research in a way that is not currently well supported in the CSE community.

Finally, a critical role that testing plays in research software is that it aids in the reproducibility of the numerical results of the research. For some classes of algorithms and methods, it is possible for the automated test suite to actually produce the results reported in publications. In other cases where the results require special hardware and are very expensive to run, automated tests can test a "dumbed down" version that, with a simple change to the inputs, can reproduce the full expensive calculations. Of course testing alone is not sufficient to achieve reproducibility, but one can argue that it is a necessary component of reproducibility.

4.4.2   Role of Testing in Development Productivity

Some of the more significant benefits of automated testing are those that improve development productivity. While most automated tests in CSE codes tend to be at the system level (e.g., a full finite-element simulation), there are numerous advantages to also writing finer-grained unit and integration tests, for better productivity. Here, development productivity includes not only productivity in writing an initial implementation but also productivity in future modifications of the software. Some of the universal advantages for finer-grained testing are very well described in [167].

While finer-grained testing has proven its effectiveness in other domains [160, 166, 177, 187], it is even more useful and important in computational codes. Each advantage of finer-grained tests is briefly explained below.

Finer-grained tests rebuild quickly and rerun quickly and better localize errors when they fail. Developers will likely spend an hour or more changing code before they rebuild and rerun the system-level tests. During that time the developer may have written or changed 100 lines or more of code. If a system-level test fails, then it can take a long time to find the faulty code. In contrast to system-level tests, even higher-level integration tests that cover a section of code can typically be rebuilt in under a minute and can usually run in just a few seconds. That is fast enough to rerun after just a few minutes of coding or refactoring work that involve far fewer lines of code. Changes can be made in smaller batches with much less risk and less time spent debugging. Additionally, if one of these tests fails, there is less code to inspect to find the problem. This can make the development cycle more robust and massively speedier, especially during a refactoring effort [167, 168].

Finer-grained computational tests allow much tighter floating-point tolerances and better portability. This property is especially useful in CSE codes where floating-point computations generally dominate. Typical system-level tests may involve millions (or billions) of floating-point operations, whereas fine-grained tests on a focused computational routine may only involve a few dozen floating-point operations. They also tend to be much more robust across different platforms. These tight tolerances can help to catch and localize numerical defects in a way that necessarily looser tolerances for system-level tests cannot. For example, a subtle defect in the implementation of a quadrature rule for a finite element method may be very difficult to detect in a system-level test that solves a PDE over an entire mesh, since the test has to allow for inexact linear and nonlinear solver tolerances and incurs a lot of round-off error. Alternatively, a fine-grained test for the quadrature rule for a single element can easily and accurately detect most such defects because of the ability to impose near machine-level relative error tolerances. Finer-grained tests can more easily be constructed to test the boundaries of ill-conditioning and the numerical stability of smaller computational units. For example, finer-grained tests for single element calculations can easily generate various types of ill-conditioned elements with very small angles and then test how robust the element-level calculations are when faced with these ill-conditioned corner cases. Detecting such problems in a full simulation in a portable way is extremely difficult. Creating entire meshes that expose all of the various types of ill-conditioned elements is very hard and isolating the impact of these elements is equally difficult in system-level tests. Codes that have only system-level tests based on necessarily looser tolerances tend to allow subtle defects to creep into the code.

Finer-grained tests force more modular design (leading to better reuse and parallel development). That is because the process of getting a single class or a small number of classes or functions into a unit-test harness requires breaking entangling dependencies that often exist in software that is not unit tested. The benefits of modular design are numerous. The more modular classes and functions are, the easier it is for different developers to work on different parts of the system at the same time without stepping on each other's toes (i.e., merge and semantic conflicts upon integrating the different branches of development). Also, more modular code allows for easier reuse of that code in other contexts, even outside the original application code. This further accelerates productivity because it is often easier to reuse an existing piece of (working) software than to write it from scratch yourself (which is likely to be a buggy implementation).

Finer-grained tests make porting to new platforms much more efficient with lower risk and help to isolate problems with third-party libraries (TPLs) on new platforms. Here porting might involve new compilers, new processor classes, new TPL versions and implementations, etc. For example, if a large CSE code only has system-level tests, what do you do when you port to a new platform and some of the solves just fail, the solvers diverge, or the code produces radically different, possibly wrong, answers? Without finer-grained tests, one is left with a difficult and time consuming debugging effort over thousands (to hundreds of thousands) of lines of code to try to determine the cause of the problems. In contrast, with good finer-grained unit-level and integration-level tests in place, the selective failure of the finer-grained tests will pinpoint the sections of code that cause the problem.

With respect to software written for users, automated tests help in the communication with the users. For example, users can inject their require-ments directly into the development process by helping to develop acceptance tests, even before the software is written. The process of writing acceptance tests first and then implementing the changes or additions in the software to pass the acceptance tests is known as *acceptance test driven development* (ATDD) [169].

4.4.3   Role of Testing in Software Maturity and Sustainability

Finally, the most valuable role that automated testing plays in CSE software, and where the investment in automated testing pays the greatest dividends, is in the long-term maturation and sustainability of the software.

The types of tests that are the most useful or important differ based on the level of maturity or stage of development of CSE software. In the early development of research software, the most important types of tests are verification tests that demonstrate the key properties of the algorithms and methods being developed. If the methods in the research software demonstrate their effectiveness, people will want to use the software in their own efforts. As users begin to depend on the research-based software, acceptance tests can be added to help pin down the exact requirements of these new users and help to protect the behavior of the software going forward. As more features are added to the software due to user demand or new research directions, the code base naturally grows in size. To keep development on the larger code base productive, finer-grained integration and unit tests help to keep faster change/build/test cycles. They might be even more important over the long lifecycle of the software than during early development, since as mentioned in Section 4.4.2, they are also very useful when porting code to new platforms, which might require significant changes. Finally, as the software matures, the automated test suite pins down important behaviors that all of the various users and researchers depend on.

When considering the long lifetime of some CSE software, the initial investment in strong automated tests has an even larger payoff. In fact, for some types of CSE software, a strong fast initial test suite may be more valuable than the actual initial implementation of the CSE software itself. That is because, over the long lifetime of the software, the internal implementation may have been rewritten several times as the code is ported to new platforms, new demands on the software require different tradeoffs in space/time performance, and new programming paradigms and supporting libraries become available. Through all these changes, a test suite tends to see fewer changes. For example, adding high levels of threading to existing code may require a massive rewrite of the internal software, algorithms, and data structures but the tests that check the basic numerical properties of the algorithms would tend to be mostly unaffected. Therefore, it is even more important to invest in a fast strong test suite early on, since that will make future development and maintenance more productive.

Finally, a strong clear test suite (composed of many verification and acceptance tests) provides the most important type of documentation that later development teams may have access to. Often, the automated test suite may be the only correct form of documentation of a code when it is handed off to later developers, since well meaning early developers may have developed documentation about the design, behavior, and purpose of the software but did not adequately maintain it over subsequent changes. When such documentation gets too far out of sync with the code itself, it can do more harm than good. Therefore, it may be better to invest in a clean well purposed automated test suite than in design and implementation documentation that is not well maintained.

4.5 Challenges in Testing Specific to CSE

In this section, a number of challenges are discussed that are dominant in, if not unique to, CSE codes as compared to other domains. These include the use of floating-point operations, and model testing, which are unique to CSE codes with physical and mathematical models, and scalability testing, which is specific to CSE codes that need to be run at large scale.

4.5.1 Floating-Point Issues and Their Impact on Testing

High-performance, fixed-precision floating-point computations are the cornerstone of CSE software, much more so than in most other software-related domains. Even with formal floating-point standards like IEEE 754 in place, the strong need for high flop rates, along with differences in computer architectures and system software, negates the possibility of strictly defining the binary output from such programs [170]. In particular, fixed-precision floating-point computations generally do not obey basic numerical properties such as the associative, commutative or distributive properties of operations on real numbers. They only approximate these rules up to fixed-point round off. This presents great challenges in developing strong portable test suites and in performing fundamental software verification.

One typically expects to get different binary answers when porting the software to different platforms or by changing the **compiler optimization level**. For example, higher optimization levels may use more aggressive inlining resulting in operations being performed in a different order, or they may relax more rigorous rounding rules.

Another issue that impacts the results of floating-point computations is the **instruction set** of different processors. For instance, some processors offer a "fused multiple and add" operation $d = round(a * b + c)$ that produces a more accurate result than standard binary floating-point operations.

Multi-processor computation can also result in different floating-point results even for mathematically identical algorithms. For example, consider the simple summation of an array of floating-point numbers. One can easily parallelize such a summation by having each process compute a partial sum and then sum up the results across all processes. But since the numbers are now being added in a different order, this can lead to a different result.

While the above issues can result in different floating-point results, they all generally result in deterministic floating-point numbers. That is, if the CSE software and tests are well written (e.g., use the same seed for random number generators on each test run), then the code will produce the exact same binary result each time it is run. Determinism makes it easier to define test suites and to debug problems when they occur. But determinism is lost once one considers scalable high-performance **multi-threaded algorithms**. In a scalable multi-threaded program, one cannot guarantee that the same binary floating-point numbers are computed in each run of the same code. This makes it impossible for tests to use binary reproducibility as in [165].

CSE software often contains complex linear and nonlinear models, which present a number of challenges with regard to floating-point operations. For example, a set of nonlinear equations can have more than one solution [179], and algorithms that solve these equations can find any one of these solutions or no solution at all. Nonlinear models can also possess **bifurcations** [157,189], **non-convexities** [179], **ill-conditioning** [179] and other phenomena that can make the behavior of numerical algorithms on these problems quite un-predictable. Therefore, if any of these factors is present, a test may result in a solution with a difference as large as $O(1)$ in any norm one might consider com-pared to a previous solution. Even in the case of linear solvers, ill-conditioning can result in large changes in the results for small differences in the order of op-erations and how round off is performed. In addition, many of the algorithms are iterative and are terminated once a given error tolerance is achieved. This becomes a major issue when tests are defined that use loose tolerances and evaluate the final solution or look at the exact number of iterations used for a given test problem. A minor change in the order of floating-point operations can result in a tested algorithm going from, for example, 5 to 6 iterations and cause a large change in the results.

Also the use of operations like $min()$ and $max()$ can result in large changes in the output of a numerical test for even small changes in the order or round off of floating-point operations due to any of the above issues. For example, if a test checks the value and position of the maximum temperature in a discretized field of a finite-element code, a small change in floating-point op-erations can cause a large change in the position of such a value, resulting in a non-continuous change in the output of the code.

While in a non-floating-point code, by definition, **refactoring** the code does not result in any observed change in the behavior or the output of the program [168], this property, unfortunately, cannot be maintained for even the most simple refactoring in a floating-point code, even for mathematically identical code. For example, suppose one starts out with a block of code that computes z = a + b + c. If one refactors the code to create a function add() and uses it as z = add(a, b) + c then the floating-point result for z can be different depending on the compiler, the processor, the sizes of the various numbers, etc. Therefore, refactoring can become very difficult and expensive in codes with poorly designed test suites that do not take into account the realities of floating-point operations. An example of a test suite that deals with floating-point operations is given in Section 4.6.3.

4.5.2 Scalability Testing

Testing the scalability of a parallel CSE code to more (MPI) processes introduces a number of special challenges, to which an entire book could be devoted. Here, just a high-level overview of the major challenges is provided.

There are two types of scaling with respect to the number of processes. Running a CSE code with a fixed problem size while increasing the number of processes is known as **strong scaling**. This is differentiated from **weak scaling** where the problem size per process is kept constant as the number of processes, and with it the total problem size, is increased. Strong and weak scaling studies are performed a little differently. For a strong scaling study, where the total problem size is kept constant, one first performs the code on the smallest number of processes for which the problem will still fit in memory. Then the same problem is solved by gradually increasing the number of processes, typically by a factor of 2. This is continued until the work per process becomes small compared to the global communication and synchronization cost. For a weak scaling study, one will start out with the smallest number of processes for which the problem is reasonable to solve and then refine the discretization as processes are added. Here, typically the only practical limits on the number of processes are the budget in processor time that can be afforded to run the study and the amount of processors of the available hardware.

A good parallel algorithm should, in theory, show close to perfect scaling, i.e., when increasing the number of processes by a factor p it should solve the problem p times as fast in a strong scaling study, or it should solve a problem that is p times as large in the same time as the original problem when using weak scaling. Many of the most effective parallel algorithms don't scale perfectly even in theory but should still provide significant speedup as more processes are added. When these algorithms are implemented, one often does not obtain the predicted scaling. This can be due to poor coding or unexpected effects of the specific computer architecture used. Therefore, scalability testing is vital to detect and correct such problems. Below we discuss several issues that present serious challenges to such testing.

When measuring the performance of a code on a large parallel machine shared with other users, it can be difficult to get accurate scaling data. Often it is not possible to request a specific set of nodes for a test run and so different runs of the same problem can get assigned to completely different distributions of processes, resulting in large differences in latencies and bandwidths of parallel communication and with it timings. Also, fluctuations in parallel disk I/O resources shared with other user jobs can significantly affect runtimes, even on the same nodes. Such inconsistencies can be addressed by repeating the same run multiple times, but this strategy greatly increases the cost.

One of the challenges for weak scaling studies is the question on how to best scale up the global problem in a way that allows for a logical comparison between different problem sizes. For example, a refined problem can be more or less ill-conditioned and consequently behave very different at large scale. One needs to consider whether one wants to include such effects in the scaling study or not. In any case, interpreting such a scaling of the code can be difficult, especially if one is not aware of such issues a priori.

Getting access to a large number of processors on a parallel machine for longer time periods can be difficult and expensive. The cost of weak scaling studies is typically greater because the cost per process can go up (somewhat) as the number of processes is increased and, therefore, the last scaling point (e.g., going from 32,768 processes to 65,536 processes) is more expensive than all of the previous cases combined! This makes doing very large scale scalability studies (e.g., $O(100,000)$ processes) extremely expensive. Another factor that hampers scalability testing is that supercomputing facilities that give out time at no cost to research CSE projects generally want the cycles to be used for science runs and not for testing and therefore discourage routine scalability testing. Another difficulty is that supercomputers use batch submission systems where users submit requests for jobs that reserve X number of processes for a maximal wall clock time of Y hours. These requests are placed into a queue, which is prioritized based on various criteria. Generally, jobs that require more processes and time are pushed further back in the queue and therefore it can take a long time before they are selected to be run, if they are selected at all. So strategies have to be devised to submit a scaling study in a set of smaller jobs and then to aggregate the results. The large overhead and complexity of performing such studies on a shared supercomputer is often enough of a deterrent to scaling studies.

The codes with the greatest challenges for scalability testing are codes that are designed to be massively scalable, e.g., codes with structured grids. While such codes can show excellent scalability on 10,000 processes, there is no guarantee that they will continue to scale well at 100,000 processes or more. For example, communication overhead that has little impact on scalability at 10,000 processes can become a large bottleneck at 100,000 processes. Also, just the sizes of buffers and index ranges for larger problems can cause significant slowdowns or even complete failure at large scale. Such situations are difficult to test for or predict on smaller numbers of processes. Such defects could e.g., be in the MPI implementation, which makes prediction and diagnosis even more challenging. To be absolutely sure that a CSE code will run at large scale, one actually has to run it. Since this is not always possible, there are ways to mitigate the need to run full problems on larger numbers of processes. For example, one can put targeted timers in the code around certain computations and then observe the growth rates of the measured times. This can be helpful in finding code segments that are too expensive or growing more rapidly than they should. To detect problems caused by buffer sizes and index ranges, one can simulate aspects of a large problem or run very short jobs at large scale.

However, the latter test is more of a correctness test checking for hard defects than a scalability performance test.

In summary, scalability testing is typically extremely complex and expensive, requiring a lot of compute time and large numbers of processes. But this testing is critical to obtain highly efficient CSE codes that are capable to solve problems of scientific and engineering interest at large scale.

4.5.3 Model Testing

The increasing importance of modeling and simulation, in conjunction with experiments and observations, to advance scientific understanding is a key driver of CSE software development, and introduces a number of unique challenges for model development and testing. For example, the iterative nature of the scientific process causes requirements to evolve rapidly as new knowledge and understanding must be incorporated in the software quickly and reliably. This aspect of CSE underscores the importance of the hierarchical and automated testing approaches highlighted in Section 4.4. In addition, the potential computational power of exascale systems raises the expectation that the predictive skill of the models will increase significantly through improvements in model fidelity. This increasing fidelity spans several dimensions of model complexity, including grid resolution, process representation, and process coupling, and uses analysis techniques such as data assimilation and uncertainty quantification to integrate experimental and observational data. Developing these increasingly complex models and workflows benefits significantly from a hierarchical approach, in which a test suite is developed that builds a complete system or acceptance test up from unit and integration tests (e.g., constitutive laws, single processes) up to coupled processes [163]. In addition, such a test suite would include tests of model inputs at each stage or level, and would reuse inputs and components as opposed to duplicate them in separate files or code. Here we highlight model input and component testing in the context of geometric complexity, process representation, and the number of coupled processes.

In many CSE applications the modeling domain is complex, ranging from engineered systems such as fuel bundles in nuclear reactors to natural systems such as sloping and pinched-out stratigraphic layers in the subsurface. Sophisticated mesh generation techniques and software have been developed to represent these domains in simulations, including unstructured simplex or polyhedral meshes, body-fitted meshes, adaptive mesh refinement, and multiblock meshes. The mesh is critical input to the simulation and underpins what it represents. The increasing scale of simulations, from thousands to millions to billions of cells makes it increasingly impractical for users to visually inspect the mesh and determine a priori if it is consistent with the conceptual model they intended. Although some tests of mesh quality are easily automated, addressing higher-level questions of intent is much harder but just as important. For example, in an unstructured mesh it is possible to represent voids or fractures with interior faces that are very close together, but structurally separated from their neighbor, i.e., no edges connect the nodes across a fracture. Unfortunately, this cannot be readily distinguished from a mesh generation error in which two adjacent geometric objects were not correctly joined to form a single domain. Instead, in this case it is necessary to provide additional tests to users to ensure the mesh captures the geometry of their conceptual model. Here, a simple diffusion problem with linear boundary conditions could be used to verify that the mesh is properly connected, and no unintended voids are present. Thus, we can see the value of flexible functional representations of initial conditions, boundary conditions and source terms to not only support verification testing but the development of tests that probe these higher-level aspects of conceptual models.

Model complexity is also growing through a steady increase in the number and variety of processes being studied and coupled in simulations. Here the challenge for testing is to support a scientific workflow that explores the relative importance and representations of a wide range of processes in order to develop scientific understanding and build confidence in particular model configurations. In essence, the distinction between test suites used by developers and simulation campaigns used by domain scientists is blurred as we move beyond the traditional multi-physics setting where a small number of processes are coupled in a small set of predefined configurations to a dynamic environment where the configurations needed by the users cannot be enumerated a priori. To address this challenge, flexible and extensible frameworks are being explored that leverage object oriented designs with well defined abstract interfaces, automated dependency analysis, (semi)-automated process couplers [163, 180], and data management capabilities [185].

Increasing model fidelity through increasing mesh resolution is another natural approach that raises two additional challenges for testing. First, as the mesh is refined the efficiency and scaling of the underlying algorithms is stressed. In particular, in a time dependent simulation the time step will be refined accordingly to maintain accuracy, implying more time steps to reach the same target time. In addition, for processes with an elliptic component, e.g., diffusion, implicit time-integration is necessary and each time step requires now a larger system of equations to be solved. Thus, the challenges of scalability testing highlighted in Section 4.5.2 are prevalent here as well. Second, as the mesh is refined, approximations to the model equations and parameterizations of subgrid processes may need to be modified. Thus, the interaction of computational capabilities and scientific research raises the same challenges identified with increasing model complexity, as it effectively increases the number of coupled processes being studied.

Finally, an important class of acceptance tests (Section 4.2.2) for models in complex applications is benchmarking. In benchmarking, a mathematical description of a problem is laid out in sufficient detail that the simulation results of several codes can be compared using a variety of solution and performance metrics. This has numerous benefits for the community, including understanding the impact of different algorithmic choices, implementation differences, and building confidence in the capabilities of a code or set of codes. Although a number of challenges arise in benchmarking that limit its use in CSE software development, many of these could be addressed effectively through the use of frameworks that naturally support the development of a hierarchical suite of tests as noted above. For example, data from external sources, such as journal articles and input to other simulation and codes, may not be expressed in the same units that the software uses internally. Verifying the consistency of units is critical for several reasons. When inconsistencies slip through, failures may not be catastrophic but may be misleading (e.g., a front doesn't propagate through a particular interface). Performance may suffer (e.g., adaptive time-stepping may lead to unreasonably small time steps), while results are suspicious but don't clearly point to the problem. In this case, CSE software should provide developers and users with the ability to design tests to obtain a variety of diagnostic output related to the model input. In particular, time series plots of various inputs, e.g., boundary conditions, or sources, can provide developers and users with valuable visual feedback to confirm temporal relationships of inputs. Similarly, constitutive laws, such as pressure-saturation curves in subsurface flow, can be plotted at the beginning of the simulation to give visual feedback that units of the input parameters were handled correctly. With confidence that model input and configuration is identical across a suite of codes, developers and domain scientists can focus on the important question of algorithmic and implementation differences and their impact on the benchmark results.

4.6 Testing Practices

Testing should be used in many stages of the software development. The writing of tests can start as early as **before or at the beginning of code development**. In *test-driven development* or *TDD* [158,169], the software developer will design test cases for each piece of code before those pieces are actually written. This practice can be very helpful to gain clarity on the code one is about to write and has the additional advantage that it guarantees the existence of tests. While it is currently unclear whether this approach has any significant impact on programmer productivity [190], it can be worthwhile even in small teams where testing can be viewed as extra or unsustainable tax on resources, since it protects against the added cost of delayed detection of defects in the software that are more difficult and time consuming to correct.

It certainly is necessary to test **during code development** using all types of tests. Section 4.6.1 discusses how to build a test suite for a new software project as well as an already existing CSE code both during development as well as when **refactoring and adding new developments**. Once a regression suite has been developed, it should continually be evaluated and maintained, as described in Section 4.6.2.

It is useful to provide users a test suite that allows them to test a code **when building and before using it** to make sure that it runs as intended and provides correct results. Section 4.6.3 provides the example of such a regression test suite of the direct solver library SuperLU.

Software should be tested **regularly**, if possible daily. This is clearly only achievable when done in an automated fashion requiring an automated testing system or test harness; see Section 4.6.4. This section concludes with some policies for testing practices that have shown to be useful. For a few short documents on CSE software practices see also [10].

4.6.1 Building a Test Suite for CSE Codes

The ideal time to build a test suite for a piece of software is during development, when tests are devised to ensure that the software is doing what it is designed to do. After the software has reached some level of maturity one needs to ensure that any new code being added does not break any existing functionality. When there is no ongoing regular testing the process of adding new code is ad-hoc, error-prone and unnecessarily burdensome. Furthermore, any structural changes that affect a large part of the code are tedious because there is no way of verifying their ongoing correctness. Regular automated testing, mentioned in Section 4.4, is not only critical for structural changes, it can also provide huge savings in the cost of adding new code to existing software. In general, a test suite that provides sufficient coverage to the code base leads to greater confidence in results obtained using it, and ultimately to better science.

Legacy CSE software, however, often finds itself in a predicament where there are no or too few tests that can be used to demonstrate that it performs as intended and delivers correct results. If such software needs any new non-trivial development, whether structural or capability, it must first add appropriate levels of testing to the code. How to do so is also discussed in [167]. Making sure that the test suite provides adequate coverage is a challenging problem in any situation; it is particularly difficult with legacy codes. Below we discuss various aspects of building and automating a testing regime that provides sufficient coverage without placing unnecessary strain on computing resources.

During the development phase it is necessary to devise tests that give confidence to the developer that the software is behaving as it ought to. This can occur in multiple stages. The first stage is the analysis of the mathematical properties of the numerical algorithm, its stability and order of accuracy. The second stage is applying the algorithm to a physical situation and verifying that physical laws are not broken and expected properties are preserved. In some cases there may be later stages such as statistical or some other kind of analysis to evaluate the solution quality. The tests can take many flavors, such as convergence tests, confronting the numerically obtained solution of a simplified problem with an analytical or semi-analytical one, or examining some defining features that only occur if the solution is right. Sometimes these tests can also serve as regression tests, but often requirements for ongoing testing have a different focus.

The first step in formulating a continuous testing regime is to take an inventory of verification needs within the software. This process defines the code coverage requirements for the software. It implies picking all features of the code that are necessary for correct behavior. These features are not limited to code sections/units or even subsections, they also include interaction between code units. In CSE codes, where it is not always possible to eliminate lateral coupling between code sections, code unit interactions can have multiple facets. Some of these multi-faceted interactions may be features that need to be included in the inventory. One of the guiding principles in taking the inventory is to know the purpose of testing each feature. This knowledge is critical for several reasons. It reduces effort wasted in developing tests that have limited usefulness. It helps in mapping a specific testing need to the most appropriate kind of test for it, and by minimizing waste it makes sure that testing resources (human or machine) are optimally used.

The next step is to identify behaviors of the code that have detectable response to changes. Since the purpose of testing is to be able to map a failure easily to its source, it is also essential to be able to isolate the cause of detected response. When a single code unit is being tested for its functionality, the generic software engineering approach to meeting the isolation requirements is to build a unit test for it. This is also a useful practice for CSE software where possible. However, many times, breaking down the dependencies may not be a feasible or worthwhile effort. For example, most physics on a discretized mesh would need the mesh mocked up, which is less helpful than just using the existing mesh. A work-around is to use minimally combined code units. The purpose of these tests is still the same as that of unit tests - quickest map of manifestation of failure to the source of failure within a minimal set of units.

Testing for interaction between units is trickier because many permutations may be possible. Being numerical, code units may add regime of validity for a particular combination to the overall testing space. For this kind of feature testing scientists rely on one or more no–change or bounded-change tests. One very important requirement for such tests is that they should be low cost in terms of running. The verification tests that are used during the development phase of the code need not have this constraint, but the ongoing test suite does. One way to ensure that is to select tests that respond quickly to perturbations. Because of multi-faceted interactions the count of needed tests can grow rapidly. Similar challenges arise when covering features that cannot be directly tested. Cross-checking with more than one test may be needed to pinpoint the cause of failure. In both situations one is faced with the need to downselect from the number of available tests for the whole testing system to remain viable. One option is to use the matrix approach with tests and feature coverage as rows and columns of the matrix respectively. This way any overlap in coverage becomes visible and can be leveraged to reduce the number of tests. A detailed example of using the matrix approach is described in [155], and also discussed in Chapter 1 "Software Process for Multiphysics Multicomponent Codes"

The approach to adding tests needs to be somewhat different when adding new code to software that is already under the regime of regular testing. Here, the concerns are limited to testing the new functionality and its interaction with the existing code. If possible one should always add a unit test for the new code. Sometimes tweaking some of the existing tests may provide the coverage, otherwise one or more new tests may need to be added. In general it is desirable to leverage the overlap as much as possible and minimize the number of new tests added.

4.6.2   Evaluation and Maintenance of a Test Suite

Any testing regime is useful only if it is maintained, monitored regularly, and the response to failure is rapid. The maintenance of a test suite may include updating tests, benchmarks for comparison, and periodic adjustments to upgrades in the software stack of the platforms on which the tests are run. It may also include archiving and retrieval of the output of the test suite. Note that the output of the test suite is different from that of individual tests. Archiving of the test suite output can be helpful in tracing back a change in the code behavior if need arises. Sometimes, when there is a deep enough structural change in the code which affects most of the tests, having an archive and retrieval mechanism can ease the time pressure in bringing all the tests up to date.

The best kind of monitoring of individual tests is the automated kind. If monitoring of the test output is manual, the burden on the developers is too high, and it is unlikely that the practice will persist. In general, management of the test suite is an overhead, though a necessary one, for the team. Therefore, minimizing the effort expended on testing is preferable as long as it does not compromise the quality of verification. If test verification is automated, then manual inspection can be limited to only the failed tests. If the test suite is tied to a repository, manual intervention can be further reduced by correlating failure to check-ins within a certain time period and alert the concerned contributors. It may also help to assign ownership of the tests to members of the team and configure the alert system so that only the owners of failed tests need to respond.

The most useful test suite is one where all tests are successful most of the time because then it is easy to map a failure to its cause. In an environment where developments are few and/or isolated to some sections it is relatively easy to maintain success of all tests. It is much more challenging to achieve in a rapidly changing code with many parts of the code undergoing changes simultaneously. A developer tracing the cause of failure may need to spread the net wide in order to catch the source. Such teams would be well advised to institute the practice of running pre-commit test suites for all developers.

As with code, it is important to periodically review the collection of tests in the test suite to look for gaps and redundancies. Pruning the test suite is almost more important than pruning the code because redundant tests continue to use precious testing resources. And as the code base grows, some gaps may develop in testing of interaction features. The matrix approach mentioned above can be equally useful in doing both, especially if the matrix is designed to be flexible. To prune, one can simply remove deprecated features from the matrix and remove the tests that do not exclusively cover any of the remaining features. Similarly, to add tests, one can add the new features and added tests and look for remaining gaps in the matrix. New tests may need to be devised and added if gaps are found.

4.6.3   An Example of a Test Suite

For the sake of space we will describe only the regression suite of SuperLU [186] in this section. For further examples we point to Sections 1.5.1.3 and 1.5.2.3 in Chapter 1 of this book, which describe testing for the multiphysics simulation code FLASH and for Amanzi, a flow and reactive transport simulation code for environmental applications. Another good example that describes testing of an application code solving the Schrödinger equation can be found in [175].

SuperLU [186] is a general purpose library for the direct solution of sparse nonsymmetric systems of linear equations. It solves a system of linear equations $Ax = b$, using LU decomposition with partial pivoting. Its test suite consists of many unit and integration level tests that perform very fast (the whole suite can be run in a few minutes). It demonstrates both validation and acceptance testing as well as no-change (or bounded change) testing. It also shows how one can deal with floating-point issues.

The test suite pursues the following two main goals. First off, it tests whether the query functions to the underlying floating-point parameters return correct values, conforming to the IEEE 754 floating-point standard in both single and double precision; this includes tests for the machine epsilon, underflow threshold, overflow threshold, and related parameters. It also aims to provide coverage of all routines by testing all functions of the user-callable routines.

In order to achieve these goals and perform exhaustive testing, a variety of input matrices are generated with different numerical and structural properties. The linear systems are then solved using these input matrices. In addition, several numerical metrics, such as stable LU factorization, small backward error and forward errors, are verified to assert the accuracy of the solution. The SuperLU Users' Guide contains details on the types of matrices generated and the numerical metrics used for correctness verification [176].

Let $I = \{I_1, I_2, ..., I_q\}$ be a set of q input arguments of a user-callable routine. For example, I_j can be the dimension n of the linear system. The test program is structured as follows:

```
For each I₁ ∈ set of valid values {
    For each I₂ ∈ set of valid values {
        . . .
        For each I_q ∈ set of valid values {
            For each matrix type {
1.              Generate the input matrix A and right-hand side b;
2.              Call a user-callable routine with input values
                {I₁, I₂, ..., I_q};
3.              Compute the test metrics;
4.              Check whether each metric is smaller than a
                prescribed threshold;
            }
        }
        . . .
    }
}
```

With this nested loop setup, the users can perform "exhaustive" testing of a large number of input parameter configurations at installation time, running over 10,000 tests in only a few minutes.

4.6.4   Use of Test Harnesses

If one deals with a very large software code, the use of a test harness or automated test framework is essential to be able to actually set up and run the tests as well as to evaluate the test results efficiently. With a test harness, it is also possible to execute logical subsets of tests in different situations, such as pre-push, or nightly, using a single command.

Executing a test harness in an automated fashion is critical for CSE software projects with long running test suites, such as nightly or weekly, or for projects that support a variety of platforms. Increasingly, this is the case for most CSE software projects. A very basic approach to automated testing is to use a crontab on a specific machine to execute a specified command at a specified time. Newer tools allow centralized servers to execute tests on multiple platforms, and assist in load balancing and scheduling on available test resources. The test execution can be triggered by time, an event (such as a repository modification), or a manual request by a developer.

There are three common ways to report test results. The simplest approach, appropriate for developers executing pre-push testing, is to output the test results to the screen. Support for this kind of output is typically built into the test harness. A slightly more sophisticated way to report test results is to send an email to a mail list. Often the contents of the email are captured from

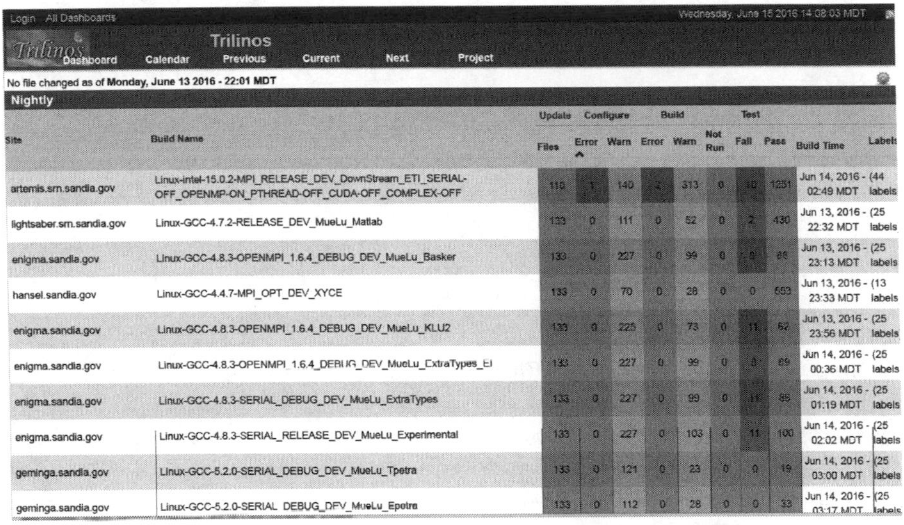
Login All Dashboards Wednesday, June 15 2016 14:08:03 MDT

Trilinos

Dashboard Calendar Previous Current Next Project

No file changed as of **Monday, June 13 2016 - 22:01 MDT**

Nightly

Site	Build Name	Update Files	Configure Error	Configure Warn	Build Error	Build Warn	Test Not Run	Test Fail	Test Pass	Build Time	Labels
artemis.srn.sandia.gov	Linux-intel-15.0.2-MPI_RELEASE_DEV_DownStream_ETI_SERIAL-OFF_OPENMP-ON_PTHREAD-OFF_CUDA-OFF_COMPLEX-OFF	110	1	140	2	313	0	10	1251	Jun 14, 2016 - 02:49 MDT	(44 labels
lightsaber.srn.sandia.gov	Linux-GCC-4.7.2-RELEASE_DEV_MueLu_Matlab	133	0	111	0	52	0	2	430	Jun 13, 2016 - 22:32 MDT	(25 labels
enigma.sandia.gov	Linux-GCC-4.8.3-OPENMPI_1.6.4_DEBUG_DEV_MueLu_Basker	133	0	227	0	99	0	9	88	Jun 13, 2016 - 23:13 MDT	(25 labels
hansel.sandia.gov	Linux-GCC-4.4.7-MPI_OPT_DEV_XYCE	133	0	70	0	28	0	0	553	Jun 13, 2016 - 23:33 MDT	(13 labels
enigma.sandia.gov	Linux-GCC-4.8.3-OPENMPI_1.6.4_DEBUG_DEV_MueLu_KLU2	133	0	225	0	73	0	11	62	Jun 13, 2016 - 23:56 MDT	(25 labels
enigma.sandia.gov	Linux-GCC-4.8.3-OPENMPI_1.6.4_DEBUG_DEV_MueLu_ExtraTypes_EI	133	0	227	0	99	0	3	89	Jun 14, 2016 - 00:36 MDT	(25 labels
enigma.sandia.gov	Linux-GCC-4.8.3-SERIAL_DEBUG_DEV_MueLu_ExtraTypes	133	0	227	0	99	0	11	86	Jun 14, 2016 - 01:19 MDT	(25 labels
enigma.sandia.gov	Linux-GCC-4.8.3-SERIAL_RELEASE_DEV_MueLu_Experimental	133	0	227	0	103	0	11	100	Jun 14, 2016 - 02:02 MDT	(25 labels
geminga.sandia.gov	Linux-GCC-5.2.0-SERIAL_DEBUG_DEV_MueLu_Tpetra	133	0	121	0	23	0	0	19	Jun 14, 2016 - 03:00 MDT	(25 labels
geminga.sandia.gov	Linux-GCC-5.2.0-SERIAL_DEBUG_DEV_MueLu_Epetra	133	0	112	0	28	0	0	33	Jun 14, 2016 - 03:17 MDT	(25 labels

Figure 4.1: Trilinos dashboard.

the direct output described previously. Sometimes the email is generated by a project test results dashboard, the most sophisticated approach for reporting test results. A test results dashboard tool can commonly display results from a range of dates (typically limited by total database size, or team preference), detect changes in pass/fail conditions, and allow the test results to be sorted and searched. It enhances the visibility of failing builds and tests. An example of such a dashboard is illustrated in Figure 4.1, which shows the output of a dashboard for Trilinos [188] using the test harness CTest/CDash [162, 164]. Different colors indicate the status of the tests, with gray indicating passed tests, dark gray failed tests and light gray warnings. Additional dashboards can be accessed online at [8].

Other software projects may use self-developed systems, such as the *hypre* project [172], which uses a system of scripts that sends emails to the *hypre* developers indicating whether there are any issues and pointing to the directories in which they occurred. These can then be further investigated. Other useful testing frameworks are Jenkins [335] and the Atlassian tool Bamboo [156]. Again, the actual size of the software and the number of developers determine what is the best approach to use for each individual team.

There are also finer-grained testing frameworks or unit test harnesses that enable the fast writing and running of unit tests. Unit tests are considered a foundation for modern agile software development methods (e.g., test driven development) and also provide a foundation for fast efficient development and refactoring efforts. A well designed and easy to use unit test harness, such as gtest [171] or xUnit [191], can make unit testing cost effective, when tailored to the programming language and particular software being tested.

4.6.5   Policies

A software project should have solid policies on testing practices. Here, some policies that have shown to be useful and avoided issues when followed by everyone are listed.

It is important to have a consistent policy on how to **deal with failed tests**. Generally, critical issues should be fixed immediately, whereas fixing minor issues possibly can be delayed. To make sure that such issues are not delayed indeterminately and are not forgotten one needs to find an efficient method to track the issues. The tasks of fixing the bugs need to be adequately assigned to the team members, i.e., it needs to be clear who is responsible to fix the problem, particularly in a larger team. It could be the responsibility of the person who wrote the part of the code that is broken, since they should know the code best. That is where the policy to always assign a second person who is familiar with that part of the software, is useful, since they can now take over. Once the problem has been fixed it is advisable to add another regression test for this issue to avoid reintroducing it at a later time. For very large teams and integration efforts it is important to designate one or several people who will watch over the test suite, monitor results and address failures. They should ensure that these failures are addressed in a timely fashion by assigning someone to take care of the problem within a set time or fix the problem themselves.

When **refactoring and adding new features** in order to preserve code quality, it is a good policy to require running a regression test suite before checking in new code to avoid breaking the existing code. In addition one should add new regression tests to regularly test the new features.

Making sure that there is always a **second person familiar with a particular portion of the code** is another good policy. This person can then take over in case the original developer is not available or leaves the project for any reason. Should the developer leave, it is important that a replacement is trained in the knowledge of the code, or this policy will eventually break down, making it very difficult to deal with issues later, particularly if there is insufficient documentation.

A good policy is to **avoid using regression suites consisting primarily of system-level no–change tests**. While there are many instances where no–change tests can be very useful, particularly at the unit and integration test level, their use can also lead to serious issues. One problem is that when the behavior of the software changes, these tests have to be rebaselined in order to pass. This is often done without sufficient verification of the new updated gold standard outputs. Many CSE codes use regression test suites that almost completely consist of no–change system-level tests. Such test suites generally do not provide a sufficient foundation to efficiently and safely drive future development and refactoring efforts for CSE codes. Codes that have only system-level no–change tests based on necessarily looser tolerances can tend to allow subtle defects to creep into the code. This has led some teams to the extreme policy of requiring zero-diffing tests against "gold standard output" (for example, see [165]). First off, the verification that goes into the "gold standard output" can be tenuous. Even if it is solid, these tests do not allow even the most basic types of valid refactorings (to improve the design and better handle complexity) and therefore result in more complex and less maintainable software. This trend nearly always leads to the uncontrolled generation of software entropy which in turn leads to software that is very difficult to change and in many cases the eventual (slow and painful) death of the software [159, 161, 177, 181]. Also, no–change system-level tests with higher tolerances are extremely difficult to maintain across multiple platforms. High-quality finer-grained computational tests allow for better system-level testing approaches while at the same time still providing a solid verification and acceptance testing foundation in a much more portable manner. With strong finer-grained unit and integration tests in place, the remaining system-level tests can then be focused on gross integration issues and higher-level verification tests and therefore allow for looser (and more portable) tolerances.

A good policy is to require a **code review** before releasing a test suite. Such a review includes going over the test suite with the whole project or a fellow programmer who can critique it and give advice on how to improve it. Just with a paper or general research it is easy to miss any problems after having looked at the code for a long time, whereas another person might spot any issues right away. The code review can be performed in a group meeting or through an online tool such as github, which allows each reviewer to examine the code and comment. The evidence for the cost effectiveness of code reviews in the SE literature is overwhelming (see [177]), but they are often neglected or not even considered due to lack of sufficient developers or funding for the software. One issue with code reviews is how to minimize the overhead of code reviews while still being effective.

4.7 Conclusions

Automated software testing is extremely important for a variety of reasons. It does not only ensure that a code delivers correct results, but it can also significantly decrease development and maintenance costs. It facilitates refactoring and portability of the code and plays an important role in software maturity and sustainability. While these benefits apply to any type of software there are challenges that are specific to scientific software, such as the the predominant use of floating-point operations, the need to run the code at large scale on high performance computers, and the difficulty to test the underlying physics models, all of which have been discussed here. In addition, stakeholders and the key team roles for testing in a scientific software project as well as various testing practices, including the development and maintenance of test suites, the use of automated testing systems and a few helpful policies were presented. All of these components need to be considered to generate reliable, mature scientific software of high quality, which is crucial to deliver correct scientific research results.

4.8 Acknowledgments

This work is partially supported by the Director, Office of Science, Office of Advanced Scientific Computing Research of the U.S. Department of Energy under Contract No. DE-AC02-05CH11231. This material is based upon work supported by the U.S. Department of Energy, Office of Science, under contract number DE-AC02-06CH11357. This work is funded by the Department of Energy at Los Alamos National Laboratory under contracts DE-AC52-06NA25396 and the DOE Office of Science Biological and Environmental Research (BER) program in Subsurface Biogeochemical(SBR) through the Interoperable Design of Extreme-scale Application Software (IDEAS) project. This work was performed under the auspices of the U.S. Department of Energy by Lawrence Livermore National Laboratory under Contract DE-AC52-07NA27344. This manuscript has been authored by UT-Battelle, LLC under Contract No. DE-AC05-00OR22725 with the U.S. Department of Energy. The United States Government retains and the publisher, by accepting the article for publication, acknowledges that the United States Government retains a non-exclusive, paid-up, irrevocable, world-wide license to publish or reproduce the published form of this manuscript, or allow others to do so, for United States Government purposes. The Department of Energy will provide public access to these results of federally sponsored research in accordance with the DOE Public Access Plan(http://energy.gov/downloads/doe-public-access-plan). Sandia National Laboratories is a multi-program laboratory managed and operated by Sandia Corporation, a wholly owned subsidiary of Lockheed Martin Corporation, for the U.S. Department of Energy's National Nuclear Security Administration under contract DE-AC04-94AL85000.

Chapter 5

Preserving Reproducibility through Regression Testing

Daniel Hook

5.1   Introduction

This chapter describes an approach to software testing that is known to software engineers as regression testing. To the mathematically minded scientist the word "regression" is strongly associated with the statistical machinery for fitting equations and models to data. It is therefore necessary to open this chapter with an important clarification: software regression testing is not (necessarily) a statistical approach to testing and does not involve the fitting of mathematical models.[1] Simply put, a regression test is a test that is repeated over time to detect and quantify changes in the output of a piece of software. When the test output changes it indicates that there has been a *regression*, that is, that reproducibility has been lost. In the context of scientific software testing, a better name for regression testing would be *reproducibility* testing.

After a few words about scientific software testing techniques other than regression testing, the remainder of this introduction will discuss software reproducibility and the role regression testing plays in maintaining reproducibility. The next section of the chapter will describe particular challenges that are encountered when testing scientific software—including the oracle and tolerance problems—and will describe how regression testing helps with these challenges. A case study describing the regression testing carried out at Engineering Seismology Group Solutions (ESG) will then be presented to illustrate some of the benefits realized and challenges encountered when regression testing is applied to a real-world suite of analysis software. Finally, the conclusion will include a call for research into techniques that might help mitigate challenges encountered by scientists who are trying to apply regression testing to their software.

It should also be mentioned that this is not the first scientific software case study to include some description of a regression testing process: testing processes—including regression tests—used to test climate models at the UK Met Office are described in a paper by Easterbrook and Johns [194]. That paper, and some brief conversations with Easterbrook, helped to inspire parts of the regression testing work that has been carried out at ESG. However, while the Met Office study only briefly discussed regression testing as part of a larger case study, this chapter focuses particularly on regression testing and includes many details about the specific issues that practitioners should consider when implementing regression testing of scientific software.

5.1.1   Other Testing Techniques

Software testing has been a field of active and published research since at least 1979 when Myers published *The Art of Software Testing* [200], and Beizer's textbook [192] offers a thorough overview of many techniques that have been developed. However, as described by Sanders and Kelly [202, 203], many established software testing techniques are not ideally suited to the testing of scientific software due to their inability to deal with challenges like the oracle and tolerance problems encountered in the scientific software domain. In the last few years a number of software engineers and scientists have noticed this deficiency and have begun to investigate new and adapted testing techniques that are specifically targeted at scientific software—a paper

---

[1]The application of statistical methods during regression testing is not essential, but neither is it forbidden. In fact, a statistically literate scientist may find opportunities to advance the state of the art in software testing through the innovative application of statistical techniques.

from Kanewala and Bieman [198] surveys much of this work—but much of this testing research is still in its infancy: a clear set of best practices for testing scientific software still needs to be identified. This chapter intends to show that regression testing should be one of the techniques included in this set of best practices.

Note that readers who are interested in learning more about software testing techniques that are not specific to scientific software should consult reference books by Myers [200] and Beizer [192].

5.1.2   Reproducibility

For a scientific result to be considered trustworthy it is necessary that it be *reproducible*. It should be possible, at least in theory, to reproduce any scientifically valid result by following the same procedure that was used to produce the result in the first place. Reproducible results are more trustworthy because they can be independently verified, and they are more widely and deeply understood by the scientific community. Reproducible results are also important in that they act as a starting point for further research. Donoho et al [193] offer an excellent summary of the importance of reproducibility in computational science. They write, "The prevalence of very relaxed attitudes about communicating experimental details and validating results is causing a large and growing credibility gap. It's impossible to verify most of the results that computational scientists present at conferences and in papers.... Current computational science practice doesn't generate routinely verifiable knowledge."

Admittedly, Donoho et al have a broad view of reproducibility in mind— they would like to see it become common practice for researchers to publish their codes and data sets with their articles so that other scientists can test the codes and results for themselves. It is a laudable and ambitious goal. The goal of this chapter is more modest: here the aim is simply to show that regression testing is a very powerful and important tool to aid in the ongoing development of scientific software that produces reproducible results. To that end, this chapter will use a less broad definition of reproducibility; let us say that software can be described as giving reproducible results if, for a specific, fixed set of inputs, it gives a corresponding, fixed set of outputs even as the software is modified and distributed.

In some simple contexts software reproducibility is trivial to achieve: computers are designed to be deterministic machines and, unless faulty, should always compute the same result provided that the initial state and operational environment are constant. However, in most real-world contexts the initial state and operational environment are not constant.

Broadly speaking, there are three main reasons that software reproducibility is lost:

1. A developer unintentionally changes the behavior of the software, that is, someone introduces a code fault (a "bug"). This kind of change may

go undetected, but is never desired. Testing is used to help detect these faults, and once detected, such faults can be fixed.

2. The platform used to compile or execute the software changes. For example, the software might be run on a new piece of hardware, run in a different operating system, or built using a different compiler. The resulting change in the output is usually not desirable but is generally unavoidable. Testing is used to help quantify the magnitude of the change and to mitigate the risk of unacceptable inaccuracy.

3. The behavior of the software is intentionally changed to meet new requirements—perhaps to improve its accuracy. In this case a change is desired, and testing can help to track and quantify the magnitude of the improvement.

It should be noted that a rudimentary form of software reproducibility can be achieved by keeping old versions of software in a historical archive or version control system. By running the archived version in a controlled execution environment it is often possible to reproduce historic results. However, there are two downsides to this approach to achieving reproducibility. First, having an old version of the software is not generally sufficient: it is also necessary to be able to reproduce the execution environment in which the software was originally run—that may not be possible if the hardware, operating system, or workflow engine has changed. Second, this kind of version stamping does little to show how the outputs of the software have evolved over time.

A better solution is to use regression tests. Regression testing offers a convenient and powerful way to measure software output over time, and can, therefore, help scientists track software reproducibility over time. Because reproducbility is continuously monitored, even in the presence of software change, regression testing allows for software to be trusted even as it evolves to work in new environments and on new problems.

5.1.3 Regression Testing

At its core the idea behind regression testing is quite simple, even obvious: sets of automated tests with known results are applied to a piece of software on a regular schedule in order to identify those occasions when the software output differs from the historic reference values. There are a few key characteristics of the regression tests discussed in this chapter that distinguish them from other kinds of tests:

1. Regression tests are mainly designed to measure reproducibility rather than accuracy. That is, a regression test tells a tester how much the output from that test differs from the historic output, but it does not tell the tester how much the output differs from the true value[2]. This differs

---

[2]Here the true value is considered to be the output that the software would produce if there was no error in the output.

from scientific validation tests that measure accuracy by comparing the outputs with accepted "true" values.

2. Regression tests should be automated to run in a way that requires little to no human intervention. Automation allows large test sets to be run and evaluated with minimal effort in a way that is consistent over time. This is different from ad hoc verification tests that may be run by the developer during development activities.

3. Regression tests are usually lightweight tests that are chosen to run as quickly as is reasonably achievable while maintaining an acceptably high level of code coverage. That is, the goal of regression testing is to exercise the code, not to stress test the hardware or check the science. This differs from stress tests and from many validation tests. Note that other types of tests—e.g., unit tests—may also be lightweight.

4. Usually the tests are designed to test integrated software systems rather than focusing on isolated routines. This differs from unit tests that are coded alongside individual routines.[3] There is, however, some overlap between regression tests and unit tests: some regression tests may be focused on specific modules, and a suite of unit tests can be run as a valuable part of a regression testing procedure.

Regression tests, like most traditional software tests, are often evaluated on a pass/fail basis where a failure is understood to have occurred when the output from a test differs from the historical output for that test. However, it is important to note that simple binary pass/fail evaluation can easily be generalized to a nearly continuous set of scores by using a more advanced metric—such as relative error—to compare the current and historical outputs. In fact, because of the tolerance problem, such a generalization is often essential when one is testing scientific software.

5.2   Testing Scientific Software

5.2.1   The Oracle and Tolerance Problems

For any non-trivial piece of scientific software it is often very difficult or impossible for a scientist to predict precisely the output a test should

---

[3]Unit tests are generally written in a context where the programmer can determine the expected result ahead of time, thus allowing them to hard-code the correct test result directly into the test. Integration and regression tests of scientific software, on the other hand, usually involve a level of complexity such that the expected output cannot be predicted and must be measured either from an external source (for a validation test) or from the output of the program itself (for a regression test).

produce—the scientist lacks an information source—referred to as an oracle—
that can tell him or her the right answer. It is also often very difficult or
impossible for the scientist to put a strict bound on the acceptable error[4] in
the output—the scientist does not precisely know the allowable tolerance for
error or uncertainty. These two problems are known, respectively, as the *oracle*
and *tolerance* problems.

Previous studies of scientific testing have examined these problems in some
detail and have observed that having an accurate oracle and a precise tolerance
can make software testing much more effective. For example, Hook and Kelly
[196, 197] showed that many faults in sample numeric codes were not detected
when using a large set of tests and a weak tolerance, but, when that tolerance
was tightened, many of the previously undetected faults could be detected
while using a much smaller number of tests.

Scientists often rely on imprecise oracles in order to evaluate their tests
[203]. For example, a scientist who evaluates the validity of an output by
assessing it against their experience and expectations could be said to be acting
as an imprecise oracle. Experimental data used for validation also includes
uncertainty, and analytic results become imprecise when they are used to
gain insights into problems and test cases that aren't strictly analytic.

*Regression testing nicely side-steps the oracle problem by using the software
itself as the oracle.* That is, in the context of a regression test, the historic test
output is considered to be the "right" answer and, therefore, some external
oracle is not needed. The historic result is not guaranteed to be the true
answer—if, for example, the historic software had a bug then the historic
answer might be wrong—but it is a fixed reference point that can be used to
quantify change in the test outputs.

The tolerance problem must be handled a little more carefully. In some
regression testing scenarios, the tolerance problem can be overcome by
declaring that any difference between the current and the historic result is
unacceptable—that is, one allows no tolerance for deviation from the historic
results. To scientists who are used to contending with round-off errors the
zero-tolerance requirement may sound too strict, but as long as the code under test and the regression testing environment are both kept constant then
the test outputs will be constant—any change in the output indicates that
something in the code or the environment has changed. *This heightened sensitivity to perturbations makes it very easy to detect unintentional changes in
the tested execution paths.*

Unfortunately, there is a downside to the zero-tolerance condition: changing the compiler or execution platform or slightly perturbing the code can
cause many regression tests to fail, and then the tolerance problem resurfaces
as one must decide whether or not the new results are acceptably close to
the historic results. However, even when the zero-tolerance condition breaks

---

[4]Acceptable errors or inaccuracies may be due to sources such as modeling error, discretization error, and round-off error. These errors are often unavoidable and difficult to
quantify [201].

down, the record of historic results from regression tests can help one better manage the tolerance problem by providing valuable insights into the evolution of the software's accuracy. For example, the developers may observe that certain outputs are more likely to be perturbed than others—this may indicate some numerical instability that can be reduced by better solution techniques or it may, at least, indicate that tolerances on those outputs need to be more carefully chosen. These historic insights can then be called upon when one is attempting to determine appropriate test tolerances.

It also bears mentioning that there are other testing techniques that can help tame the tolerance problem. Sensitivity testing is one useful approach.

5.2.1.1   Sensitivity Testing

An input sensitivity test can be carried out by changing the inputs to a test by small amounts and then measuring the change in the corresponding outputs. The goal is to find a tolerance in the output that allows for the known uncertainty in the inputs and for the expected error (such as round-off error) that is accumulated during execution. One suggested approach, proposed and prototyped by Meng [199], is interesting because it combines interval arithmetic and automatic differentiation to identify and measure sources of numeric error at run-time.

Alternatively (or additionally), a code sensitivity test can be carried out by holding the inputs constant and, instead, making small changes to the code before measuring the resulting change in the test output. In this case, the goal is to set a tolerance such that these changes in the code are detected by the tests. An automated approach to code sensitivity testing—Mutation Sensitivity Testing—is described by Hook [196].

When doing any kind of sensitivity test the tester should remember that code faults or algorithmic deficiencies can, of course, result in inflated or muted sensitivity to perturbations. In theory, this leads to a kind of chicken-and-egg problem where the tolerance for error has to be estimated from a potentially faulty code, but, in practice, sensitivity tests can still help the tester develop some intuition and empirically derived tolerance values.

5.2.2   Limitations of Regression Testing

The first and most obvious limitation of regression testing is that, as has already been mentioned, a regression system knows only about the historic outputs and cannot check outputs against the true value. This means that regression tests cannot detect innate or preexisting problems in a code that might be due to a mistake in the initial specification or in the initial implementation of the specification.

The need to automate regression tests can also make it very difficult to use them in some applications. Automating the testing of graphical user interfaces (GUIs), while possible, can be challenging and time consuming. For that reason, it is suggested that architects of scientific software should make an effort to keep user interfaces clearly separate from the computational engine so that analysis routines can be tested without having to use a GUI to control them.

It can also be difficult to automate the testing of routines that handle input or output (I/O) to or from external sources such as sensors or other computers. Adequate testing of I/O routines can sometimes be managed by developing small routines that emulate input sources or output sinks, but care must be taken to make sure that such routines adequately mimic reality.

Test automation and output assessment may also be difficult in High Performance Computing (HPC) environments where data sets may be large and run-times very long. In such contexts one may have to develop regression tests that are artificially small or simple. For example, a finite-difference engine might have to be tested using an unusually coarse grid spacing, or a complex neural network implementation might have to be tested with a relatively meager amount of training data. It is important to remember that the primary goal of regression testing is code fault detection and not scientific validation. As long as the test can detect perturbations in the code then it is still valuable as a regression test even if it uses inputs that are not scientifically valid.

5.3   Regression Testing at ESG

Engineering Seismology Group Solutions (ESG) is a company that specializes in the monitoring and analysis of induced seismic activity around mines, oil wells, and other geotechnical installations. Software tools are essential for the acquisition, analysis, and visualization of seismic data.

The ESG software suite that is used for these activities has been developed over 20 years and, as of November 2015, is built from over 800,000 lines of C/C++ and C# code. To aid in management of the code it has been separated into a number of libraries and executables that are specialized for different tasks. Three of these libraries—comprised of 200,000 lines of C/C++ code— contain most of the routines for data storage, signal processing, and seismic analysis. These three libraries are the key components of the computational engine and are the components that are tested by the ESG regression test suite.

The Microsoft Team Foundation Server (TFS) source control system is used for code version control and change tracking at ESG. Mozilla's BugZilla is used as an issue tracker. These tools were in use before ESG developed the regression testing procedure and have facilitated the tracking of the regression test history.

Regression tests are run on every nightly build of the software. If any of the tests fail then the build is aborted and the software will not be distributed until

Table 5.1: Detected Code Faults Classified by Severity.

Severity	Count
Low	6
Moderate	13
High	9
Fatal	8
Total	36

the cause of the failure can be identified and rectified. This build procedure ensures that software with detected faults will not be distributed to beta testers and users.

The regression testing procedure at ESG was first applied to the nightly build on May 24, 2012. In the time between implementing our regression testing procedure and the writing of this chapter (November 1, 2015) there have been a total of 114 regression test failures. 36 of these failures were due to code faults—Table 5.1 lists the 36 fault related failures in four categories of severity. The other 78 failures were due to unavoidable and/or expected losses of reproducibility: 77 were due to improvements in the code and one was due to a compiler update.

5.3.1   Building the Tools

As described in the Introduction, regression tests should be automated for easy execution and evaluation. Third-party tools are available to help with test automation, but ESG decided to develop in-house testing tools for three reasons.

1. The existing code was not designed or built to be used with automated testing in mind and was, therefore, difficult to pull apart and link with third-party libraries.

2. The outputs of seismic data processing can be extensive and varied—we currently check 140 different output fields for each test. This requires a test evaluation system that is flexible and which can provide much more detailed information than a simple pass/fail result. Using ESG software leverages existing data manipulation routines to evaluate the outputs.

3. The software reads from and writes to proprietary binary files and databases which are most easily read and parsed by ESG routines.

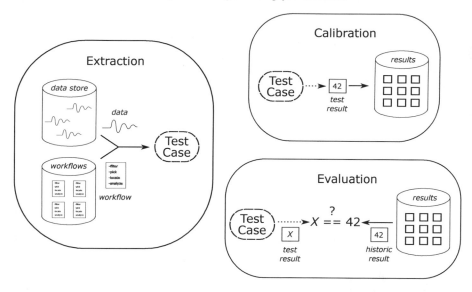

Figure 5.1: Schematic of the relationship between the three regression tester tasks.

The regression testing application supports three modes of execution: test data extraction, test calibration, and test evaluation. A schematic showing the relationship between these three tasks is shown in Figure 5.1.

In the *extraction* step the necessary data for running a test (i.e., seismic signals) is extracted from a larger data collection and the signal and seismic processing workflow is captured. Extraction only happens once for a test case. After extraction the test input data should not change; if the input data or workflow does change then it should be considered to be a new test case.

In the test *calibration* step the test case is run—i.e., the processing workflow is applied to the data—and the outputs are recorded. This is done to establish the historic results that are used to check reproducibility. Test calibration will need to be redone whenever the test outputs change for an expected or unavoidable reason—e.g., if the compiler is changed and or a more accurate solution technique is implemented. At ESG these calibration outputs are tracked by uploading them to the source control database every time that they change.

In the test *evaluation* step the test case is run and the outputs are compared with the historic outputs. Evaluation, as described in the introduction, may give a pass/fail result, a quantified error, or some sort of accuracy score. Unacceptable outputs are automatically and clearly flagged so that bad results are not accidentally overlooked. The time of the failure is recorded and, once it is determined, the cause of the failure is documented.

To develop the first version of the regression testing program it took an experienced developer roughly 75 hours. Since then it has taken an average of two or three hours per month to maintain the tests and add new testing features as they are required. Management agrees that these time costs are small compared to the amount of time that would have been spent on testing, debugging, and tech support had these faults not been detected during the build process.

5.3.1.1   Key Lesson

- Modifying legacy code can be very time consuming. If possible, try to design and build code with testing in mind so that the testing engine can be attached to the software with minimal effort. It is particularly important to keep a clear separation between the user interface and the computational engine so that you can easily replace user interfaces with a programmatic interface such as a command-line interface.

5.3.2   Selecting the Tests

Broadly speaking, the regression tests at ESG can be classified as either *code module verification* tests or *real-world validation* tests.

Code module verification tests originate from ESG's software developers, and are used to check that the functionality of specific code routines and functions are not changing. These tests are usually focused on a relatively small amount of code (somewhat like unit tests), and are intentionally selected in an effort to cover the important analysis code within a tested module. In the case of a regression failure, these tests often help us pinpoint the module that is at the root of the problem. These module tests are more flexible than real-world validation tests in that the input data and executed workflow need not be realistic. For example, the input data for a test of a signal filter might be an ideal impulse even though one would never see an ideal impulse in real seismic data. New code module tests are added when new data storage/retrieval or processing modules are added to the software or when existing modules are significantly changed.

Real-world tests, on the other hand, are chosen by domain specialists from ESG who work outside the software group. These tests are less focused than module tests—they usually involve many code modules—but they are useful to help us demonstrate that our software is still producing realistic results for real analysis problems. Like integration tests, they often involve execution states that may not be explored by simple single module tests. For example, a workflow for a real-world test may include a module to do signal clean-up, a module to identify phase arrivals, and a module to locate the event source. At ESG, the real-world tests are added and updated every year to ensure that the tests remain relevant to the analysis work that is currently underway at the company and our clients.

5.3.2.1 Key Lessons

- Focused code module tests are important to help pinpoint the root cause of a change in output. Real-world test cases are important to provide confidence that the software is working as expected on real data.

- Regular maintenance of regression test sets is important. If tests are not kept up-to-date with changes in code and in the application domain then test effectiveness will suffer.

5.3.3   Evaluating the Tests

A zero tolerance (strict equality) condition is used at ESG to evaluate the regression test outputs from the regular builds. If any change is observed in a checked[5] output then the test is said to have failed and the build will be discarded. As discussed earlier, this strict tolerance allows the tests to be very sensitive to any changes in the tested code, but does cause "false" failures when the code is improved or the execution platform is changed.

To help diagnose test failures a test report is created with every failed test. This report includes the observed difference in every checked output. For numerical outputs, discrepancies are reported as signed differences or relative errors depending on the nature of the numeric value. Differences in output strings are reported by printing the two strings.

The tests can also be run using a special non-zero tolerance mode in which output differences less than a user specified tolerance are ignored. When small discrepancies are expected—for example, when the compiler is upgraded—this special mode can be used to confirm that the tests are not exhibiting an error worse than a desired tolerance. After using this mode to confirm that the errors are reasonable the tests are then re-calibrated so that the differences are eliminated.

Note that the collection of regression test failure logs and calibration points can be used as a kind of changelog that clearly shows when developers have made changes to code that will impact reproducibility. This traceability has proven to be very useful for both internal use—it helps the software team manage and understand changes—and for external use when compiling lists of changes for clients. By storing historic test results in the source control database after every calibration ESG also has the ability to look back in time at old outputs and to quantify the change in outputs over time.

5.3.3.1 Key Lessons

- Make sure that regression testing tools can evaluate the test outputs in a way that is flexible. At a bare minimum it must be possible to measure

---

[5]Some of the ESG software outputs are expected to change (for example, time of execution) and are, therefore, not checked by the regression testing engine.

the relative or absolute error in the outputs—a pass/fail criterion is not sufficient to understand or evaluate the test results.

- Make it easy to identify which outputs of which tests have unacceptable results—making the failures obvious will make it easier to find the root cause of the failures.

- Zero tolerance test evaluation can result in false test failures and, therefore, requires the tester to spend some time examining the innocuous changes that led to these failures. However, the value of the increased sensitivity to code faults should not be overlooked.

- Test failures should be taken seriously. There is a temptation to assume that small changes in outputs are due to round-off errors, but this assumption should always be confirmed. Some of the code faults detected by the ESG regression tests only caused small perturbations in the test outputs, but had the potential to cause significant errors in certain scenarios.

- Make it easy to recalibrate your tests. You will have to do it often due to desirable or unavoidable changes to the code or environment.

5.3.4   Results

As of the writing of this chapter, regression testing has been used at ESG for 680 weekdays (ESG's nightly builds are not run on the weekends). As shown in Table 5.1, 36 code faults were detected by the regression tests and 22 of these faults could have significantly hurt the accuracy of our software's outputs while 8 of them could have resulted in software crashes.

For the sake of comparison, it was noted that in the time since implementing regression testing there have been 28 bugs reported in BugZilla for the three libraries that are being tested by the regression tester. (Note that bugs that are caught by regression tests are not included in BugZilla.) An examination of the descriptions of the 28 BugZilla bugs suggests that at least 23 of them are innate bugs, that is, they are due to problems in the initial specification or implementation of an algorithm and so are not detectable by regression tests. At ESG, this suggests that the rate at which code faults are introduced during the modification of existing software is comparable to the rate at which they are built into new developments. Regression testing has proven its value by helping ESG detect more than half of the bugs reported in the libraries in the last 680 days, and these bugs were detected before they were distributed to any beta testers or users.

The other interesting observation is that there were 36 faults (i.e., mistakes) per 77 improvements that broke reproducibility. This suggests that for every 10 improvements made to existing code routines developers have made roughly 5 mistakes—if testing hadn't been applied to detect these faults ESG would have taken 1 step back for every 2 steps forward. Even if these results are not representative in a wider context, it still seems reasonable to hypothesize that developers make mistakes at a rate that is comparable to the rate at which they make improvements: that is why it is critically important to inspect and test scientific code.

5.4　Conclusions and Future Work

Among software engineers, regression testing is generally considered to be a quality assurance process that is of critical importance when developers want to avoid losses of reproducibility. Furthermore, by taking advantage of historic results, regression testing allows software testers to side-step two of the biggest problems that are encountered when testing scientific software: the oracle and tolerance problems. For this reason, regression testing is of even more value to scientific software developers than it is to developers of software in many other domains.

The case study described in this chapter demonstrates that regression testing can help developers produce software with reproducible outputs. At ESG, 36 reproducibility breaking faults were detected by the regression tests in 680 days. While it is impossible to say how many of these faults would have been missed were it not for the regression tests, it is certain that without the tests the faults would have been harder to detect and that they would have been more costly to repair; it is also probable that the faults would have caused problems for end-users before they were detected. Regression testing improves a development team's ability to detect faults introduced into an existing code, and it detects these faults before the problematic code reaches beta testers, in-house users, or third-party clients.

The case study has also demonstrated another benefit of the regression testing process: it facilitates the monitoring and measurement of changes in software outputs. In the case study, 78 regression test failures were due to unavoidable or desirable breaks in reproducibility. The occurrence and magnitude of these output changes is clearly indicated and quantified when the regression tests are re-calibrated. Regression testing improves a development team's ability to track how their software's behavior on concrete test cases has changed over time, and these records can be useful when discussing software changes with clients and end-users. This kind of traceability is a boon to scientists who are often required to prove the historical validity of their results and processes.

Finally, the case study demonstrated that regression testing can be applied to a large piece of scientific software without sacrificing productivity. Managers and developers at ESG all agree that the 75 hours spent implementing the regression testing process and the 2 or 3 hours per month spent maintaining the tests are insignificant when compared to the many hours of debugging and troubleshooting that would have been spent if the faults had not been detected before beta testing and the software's release.

When developers are working with software that is amenable to test automation, regression testing activities are of demonstrable value, but what about contexts where test automation is more difficult? For example, it may be challenging to automate the testing of a software system that includes large amounts of complex legacy code or a system that is designed to be applied to very large data sets. In such contexts the developers may have to step back and consider if it is worth re-working the architecture of their system in order to make at least some parts of the system testable. Perhaps testing could be focused on some key units or routines that are known to be prone to errors, or maybe some artificial data sets could be created to exercise only key parts of the code. Further research into more advanced regression testing techniques may also be needed. While such work may be time consuming, this chapter suggests that the resulting improvements in reproducibility and traceability will pay dividends.

Some areas where further research and development is needed include the following:

- Studies of test selection techniques that are specifically targeted to scientific software are needed. Some initial work by Gray and Kelly [195] suggests that randomly selected tests have some utility when testing scientific codes, but further work remains to be done and is needed. At this point in time, no work targeted specifically at test selection for scientific software regression testing is known to exist.

- Work could be done to develop techniques that use historical regression test results to help tame the tolerance problem. A zero-tolerance condition is not always appropriate—e.g., when changing compiler options—and it can be difficult to know what tolerance should be used for tests in such cases. Perhaps a combination of sensitivity testing, statistical techniques, and regression histories could be used to help determine appropriate tolerances.

- Case studies of regression testing techniques being applied in diverse and varied scientific contexts would be valuable. Developers and managers at ESG have been strongly convinced of benefits of regression testing. Case studies from scientific software developers in other fields and/or using different tools would help to reinforce the value of reproducibility testing in these other contexts.

- Test automation can be very challenging when dealing with large scientific systems that run in complex execution environments. Test automation tools that acknowledge the oracle and tolerance problems and other challenges of the scientific computing world need to be developed.

Chapter 6

Building a Function Testing Platform for Complex Scientific Code

Dali Wang, Zhuo Yao, and Frank Winkler

6.1 Introduction

Complex scientific code is defined as complicated software systems that have been adopted by specific communities to address scientific questions. Many scientific codes were originally designed and developed by domain scientists without first implementing basic principles of good software engineering practices. Software complexity has become a barrier that impedes further code development of these scientific codes, including adding new features into the code, validating the knowledge incorporated in the code, and repurposing the code for new and emerging scientific questions. In this chapter, we describe innovative methods to: (1) better understand existing scientific code, (2) modularize complex code, and (3) generate functional testing for key software modules. In the end, we will present our software engineering practices within the Accelerated Climate Modeling for Energy (ACME) and Interoperable Design of Extreme-scale Application Software (IDEAS) projects. We believe our methods can benefit the broad scientific communities that are facing the challenges of complex code.

6.2 Software Engineering Challenges for Complex Scientific Code

Software testing is an essential part of software development and is an important verification activity to reveal program failures. One of the common strategies is to generate test cases by sampling the execution space, either randomly, or aiming at specific objectives that derive from the expected behavior, the program structure, or some information about software faults [218]. Many automated test generation techniques are proposed and used to improve testing effectiveness and efficiency [208, 210]. In development situations, many software developers and testers are responsible for verifying the functional correctness of code. However, for large complex scientific software code, there is an extra need to check that sub-modules actively impact other dependent modules of the source code and additional needs to check the system constraints to verify the test procedures. More importantly is to make the module validation and verification more convenient. As the present time, scientific code has become increasingly complicated; it is very difficult to write a characterized test case. In scientific code, tests may not exist for the changes that are needed. To validate scientific code and to facilitate new feature development, we must bolster the area we want to change with tests to provide some kind of safety net. From this perspective, a unit test has three advantages over large tests: (1) error localization, (2) short execution time and, (3) coverage.

6.3 The Purposes of Function Unit Testing for Scientific Code

In computer programming, unit testing is defined as a software testing method by which individual units of source code, sets of one or more computer program modules together with associated control data, usage procedures, and operating procedures, are tested to determine whether they are fit for use [216]. For generic software code, the unit testing has been proven as an efficient method for code design, optimization, debugging, and refactoring [213]. There are several existing language-specific unit testing frameworks, such as JUnit [204], CUnit [205], and FUnit [206], etc. Our unique *function unit testing* concept targets scientific code where the unit testing cases are sparse, and aims to facilitate and expedite the scientific module validation and verification via computational experiments.

Specifically, after experimenting with many testing tools in scientific code, we had repeated issues with tool scalability and usability. Based on previous experiences, we wanted to build a test platform that would: (1) be widely used by developers and module builders to fix problems and collect variables, (2) integrate smoothly into the existing workflow, (3) empower developers and module builders to write and deploy their own test case and track specific variables, and (4) produce test suites automatically and provide validation using benchmark testing cases. The ultimate goal of this effort is to generate key scientific function modules from large scale scientific code, so that those function units can be reconfigured and reassembled together to expedite new computational experiment design for model validation and verification. Due to the interests of general readers of this book, we are focusing on the functional testing framework establishment, instead of scientific experiment design using those functional units.

6.4   Generic Procedure of Establishing Function Unit Testing for Large-Scale Scientific Code

This section describes our methodology of function testing generation using traditional software development tools and concepts in computer science, particularly high performance computing research. Figure 6.1 shows the system architecture and workflow of the framework. First, after the software analysis, we can identify the software dependency information (such as external software libraries) to set up a *Unit Test Environment*, which includes a generic *Unit Test Driver* and a collection of *Unit Test Module*. Then, we identify the source code and entrance and exit of a target *Function Unit*, and generate a *Unit Test Module* for the target *Function Unit*. The *Unit Test Module* contain two major phases: *Initiation* and *Run*. In the *Initiation* phase, the memory blocks are allocated and the values are initialized. In the *Run* phase, the target *Function Unit* get executed. After that we augment the *Data Collector* into both the scientific code and the *Unit Test Module* to capture the input and output data streams of target *Function Unit*. The *Input Streams* from the

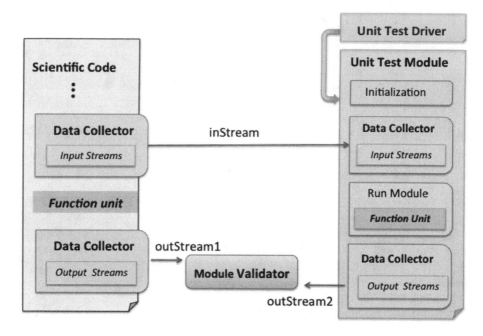

Figure 6.1: The major software component and workflow of the ACME Land Model ALM functional testing.

Data Collector inside of scientific code are used to driver the *Function Unit* inside the *Unit Test Module*. Two *Output Streams* from the *Data Collector* are sent to *Module Validator* to verify the correctness of *Unit Test Module* within the *Unit Test Environment*. Our methods contain the following steps:

6.4.1   Software Analysis and Testing Environment Establishment

Complex scientific code may contain many source code files and code dependencies can be very difficult to be investigated manually. Fortunately, there are several software development tools (such as debugging and profiling tools) that can be used for this purpose. Most modern computing language compilers also collect intensive information, which can be repurposed for software analysis. In many practices, those computing technologies and tools are used to generate scientific workflow and internal data dependencies within scientific code, especially within data structure maps, control flow charts, and software module dependency graphs. It is also important to get overview information on computational characteristics (such as function information, computational intensity, and communication patterns of scientific code), since this information can provide deep understanding of the runtime behaviors of scientific code. Many external libraries, numerical libraries or parallel computing libraries, are widely used in scientific models. These external libraries are generally kept when a function testing environment is created. A generic unit testing driver will also be created in the testing environment, so that it can initialize the unit testing procedure seamlessly.

6.4.2   Function Unit Test Module Generation

For clarity of demonstration, we define a specific scientific function (could be represented by single or a group of individual software subroutines) as a *Function Unit*. The key step of a function test procedure is the generation of an individual *Unit Test Module* from the source code. For any target *Function Unit* of interest, an associated *Unit Test Module* can be generated automatically. Each *Unit Test Module* contains two phases: *Initiation* and *Run*. The original source code of the target *Function Unit* is copied into the *Unit Test Module*, therefore, the format of all the input and output data streams are unchanged. All the *Unit Test Modules* can be initialized and executed via the generic unit testing driver.

6.4.3   Benchmark Test Case Data Stream Generation Using Variable Tracking and Instrumentation

There are many data transformations between modules and a great deal of data structure initialization works in the beginning of the legacy code. To eliminate the data dependence problems and solve data initialization problems, we have adopted a recursive compiler-based code analyzer, which analyzes unit module'AZs data flow and also processes submodels' initialization problems to make the single unit able to run. Thus, another key step within the function testing procedure is to collect the data streams in and out of any target *Function Unit* of interest during model simulation. Based on the information from software analysis, an automated procedure (using variable tracking and code instrumentation) can be developed to insert code segments into the source code, and to capture all the data streams in and out of the target *Function Unit*. In general, there are always some benchmark cases for any specific scientific code, so that by using a benchmark testing case, necessary data streams for any target *Function Unit* can be captured automatically.

6.4.4   Function Unit Module Validation

The next step in the testing procedure is to validate the results of a *Function Test Module* using the original data streams captured from the benchmark test case simulations. The validation step is very straightforward, that is the input data streams from the simulation case is used as the input data stream to test the *Unit Test Module*, and the output data streams from the *Unit Test Module* is also collected and then compared with output data streams collected from the original benchmark case simulation. If the two results match, the code integrity of the targeted *Unit Test Module* within a unified testing environment is validated.

6.5 Case Study: Function Unit Testing for the ACME Model

Over the past several decades, researchers have made significant progress in developing high fidelity earth system models to advance our understanding on earth systems, and to improve our capability of better projecting future scenarios. The Community Earth System Model (CESM, http://www2.cesm.ucar.edu) is one of the leading earth system models. Since 2014, U. S. Department of Energy (DOE) has branched off the CESM main repository and created its own model, under a nation-wide project, called Accelerated Climate Modeling for Energy (ACME). It is the only major national modeling project designed to address DOE mission needs to efficiently utilize DOE leadership computing resources now and in the future. The ACME model contains several key models which include atmosphere, ocean, sea ice, land, and glacier.

6.5.1 ACME Component Analysis and Function Call-Tree Generation

Due to the complexity of ACME, performance analysis is crucial to support ACME developers in identifying performance limiters as well as optimizing several code parts. There are several matured measurement infrastructures that can be used to collect the performance data such as function and library calls, communication events, and hardware counters that must be recorded during run time. Score-P [214] is a measurement infrastructure for collecting such performance data. It collects those events during the execution and creates either a profile in the CUBE4 format, or trace files, using the parallel Open Trace Format Version 2 (OTF2). Profiling is based on aggregating performance data, which allows a statistical view on a program run. Unlike profiling, the tracing approach records all events of an application run with precise time stamps and a number of event type specific properties. Profile analysis can be performed with Cube [207] that visualizes a call-tree of all functions. A more in-depth analysis based on trace data can be conducted with Vampir [215], a powerful performance analysis tool that offers intuitive parallel event trace visualization with many displays showing different aspects of the parallel performance behavior. Vampir displays the whole run time behavior of a parallel application. We used Score-P to get a better understanding of the software structure of ACME by profiling and tracing a coupled ACME benchmark case. Furthermore, we implemented scripts for code instrumentation and run time configuration that make it more convenient for application developers to do performance analysis on ACME using Score-P and Vampir.

To get a first overview of the software structure of ACME we used profiling to generate a call-tree of all functions of a coupled ACME benchmark case. The call-tree analysis of ACME helped to better understand the software structure within the whole earth system modeling framework. A benchmark simulation case within ACME development suite is used in our study. During the run of a three-day simulation on the Titan machine at Oak Ridge National Laboratory, Score-P collected profile data of 2626 different function calls. The total number of function visits was about 420 billion resulting in a profile size of 1GB. It has been shown that the Score-P Tool Cube [207], a profile browser, can handle such huge data to perform a call-tree analysis. Within this profile browser (Fig. 6.2), users can get not only the detailed performance information on each subroutine, but also the function call sequence of each new individual subroutine. This will help application developers with further code developments as well as porting several kernels to accelerators.

6.5.2   Computational Characteristics of ACME Code

By using the profiling and tracing capability, we are able to get the detailed computational characteristics of scientific code. In our research, we use performance analysis tool to get the detailed information on ACME simulation. Different timeline displays show application activities and communication along a time axis. Statistical displays, which focus on the current zoom-level, provide profiled results. It has been shown that Score-P can generate trace files of several parts of ACME that can be visualized using Vampir. Analogous to the profile data, (see Section 6.5.1), we generated a trace file of a three-day simulation of a coupled ACME benchmark case on the Titan machine. The run took about 9 minutes resulting in a trace file size of 644 GB. Due to a large amount of different functions we used a function grouping feature of Vampir that allows users to assign arbitrary functions to an owner-defined function group. All recorded user functions were matched with the following components: *physics, dynamics, chemistry_ modal_ aero, chemistry_ mam3, chemistry_ mozart, chemistry_ aerosal, land, ice.* Using Vampir's grouping feature, application developers can better analyze different computation phases of user functions together with communication over the processes. Figure 6.3 shows a Vampir visualization of the generated trace file. The *Master Timeline* of Vampir shows a colored sequence of different functions. Each color represents a function group, which is Message Passing Interface (MPI) or one of the ACME components. Vampir's *Function Summary* represents timing data over all processes of each component; see Figure 6.3. The two components *physics* (114,668 s) and *dynamics* (56,207 s) have the largest proportion in our simulation run. We have shown that application developers can get detailed performance data of specific ACME components by using Score-P and

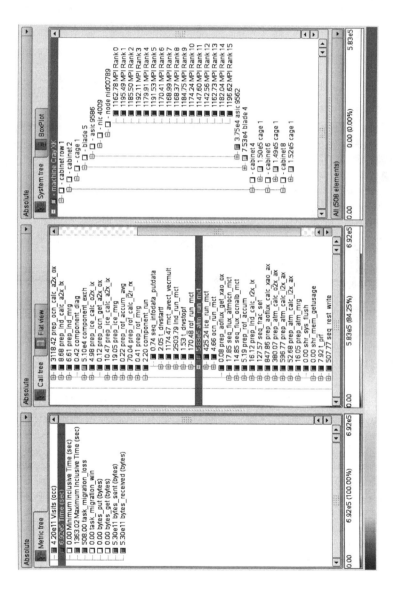

Figure 6.2: Cube visualization showing the call-tree of a three-day ACME simulation running on 32 nodes (508 cores) of the Titan machine.

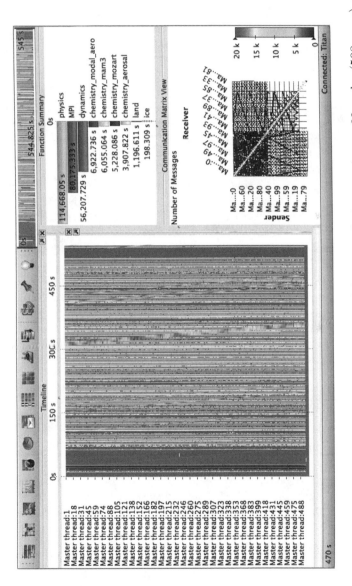

Figure 6.3: Vampir's trace visualization showing a three-day ACME simulation running on 32 nodes (508 cores) of the Titan machine.

Vampir. This also helps to maintain the code since new components, models or methods are added to the ACME code regularly.

6.5.3   A Function Unit Testing Platform for ACME Land Model

Based on the previous software analysis result, we can build a specific function testing platform for any target function unit. In this section, a function unit testing platform for the ACME land model (ALM) is presented to demonstrate the system architecture and related working procedure.

The ALM is designed to understand how natural and human changes in ecosystems affect climate. It simulates surface energy, water, carbon, nitrogen fluxes, and state variables for both vegetated and non-vegetated land surfaces [209, 212]. The ALM contains many submodes related to land biogeophysics, biogeochemistry, hydrological cycle, human dimension and ecosystem dynamics; see Figure 6.4. The structure of each submode is generally organized by software modules or subroutines based on natural system functions such as carbon-nitrogen cycles, soil temperature, hydrology and photosynthesis [217]. Each module or subroutine interacts with a list of variables that are globally accessible or subroutine-explicit. The whole ALM consists of more than 1,800 source files and over 350,000 lines of source code. The software system adopts many external numerical libraries and parallel computing technologies in order to enhance the model's computing performance. However, the software overhead and the complexities of the model structure become a barrier that hinders model interpretation and further improvements. Due to the difficulties in software configuration, it usually requires extensive effort for field scientists and modelers to design experiments and validate model results.

6.5.3.1   System Architecture of ALM Function Test Framework

The centerpiece of the ALM function test framework is a collection of individual *Unit Test Modules*, generated from the source code of any target *Function Unit* of interest. The *Function Unit* in this case is the software function related to biogeophysical and biogeochemical processes within the ecosystem. To generate an appropriate *Unit Test Module*, the first step is to set up a correct *Unit Test Environment* that incorporates the necessary software dependency on external software libraries, such as parallel computing and numerical libraries. We then can create a generic *Unit Test Driver* whose main purpose is to configure the proper testing environment for the unit testing. Each *Unit Test Module* contains two phases: *Initiation* and *Run*.

Necessary memory blocks are allocated and initialized in the *Initiation* phase. The original source code of the target *Function Unit* is copied into the *Unit Test Module* and the format of all the input and output data streams are unchanged. Another key component within the function testing framework is the *Data Collectors*, which is generated based on the information from

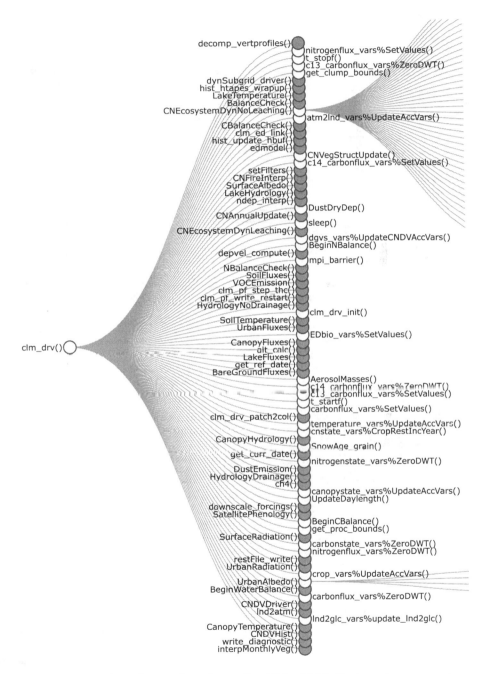

Figure 6.4: The software function call within ALM. Each node represents a software function call.

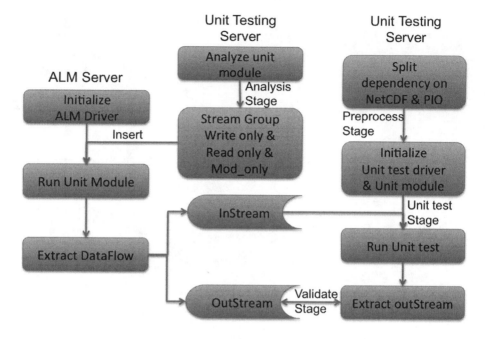

Figure 6.5: Overview of the ALM unit testing platform.

software analysis and call-tree generation process in (subsection 6.5.1). The main function of the *Data Collector* is to collect and package data streams in and out of the target *Function Unit*, or from another *Data Collector*. The last software component in the testing framework is called *Module Validator*, which is designed to identify the differences between multiple data streams among the specific data formats, and validating that the two module outputs are the same.

6.5.3.2 Working Procedure of the ALM Function Test Framework

The function test framework is a software system that allows modelers and field scientists to test particular biogeophyiscal or biogeochemical functions in ALM [211, 219].

The ALM source code runs on the Oak Ridge National Laboratory Institutional Cluster (OIC), a multiprogrammatic heterogeneous federated cluster on the Red Hat®Enterprise Linux®(RHEL) 6 64-bit system. The unit testing platform runs on a laptop with four processors (2.67 GHz Intel i7) and 4 GB of memory, running 32-bit Ubuntu GNU®/Linux®12.04. The ALM unit testing platform (Figure 6.5) has four stages: *analysis, preprocess, unit testing,* and *validate.*

At the analysis stage, there is a compiler-based dataflow analyzer; its goal is to split the data dependency between modules. It analyzes and stores dataflow using a dataflow generation algorithm. When this analyzer, run on a unit testing server, receives original source module code, it first collects all submodules, and then data groups go through it and its submodules based on a depth-first traversal algorithm. It then inserts all data declaration and output function to the beginning and ending of the original module to be a data collector. As an example of this process, the *CNEcosystemDynNoLeaching* module calls 38 subroutines, and 17 of them have expanded subroutines. To make this unit able to run without any prerequisite variable initialization problems, the analyzer will find and analyze all subroutines' initialization methods and extract three data groups (*read_only*, *write_only*, *mod_only*). The analyzer combines and divides *CNEcosystemDynNoLeaching*'s data groups with its subroutines' data groups into two parts based on their roles: the input data part that includes the *read_only*, the *write_only*, and the *mod_only* groups; and the output data part that includes the *write_only* and the *mod_only* groups. After grouping, the analyzer inserts the data output methods to the *CNEcosystem-DynNoLeaching* module.

The main purpose of the preprocess stage is to separate dependency on the parallel IO library (PIO) to make the unit test platform more portable. Technically, the following steps are implemented in our effort: (1) identify the dependency needs to be separated, because the cost in the unit test period with PIO is too high; and (2) add a new class that includes easy IO operation and replace all PIO functions with new IO functions. The result is a platform that makes it easy to deal with data collection from the original ALM simulation code.

At the unit testing stage, the unit test driver simulates a module's working background to run all unit modules. The behaviors of the test driver include: (1)initializing global parameters and constants, (2)defining variables used for subroutines and sets values based on original ALM code configuration, (3)connecting ALM simulation and loading submodules and input data collected from the ALM using override methods described previously, and (4)running unit test and creating a new output file.

At the validate stage, we compare the result from the unit test with the results from the original code simulation to validate if the unit modules ran correctly. As with the *CNEcosystemDynNoLeaching* module example: this unit has one data output from ALM and one data output from the unit testing stage. To make sure the platform is reliable and the unit module generated from the last stage is useful and correct, the Python validation tool will compare every single variable in these two files.

6.6   Conclusion

In this chapter, we have presented a unique approach to complex large-scale scientific code with sparse unit test cases. Based on the advanced development tools and modern compilers, we can build function testing platform for scientific code, so that model developers and users can better understand existing scientific code, and develop comprehensive testing cases for key scientific function modules, so that the science module builders are able to better understand existing scientific code and to make module validation more convenient. In the chapter, we also present our software engineering practices to develop a function testing platform for the land model within the Accelerated Climate Modeling for Energy (ACME). This practice is also part of code refactoring method research within the Interoperable Design of Extreme-scale Application Software (IDEAS) project. We believe our methods can be beneficial to the broad scientific communities that are facing the challenges of complex code.

Chapter 7

Automated Metamorphic Testing of Scientific Software

Upulee Kanewala, Anders Lundgren, and James M. Bieman

Scientific programs present many challenges for testing that do not typically appear in application software. These challenges make it difficult to conduct systematic testing on scientific programs. Due to a lack of systematic testing, subtle errors, errors that produce incorrect outputs without crashing the program, can remain undetected.

One of the greatest challenges for conducting systematic testing is the lack of automated *test oracles*. A test oracle determines whether the output produced by a test case is correct according to the expected behavior of the program. Many scientific programs lack *test oracles* since often these programs are written to find answers that are previously unknown or they produce complex outputs for which creating oracles are practically difficult. In such situations scientists conduct testing using a selected set of inputs and check whether the outputs are correct for only those inputs. This makes it difficult to detect subtle errors.

Metamorphic testing is a method for automating the testing of programs without *test oracles*. This technique operates by checking whether the program behaves according to a certain set of properties called *metamorphic relations*. A metamorphic relation is a relationship between multiple input and output pairs of the program. In this work, we used metamorphic testing to conduct automated unit testing on several open source scientific programs as well as a scientific program developed in-house called SAXS. SAXS generates protein structures using small angle x-ray scattering data.

We used a novel machine learning based method for automatically predicting metamorphic relations for the functions in these scientific programs. Then we used these predicted metamorphic relations as *test oracles* to conduct automated unit testing on the programs. We were able to identify 90%–99% of the automatically inserted faults using this approach.

7.1   Introduction

Custom scientific software is widely used in science and engineering. Such software plays an important role in critical decision making in fields such as the nuclear industry, medicine and the military. In addition, results obtained from scientific software are used as evidence for research publications. Despite the critical usage of such software, many studies have pointed out a lack of systematic testing of scientific software [221]. Especially, *unit testing* is an important part of systematic testing, where the smallest testable parts of the application are individually tested to ensure they are working correctly. Several studies have pointed out a lack of automated unit testing in scientific software development [222–224].

Due to this lack of systematic testing, subtle program errors can remain undetected. These subtle errors can produce seemingly correct outputs without causing the program to crash. There are numerous reports of subtle faults in scientific software causing losses of billions of dollars and the withdrawal of scientific publications [225].

One of the greatest challenges for conducting systematic automated testing is the lack of automated *test oracles*. Systematic testing requires an automated test oracle that will determine whether a test case output is correct according to the expected behavior of the program. But for many scientific programs such automated test oracles do not exist for two main reasons: (1) Scientific programs are often written to find answers that are previously unknown. Therefore test oracles do not exist for such programs. (2) Scientific software often produces complex outputs or perform complex calculations. This makes developing oracles practically difficult for these programs. Weyuker identified software that faces these types of problems as *non-testable* programs [226].

Metamorphic testing (MT) is a testing technique that can be used to test non-testable programs. This technique operates by checking whether the program behaves according to a set of properties called *metamorphic relations (MR)*. A metamorphic relation specifies how your output should change according to a specific change that you make to the inputs. A violation of a metamorphic relation during testing indicates that the program might contain a fault.

One of the challenges for automating the MT process is the task of identifying MRs. Usually MRs that should be satisfied by a program under test are identified manually by the programmer using her domain knowledge about the program. But, in this work we use *MRpred*: a novel automated method for predicting likely MRs for a given program [227]. MRpred uses a supervised machine learning approach to train a classifier that can predict MRs for a previously unseen function. Through the use of MRpred, we were able to automate the entire MT based unit testing process.

In this chapter, we present the results of a case study that we conducted to evaluate the effectiveness of the automated unit testing approach based on MT. We used four scientific libraries in our evaluation including a custom scientific library that is developed in-house. In each of the code libraries, we were able to identify about 90%–99% of automatically inserted faults through automated unit testing. Our results also show that MRs differ in fault findings effectiveness perform differently in identifying faults. MRs that make changes to individual input values perform best for the scientific libraries used in this study. Further, faults introduced by altering assignment operators and faults introduced reported the highest detection effectiveness.

The remainder of this chapter is organized as follows: Section 7.2 describes the oracle problem in scientific software testing, root causes of the oracle problem, approaches used by practitioners to alleviate the oracle problem and their limitations. Section 7.3 describes the MT process and its applications for testing scientific software. Section 7.4 describes the MRpred approach used for automatic prediction of MRs. Section 7.5 describes the experimental setup of the case studies and Section 7.6 describes the results. Finally, we present our conclusions and future work in Section 7.7.

7.2   The Oracle Problem in Scientific Software

In this section we describe the software testing process and the importance of automated oracles. Then we describe why most scientific software face oracle problems. We conclude this section with techniques used by scientists to alleviate the oracle problem and the limitations of these techniques.

Software testing is the process of executing a software to check whether it behaves according to its specification [228]. Therefore testing requires a *test oracle*, a mechanism to determine whether outputs obtained by executing the program are correct. A simple software testing process involves (1) creating a test input (often referred as a test case) (2) executing the program using the test input and get an output (3) verifying that the output is correct using a test oracle. Usually these steps are repeated multiple times until a certain *test criteria* are met.

In order to perform testing systematically and efficiently you need to automate the above steps as much as possible. This requires a test oracle that is able to determine the correctness of an output for a given test input. But scientific software often does not have an automated test oracle.

Researchers have identified several characteristics in scientific software that makes it challenging to create a test oracle [221]:

1. Some scientific software is written to find answers that are previously unknown. Therefore only approximate solutions might be available [226, 229–232].

2. It is difficult to determine the correct output for software written to test scientific theory that involves complex calculations or simulations. Further, some programs produce complex outputs making it difficult to determine the expected output [226, 233–240].

3. Due to the inherent uncertainties in models, some scientific programs do not give a single correct answer for a given set of inputs. This makes determining the expected behavior of the software a difficult task, which may depend on a domain expert's opinion [241].

4. Requirements are unclear or uncertain up-front due to the exploratory nature of the software. Therefore developing oracles based on requirements is not commonly done [233, 239, 242, 243].

5. Choosing suitable tolerances for an oracle when testing numerical programs is difficult due to the involvement of complex floating point computations [222, 238, 244, 245].

Scientific software developers have used different approaches to overcome these challenges. We describe those approaches and their limitations as follows:

1. A *pseudo oracle* is an independently developed program that fulfills the same specification as the program under test [226, 234, 241, 242, 246–250]. For example, Murphy *et al.* used pseudo oracles for testing a machine learning algorithm [235].
   Limitations: A pseudo oracle may not include some special features/treatments available in the program under test and it is difficult to decide whether the oracle or the program is faulty when the answers do not agree [251]. Pseudo oracles make the assumption that independently developed reference models will not result in the same failures. But Brilliant *et al.* found that even independently developed programs might produce the same failures [252].

2. Solutions obtained analytically can serve as oracles. Using analytical solutions is sometimes preferred over pseudo oracles since they can identify common algorithmic errors among the implementations. For example, a theoretically calculated rate of convergence can be compared with the rate produced by the code to check for faults in the program [237, 241, 246].
   Limitations: Analytical solutions may not be available for every application [251] and may not be accurate due to human errors [234].

3. Experimentally obtained results can be used as oracles [234, 237, 241, 242, 248, 253].
   Limitations: It is difficult to determine whether an error is due to a fault in the code or due to an error made during the model creation [251]. In some situations experiments cannot be conducted due to high cost, legal or safety issues [231].

4. Measurement values obtained from natural events can be used as oracles.
   Limitations: Measurements may not be accurate and are usually limited due to the high cost or danger involved in obtaining them [237, 254].

5. Using the professional judgment of scientists [234, 245, 254, 255].
   Limitations: Scientists can miss faults due to misinterpretations and lack of data. In addition, some faults can produce small changes in the output that might be difficult to identify [255]. Further, the scientist may not provide objective judgments [234].

6. Using simplified data so that the correctness can be determined easily [226].
   Limitations: It is not sufficient to test using only simple data; simple test cases may not uncover faults such as round-off problems, truncation errors, overflow conditions, etc [256]. Further such tests do not represent how the code is actually used [234].

7. Statistical oracle: verifies statistical characteristics of test results [257].
   Limitations: Decisions by a statistical oracle may not always be correct.

Further a statistical oracle cannot decide whether a single test case has passed or failed [257].

8. Reference data sets: Cox *et al.* created reference data sets based on the functional specification of the program that can be used for black-box testing of scientific programs [258].
   Limitations: When using reference data sets, it is difficult to determine whether the error is due to using unsuitable equations or due to a fault in the code.

7.3   Metamorphic Testing for Testing Scientific Software

Metamorphic testing (MT) is a testing technique that exploits the relationships among the inputs and outputs of multiple executions of the program under test. These relationships are called metamorphic relations (MRs). MT has been proven highly effective in testing programs that face the oracle problem, for which the correctness of individual output is difficult to determine [236, 259–263]. In this section we explain the MT process and its applications for testing scientific software.

7.3.1   Metamorphic Testing

Metamorphic testing (MT) was introduced by Chen et al. [264] as a way to test programs that do not have oracles. MT operates by checking whether a program under test behaves according to an expected set of properties known as *metamorphic relations*. A metamorphic relation specifies how a particular change to the input of the program should change the output.

The following is the typical process for applying MT to a given program:

1. Identify an appropriate set of MRs that the program under test should satisfy.

2. Create a set of initial test cases using techniques such as random testing, structural testing or fault based testing.

3. Create follow-up test cases by applying the input transformations required by the identified MRs in Step 1 to each initial test case.

4. Execute the corresponding initial and follow-up test case pairs to check whether the output change complies with the change predicted by the MR. A run-time violation of a MR during testing indicates a fault or faults in the program under test.

Since metamorphic testing checks the relationship between inputs and outputs of multiple executions of the program being tested, this method can be used when the correct result of individual executions are not known.

```
public static double findGyrationRadius(double[] atomsXCoords,
                    double[] atomsYCoords, double[] atomsZCoords){
   double fSum=0;
   for(int i=0;i<atomsXCoords.length;i++){
      for(int j=0;j<atomsXCoords.length;j++){
         double dx=atomsXCoords[j]-atomsXCoords[i];
         double dy=atomsYCoords[j]-atomsYCoords[i];
         double dz=atomsZCoords[j]-atomsZCoords[i];
         fSum+=(dx*dx)+(dy*dy)+(dz*dz);
      }
   }
   double fRadius=1.0/(2*atomsXCoords.length*atomsXCoords.length)*fSum;
   return Math.sqrt(fRadius);
}
```

Figure 7.1: Function from the SAXS project described in Section 7.5.1 used for calculating the radius of gyration of a molecule.

Consider the function in Figure 7.1 that calculates the radius of gyration of a molecule. Randomly permuting the order of the elements in the three input arrays should not change the output. This is the *permutative* MR in Table 7.3 on Page 167. Therefore, using this metamorphic relation, follow-up test cases can be created for every initial test case and the outputs of the follow-up test cases can be predicted using the initial test case output.

Figure 7.2 shows an automated JUnit[1] test case written for testing the function in Figure 7.1 using the permutative MR. The initial test case is generated randomly by generating three array inputs. Other automated test generation approaches, such as the coverage based test generation can be used to generate the initial test cases as well. This randomly generated initial test case is executed on the function under test. Next, based on the input relationship specified by the permutative MR, a follow-up test case is created by randomly permuting the elements in the three array input and this follow-up test case is also executed on the function under test. Finally, based on the output relationship specified by the permutative MR, an *assertEquals* statement is created to check whether the outputs of the initial and follow-up test cases are equal within a given tolerance specified by the domain. As shown with this test case, this MR based testing approach allows to generate test cases automatically and verify relationships between multiple outputs without any manual intervention.

7.3.2 Applications of MT for Scientific Software Testing

MT was used for testing scientific applications in different areas such as machine learning applications [260, 265], bioinformatics programs [236], programs solving partial differential equations [251] and image processing appli-

---

[1]http://junit.org/

```
@Test
public void findGyrationRadiusRandTest() {
Random rand=new Random();
int arrLen=rand.nextInt(MAXSIZE)+1;

//initial test cases
  double[] iX=new double[arrLen];
  double[] iY=new double[arrLen];
  double[] iZ=new double[arrLen];

  for(int k=0;k<arrLen;k++){
    iX[k]=rand.nextDouble();
    iX[k]=rand.nextDouble();
    iX[k]=rand.nextDouble();
    }

  //Executing the initial test case on the function under test
  double intialOutput=SAXSFunctions.findGyrationRadius(iX, iY, iZ);

  //create follow-up test cases by randomly permuting the array
    elements
  double[] fX=permuteElements(iX);
  double[] fY=permuteElements(iY);
  double[] fZ=permuteElements(iZ);

  //Executing the follow-up test case on the function under test
  double followUpOutput=SAXSFunctions.findGyrationRadius(fX, fY, fZ);

  assertEquals(intialOutput,followUpOutput,eps);}
```

Figure 7.2: JUnit test case that uses the permutative MR to test the function in Figure 7.1.

cations [266]. When testing programs solving partial differential equations, MT uncovered faults that cannot be uncovered by special value testing [251].

MT can be applied to perform both unit testing and system testing. Murphy *et al.* developed a supporting framework for conducting metamorphic testing at the function level [267]. They used the Java Modeling Language (JML) for specifying the metamorphic relations and automatically generating test code using the provided specifications.

Statistical Metamorphic testing (SMT) is a technique for testing non-deterministic programs that lack oracles [268]. Guderlei et al. applied SMT for testing an implementation of the inverse cumulative distribution function of the normal distribution [268]. Further, SMT was applied for testing non-deterministic health care simulation software [230] and a stochastic optimization program [261].

One of the challenges faced when applying MT is the enumeration of a set of metamorphic relations that should be satisfied by a program. This is a critical initial task in applying metamorphic testing. A tester or developer has to manually identify metamorphic relations using her knowledge of the program under test; this manual process can miss some important metamorphic relations that could reveal faults. Recently we proposed a novel technique based on machine learning for automatically detecting metamorphic relations [227,269]. In the next section we present the details of this approach.

7.4 MRpred: Automatic Prediction of Metamorphic Relations

In this section we present the details of MRpred: the approach that we developed to automatically predict metamorphic relations for a given function [269]. We first present a motivating example that demonstrates the intuition behind developing this novel graph kernel based approach. Then we explain the details of the method followed by an evaluation of the effectiveness of predicting MRs.

7.4.1 Motivating Example

Figure 7.3 displays a function that finds the maximum value of an array. Figure 7.4 displays a function that calculates the average of an array. Figure 7.5 displays a function for calculating the cumulative difference between consecutive array elements. All these functions take a double array as the input and produce a double value as the output. Figure 7.6 depicts the control flow graphs (CFGs) of the three functions without the error handling code. Consider the permutative metamorphic relation, which states that if the elements in the input are randomly permuted, the output should remain the same. The functions *max* and *average* satisfy the permutative metamorphic relation, but it is not satisfied by the *calcRun* function.

Consider the CFGs for the functions *max* and *average*. They both have very similar overall structures and they both satisfy the permutative metamorphic relation. So functions that have similar CFGs may have similar MRs. But the overall structure of the *calcRun* function's CFG is also similar to both these CFGs as well. For example, all of them have a single loop that traverses through the input array. But the *calcRun* function does not satisfy the permutative metamorphic relation. Therefore by only looking at the similarities in overall structure of the CFGs, we cannot effectively determine the metamorphic relations satisfied by them.

By observing the three CFGs in Figure 7.6 it can be observed that the satisfiability of the permutative metamorphic relation is determined by the differences in the operations performed inside the loop. While *max* performs a comparison over the array elements, *calcRun* performs a calculation between consecutive array elements. If we only consider high level properties of the function such as number of loops or types of operations we would not be able to capture this difference. Therefore it is important to include information about the sequence of operations performed in a control flow path in the features used for creating the machine learning models, and to include properties of individual operations in the function. Based on this intuition, we developed a novel method based on graph kernels for implicitly extracting features from

```
double max(double[] a) {
  int size = a.length;
  if (size==0) error;
  double max = a[size −1];
  for (int i = size −1; −−i >= 0;)
    if (a[i] > max) max = a[i];
}
return max;
}
```

```
double average(double[] a) {
  int size = a.length;
  if (size==0) error;
  double sum = 0;
  for (int i = 0; i < size;i++) {
    sum=sum+a[i];
  }
  double avg=sum/size;
  return avg;
}
```

Figure 7.3: Function for finding the maximum element in an array.

Figure 7.4: Function for finding the average of an array of numbers.

```
double calcRun(double[] a) {
  int size = a.length;
  if (size < 2) error;
  double run = 0;
  for(int i=1; i<size; ++i) {
    double x = a[i] − a[i−1];
    run += x*x;
  }
  return run;
}
```

Figure 7.5: Function for calculating the running difference of the elements in an array.

graph based representations. Graph kernels allow to incorporate similarities between operations in the functions as explained in Section 7.4.4.1.

7.4.2 Method Overview

MRped uses machine learning methods to train binary classifiers for predicting metamorphic relations. Figure 7.7 shows an overview of this approach. During the *training phase*, we start by creating a graph based representation that shows both the control flow and data dependency information of the functions in the *training set*, which is a set of functions associated with a label that indicates if a function satisfies a given metamorphic relation (positive example) or not (negative example). Then we compute the graph kernel which provides a similarity score for each pair of functions in the training set. Then the computed graph kernel is used by a support vector machine (SVM) to create a predictive model. During the *testing phase*, we use the trained model

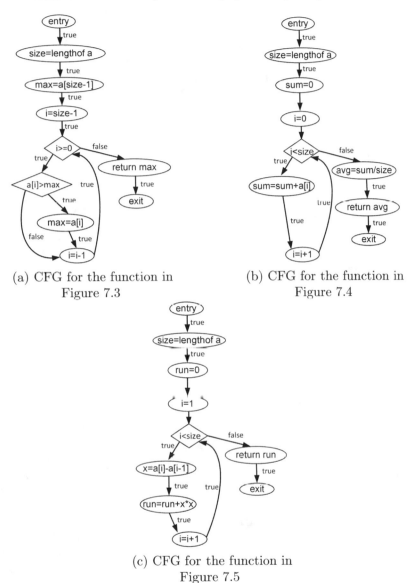

(a) CFG for the function in
Figure 7.3

(b) CFG for the function in
Figure 7.4

(c) CFG for the function in
Figure 7.5

Figure 7.6: CFGs for the functions max, average, and calcRun.

to predict whether a previously unseen function satisfies the considered meta-morphic relation. More detailed discussion about this approach can be found in our previous work [269].

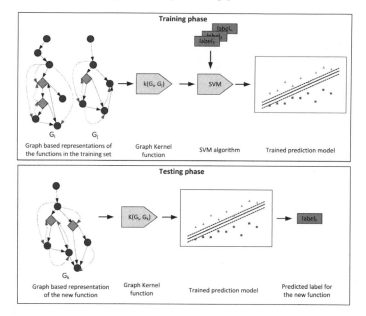

Figure 7.7: Overview of the approach.

7.4.3   Function Representation

We used the following graph-based representation of a function that contains both control flow information and data dependency information: the graph $G_f = (V, E)$ of a function f is a directed graph, where each node $v_x \in V$ represents a statement x in f. Each node is labeled with the operation performed in x, denoted by $label(v_x)$. An edge $e = (v_x, v_y) \in E$ if x, y are statements in f and y can be executed immediately after executing x. These edges represent the control flow of the function. An edge $e = (v_x, v_y) \subset E$ if x, y are statements in f and y uses a value produced by x. These edges represent the data dependencies in the function. The label of an edge (v_x, v_y) is denoted by $label(v_x, v_y)$ and it can take two values: "cfg" or "dd" depending on whether it represents a control flow edge or a data dependency edge, respectively. Nodes $v_{start} \in V$ and $v_{exit} \in V$ represent the starting and exiting points of f [270].

We used the *Soot*[2] framework to create this graph based representation. *Soot* generates control flow graphs (CFG) in *Jimple* [271], a typed 3-address intermediate representation, where each CFG node represents an atomic operation. Consequently, each node in the graph is labeled with the atomic operation performed. Then we compute the definitions and the uses of the variables in the function and use that information to augment the CFG with edges representing data dependencies in the function. Figure 7.9 displays the graph based representation created for the function in Figure 7.8.

---

[2]http://www.sable.mcgill.ca/soot/

```
public static int addValues(int a[])
{
                int sum=0;
                for(int i=0;i<a.length;i++)
                {
                        sum+=a[i];
                }
                return sum;
}
```

Figure 7.8: Function for calculating the sum of elements in an array.

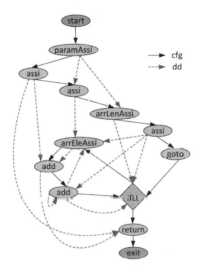

Figure 7.9: Graph representation of the function in Figure 7.8.

7.4.4 Graph Kernels

We define a *random walk kernel* for the graph representations of the functions presented in Section 7.4.3: We describe the details of this kernel next.

7.4.4.1 The Random Walk Kernel

Random walk graph kernels [272,273] count the number of matching walks in two labeled graphs. In what follows we explain the idea, while more details are provided in our previous work [269]. The value of the random walk kernel between two graphs is computed by summing up the contributions of all walks in the two graphs. Each pair of walks is compared using a kernel that computes the similarity of each step in the two walks, where the similarity of each step is a product of the similarity of its nodes and edges. This concept is illustrated in Figure 7.10. Computing this kernel requires specifying an edge kernel and a node kernel. We used the following approach for determining the kernel value between a pair of nodes. We assign a value of 0.5, if the node labels represent two operations with similar properties, even if they are not identical. The kernel value between pair of edges is determined using their edge labels, where we assign a value of one if the edge labels are identical zero otherwise.

7.4.5   Effectiveness of MRpred

We evaluated the prediction effectiveness of MRpred using the functions in the code corpus described in 7.5.1. We used 10-fold stratified cross validation to obtain the results shown in Figure 7.11. In 10-fold cross validation the data set is randomly partitioned into 10 subsets. Then nine subsets are used to build the predictive model (training) and the remaining subset is used to evaluate the performance of the predictive model (testing). This process is repeated 10 times in which each of the 10 subsets is used to evaluate the performance. In stratified 10-fold cross validation, the 10 folds are partitioned in such a way that the folds contain approximately the same proportion of positive instances (functions that exhibit a specific metamorphic relation) and negative instances (functions that do not exhibit a specific metamorphic relation) as in the original data set. Results are generated by averaging over 10 runs of cross validation.

Figure 7.11 shows the effectiveness of predicting the six MRs listed in Table 7.3. We used the area under the receiver operating characteristic curve (AUC) to measure the effectiveness. AUC measures the probability that a randomly chosen negative example will have a lower prediction score than a randomly chosen positive example [274]. Therefore a higher AUC value indicates that the model has a higher predictive ability.

According to the cross validation results, permutative and additive MRs reported the highest prediction accuracy, while the inclusive MR reported the lowest prediction accuracy. Five MRs reported an AUC higher than 0.80 showing that MRpred is highly effective in identifying likely MRs[3].

7.5   Case Studies

We conducted a case study to evaluate the effectiveness of the MT based unit testing approach for testing scientific software. In this section we present the setup of the case study.

---

[3]More in-depth analysis of MRpred can be found in our previous work [269].

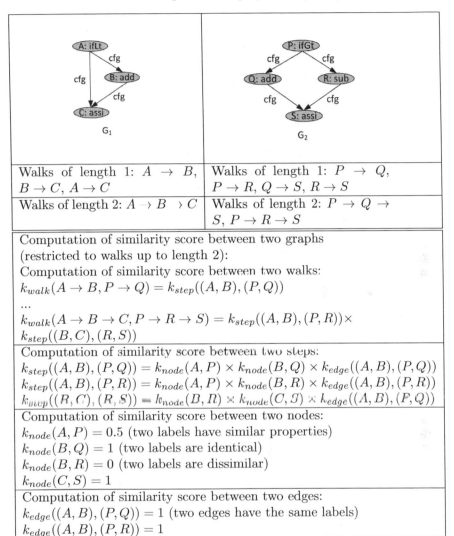

Walks of length 1: $A \rightarrow B$, $B \rightarrow C$, $A \rightarrow C$	Walks of length 1: $P \rightarrow Q$, $P \rightarrow R$, $Q \rightarrow S$, $R \rightarrow S$
Walks of length 2: $A \rightarrow B \rightarrow C$	Walks of length 2: $P \rightarrow Q \rightarrow S$, $P \rightarrow R \rightarrow S$

Computation of similarity score between two graphs (restricted to walks up to length 2):
Computation of similarity score between two walks:
$k_{walk}(A \rightarrow B, P \rightarrow Q) = k_{step}((A, B), (P, Q))$
...
$k_{walk}(A \rightarrow B \rightarrow C, P \rightarrow R \rightarrow S) = k_{step}((A, B), (P, R)) \times k_{step}((B, C), (R, S))$

Computation of similarity score between two steps:
$k_{step}((A, B), (P, Q)) = k_{node}(A, P) \times k_{node}(B, Q) \times k_{edge}((A, B), (P, Q))$
$k_{step}((A, B), (P, R)) = k_{node}(A, P) \times k_{node}(B, R) \times k_{edge}((A, B), (P, R))$
$k_{step}((B, C), (R, S)) = k_{node}(B, R) \times k_{node}(C, S) \times k_{edge}((A, B), (P, Q))$

Computation of similarity score between two nodes:
$k_{node}(A, P) = 0.5$ (two labels have similar properties)
$k_{node}(B, Q) = 1$ (two labels are identical)
$k_{node}(B, R) = 0$ (two labels are dissimilar)
$k_{node}(C, S) = 1$

Computation of similarity score between two edges:
$k_{edge}((A, B), (P, Q)) = 1$ (two edges have the same labels)
$k_{edge}((A, B), (P, R)) = 1$

Figure 7.10: Random walk kernel computation for the graphs G_1 and G_2.

7.5.1   Code Corpus

To measure the effectiveness of our proposed methods, we built a code corpus containing functions that take numerical inputs and produce numerical outputs. Since method-level mutation testing was used to create faulty versions

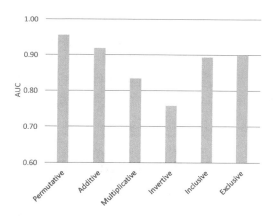

Figure 7.11: Effectiveness of MRpred in predicting MRs.

of these functions, we only use the procedural-style static Java methods from these libraries.

1. **SAXS**[4] is a systematic modeling and analysis framework for evaluation and interpretation of small angel x-ray scattering experimental data.The framework is based on a systematic development and analysis of models and a statistical analysis of the effects of uncertainty and error in models and experimental data.

2. **Colt**[5] is a scientific computing library developed by CERN. It was created to address the computational needs of high energy physics research, with an emphasis on scalability and ease of application. The library includes functionality from several domains of mathematics, including statistical reasoning, linear algebra, and pseudorandom generation.

3. **The Apache Commons Mathematics**[6] package is part of the open source Apache Commons project, which provides many modular additions to the Java API. The math components focus on common mathematical procedures not provided in `java.lang.Math`.

4. Finally we used the set of methods that we used in our previous study [227]. We will refer to this set of methods the "MethodCollection2." MethodCollection2 is composed of sorting, searching and comparative functions for numerical arrays, as well as some simple set operations and statistical calculations.

---

[4]http://www.cs.colostate.edu/hpc/SAXS/index.php
[5]https://dst.lbl.gov/ACSSoftware/colt/
[6]https://commons.apache.org/proper/commons-math/

We list the specific functions we used from the above four code libraries in Table 7.1. These functions and their graph representations can be accessed via the following URL: `http://www.cs.colostate.edu/saxs/MRpred/functions.tar.gz`. These functions and code libraries were selected to cover wide range of numerical calculations commonly found in scientific software. Thus, functions in the code corpus perform various calculations using sets of numbers such as calculating statistics (e.g. average, standard deviation and kurtosis), calculating distances (e.g. Manhattan and Chebyshev) and searching/sorting. Table 7.2 displays the LOC and the average McCabe's complexity for the functions in different libraries in the code corpus. Lines of code of these functions varied between 5 and 54, and the cyclomatic complexity varied between 1 and 11. The number of input parameters to each function varied between 1 and 5.

7.5.2   Metamorphic Relations

We used MRpred to predict likely metamorphic relations for the functions in the above mentioned code corpus. MRpred made predictions for the six MRs listed in Table 7.3 that are commonly found in numerical programs such as the ones in our code corpus.

7.5.3   Setup

We used mutation analysis [275] to measure the effectiveness of the predicted metamorphic relations from MRpred in detecting faults. Mutation analysis operates by inserting faults into the program under test such that the created faulty version is very similar to the original version of the program [276]. A faulty version of the program under test is called a *mutant*. If a test identifies a mutant as faulty that mutant is said to be *killed*.

Mutation analysis was conducted on 100 functions from the code corpus. We used the μJava[7] mutation engine to create the mutants for the functions in our code corpus. We used only method level mutation operators [277] to create mutants since we are only interested in the faults at the function level. Each mutated version of a function was created by inserting only a single mutation. Figure 7.12 shows an example mutant generated by the tool.

μJava generates method-level mutants by modifying the source code of the methods under consideration using 19 separate mutation operators. The main method level mutation categories supported by μJava are described in Table 7.4. Mutants that resulted in compilation errors, run-time exceptions or infinite loops were removed before conducting the experiment.

For each of the mutants used in the experiment, we used MRpred to get a set of predicted metamorphic relations. These predicted metamorphic relations are used to conduct automated unit testing on the mutants. For each

---

[7]`https://cs.gmu.edu/ offutt/mujava/`

TABLE 7.1: Functions Used in the Experiment

Open source project	Functions Used in the Experiment
SAXS	scatterSample, findGyrationRadius, calculateDistance, discreteScatter
Colt Project	min, max, covariance, durbinWatson, lag1, meanDeviation, product, weightedMean, autoCorrelation, binarySearchFromTo, quantile, sumOfLogarithms, kurtosis, pooledMean, sampleKurtosis, sampleSkew, sampleVariance, pooledVariance, sampleWeightedVariance, skew, standardize, weightedRMS, harmonicMean, sumOfPowerOfDeviations, power, square, winsorizedMean, polevl
Apache Commons Mathematics Library	errorRate, scale, eucleadianDistance, distance1, distanceInf, ebeAdd, ebeDivide, ebeMultiply, ebeSubtract, safeNorm, entropy, g, calculateAbsoluteDifferences, calculateDifferences, computeDividedDifference, computeCanberraDistance, evaluateHoners, evaluateInternal, evaluateNewton, mean, meanDifference, variance, varianceDifference, equals, checkNonNegative, checkPositive, chiSquare, evaluateWeightedProduct, partition, geometricMean, weightedMean, median, dotProduct
Functions from the previous study [227]	cosineDistance, manhattanDistance, chebyshevDistance, tanimotoDistance, hammingDistance, sum, dec, errorRate, reverse, add_values, bubble_sort, shell_sort, sequential_search, selection_sort, array_calc1, set_min_val, get_array_value, find_diff, array_copy, find_magnitude, dec_array, find_max2, insertion_sort, mean_absolute_error, check_equal_tolerance, check_equal, count_k, clip, elementwise_max, elementwise_min, count_non_zeroes, cnt_zeroes, elementwise_equal, elementwise_not_equal, select

function f we randomly generated 10 initial test cases. Then, we created follow-up test cases using the metamorphic relations predicted by MRpred for f, for each of the initial test cases. Finally we checked whether the corresponding metamorphic relations were satisfied when the initial and follow-up test case pairs are executed on the mutant. A mutant of f is killed, if at least one pair of test cases fail to satisfy the corresponding metamorphic relation.

Table 7.2: Details of the Code Corpus

Library	LOC	McCabe's Complexity (average)
SAXS	350	4.25
Colt	953	2.46
Apache Math	885	3.78
MethodCollection2	516	2.93

Table 7.3: The Metamorphic Relations Used in This Study

Relation	Change made to the input	Expected change in the output
Permutative	Randomly permute the elements	Remain constant
Additive	Add a positive constant	Increase or remain constant
Multiplicative	Multiply by a positive constant	Increase or remain constant
Invertive	Take the inverse of each element	Decrease or remain constant
Inclusive	Add a new element	Increase or remain constant
Exclusive	Remove an element	Decrease or remain constant

7.6 Results

In this section we present the results of our case studies. We first discuss the overall fault detection effectiveness using the automated unit testing approach that we discussed in this Chapter. Then we discuss the fault detection effectiveness of different MRs and the effectiveness of this approach in detecting faults in different categories.

7.6.1 Overall Fault Detection Effectiveness

First we present the overall fault finding effectiveness across the four code libraries in our code corpus. We present the aggregated results obtained using all the predicted metamorphic relations by MRpred to conduct unit testing on the functions in the code corpus. Fault finding effectiveness is measured through the percentage of faulty versions identified using the predicted MRs. Figure 7.13 shows the overall fault finding effectiveness across the four libraries.

Software Engineering for Science

```
(line 135) double_entropy(double):(double) k[i] / sum_k => (double) k[i] * sum_k
Original
127     {
128         double h = 0d;
129         double sum_k = 0d;
130         for (int i = 0; i < k.length; i++) {
131             sum_k += (double) k[i];
132         }
133         for (int i = 0; i < k.length; i++) {
134             if (k[i] != 0) {
135                 final double p_i = (double) k[i] / sum_k;
136                 h += p_i * Math.log( p_i );
137             }
138         }
139         return -h;
140     }
141
Mutant
127     {
128         double h = 0d;
129         double sum_k = 0d;
130         for (int i = 0; i < k.length; i++) {
131             sum_k += (double) k[i];
132         }
133         for (int i = 0; i < k.length; i++) {
134             if (k[i] != 0) {
135                 final double p_i = (double) k[i] * sum_k;
136                 h += p_i * Math.log( p_i );
137             }
138         }
139         return -h;
140     }
```

Figure 7.12: A faulty mutant produced by μJava.

Table 7.4: Categories of Mutations in μJava

Category	Description
Arithmetic	Replacement/insertion/deletion of an arithmetic operator
Relational	Replacement of a relational operator
Conditional	Replacement/insertion/deletion of conditional operators
Shift	Replacement of a shift operator
Logical	Replacement/insertion/deletion of a logical operator
Assignment	Replacing an assignment operator
Deletion	Delete an operator, variable or condition

Fault finding effectiveness of all the four libraries were above 90%. In Colt functions, 99% of the faulty versions could be found through automated MT based unit testing.

7.6.2 Fault Detection Effectiveness across MRs

Next we look at the fault detection effectiveness across different MRs. For this we computed the number of faulty versions detected by each MR when it is used by itself for testing the function. Figure 7.14 shows the percentage of faulty versions detected by the six MRs used in this study.

The highest percentage of faulty versions were detected by the additive and multiplicative MRs. Both of these MRs make changes to individual

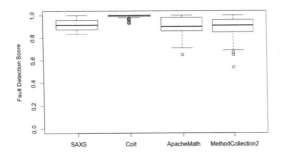

Figure 7.13: Overall fault detection effectiveness.

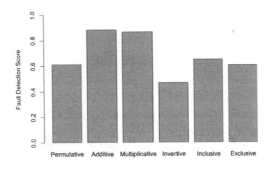

Figure 7.14: Fault detection effectiveness across MRs.

values in inputs. Invertive MR reported the lowest fault finding effectiveness. One possible reason for the difference in performance across the MRs is the prediction accuracy reported by MRPred for predicting the corresponding MR. For example invertive MR reported the lowest prediction accuracy as shown in Figure 7.11. This might be one reason for the low fault detection score for the inclusive metamorphic relations.

Figure 7.15 shows the fault detection effectiveness for each MR for the four code libraries used in this study. For MethodCollection2 and Colt functions, additive and multiplicative MRs performed best. For SAXS permutative and multiplicative MRs performed best. For SAXS additive MR was not predicted as a likely MR. Therefore it is not used for testing. For ApacheMath, multiplicative and invertive MRs performed best. It should be noted that apart from SAXS for all the other libraries additive and multiplicative MRs gave good fault finding effectiveness.

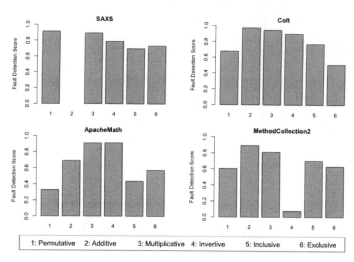

Figure 7.15: Fault detection effectiveness across MRs.

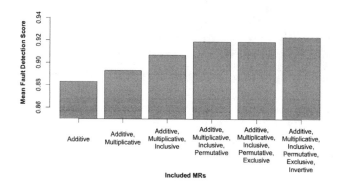

Figure 7.16: Fault detection effectiveness of multiple MRs.

Figure 7.16 shows the variation of fault detection effectiveness as we add new MRs to the set of MRs used for testing. We start testing with the additive MR that reported the highest fault detection effectiveness. Then we added the other five MRs in the order of their fault finding effectiveness as reported in Figure 7.14. There is a considerable increase in the fault finding effectiveness as the multiplicative, inclusive and permutative MRs are added to the set of MRs used for testing. The fault detection effectiveness did not improve when

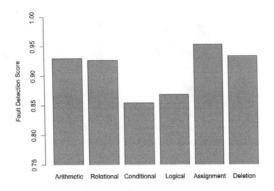

Figure 7.17: Fault detection effectiveness across different fault categories.

the exclusive MR is added. Further, the addition of the inclusive MR does not improve the fault detection effectiveness significantly. These results show that testing using the most effective MRs first will result in achieving a higher overall fault detection effectiveness quickly. This will be especially useful when there are limitations on the testing time or budget.

7.6.3   Effectiveness of Detecting Different Fault Categories

Finally we look at the effectiveness of the MT based automated unit testing approach for detecting faults in different fault categories. μJava supports the insertion of faults in seven fault categories as listed in Table 7.4. For our code corpus mutants in the shift operator category were not generated, since none of the functions used any shift operators. Figure 7.17 shows the effectiveness of detecting faults in the other six categories.

As shown in Figure 7.17, faults in the assignment category reported the highest detection percentage. Faults in this category refers to faults made with the basic assignment operator (i.e. assigning the value of the right side expression to the left side variable in Java) and faults made with short cut assignment operators (i.e. (1) +=, (2) -=, (3) *=, (4) /=, (5) %=, (6) &=, (7) |=, (8) ∧ =, (9) «=, (10) »=, and (11) »>=). μJava creates these faults by replacing these operators with another in the same category. Therefore the results suggest that the set of MRs that we used in this study are highly effective in identifying faults related to assignment operator replacement.

The lowest effectiveness was reported for faults associated with conditional operators as shown in Figure 7.17. These faults are created by inserting, deleting and replacing conditional operators (i.e. binary conditional operators - (1) &&, (2) ||, (3) &, (4) |, and (5) ∧. Unary conditional operators - !.) in Java.

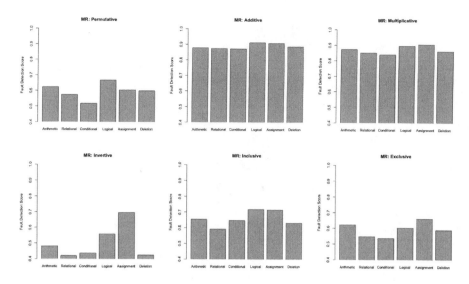

Figure 7.18: Fault detection effectiveness across fault categories for individual MRs.

Figure 7.18 shows the effectiveness of detecting faults in different categories with individual MRs used in this study. Consistent with the results presented in Figure 7.14, additive and multiplicative MRs were most effective in identifying faults in all the six categories. Invertive MR was the least effective in identifying faults in five categories except the assignment operator faults.

7.7   Conclusions and Future Work

A lack of automated systematic testing in scientific software has contributed towards missed subtle errors in this software. One of the major challenges for conducting automated testing in scientific software is the oracle problem. In this chapter we demonstrated a novel automated testing approach based on metamorphic testing to conduct automated unit testing on a set of functions obtained from several scientific libraries.

Our results show that this MT based automated unit testing approach is highly effective in detecting faults. This method was able to identify 90%–99% of automatically inserted faults in the code libraries used in this study. We also found that this approach is effective in identifying faults in different categories. With the set of metamorphic relations we used in this study, detecting assignment operator faults was most effective while detecting conditional operator faults was least effective. Further, among the six MRs used in this study, additive and multiplicative MRs were most effective in identifying faults in all the categories.

This study showed that certain MRs are more effective in identifying faults. In the future we plan to investigate this further and develop techniques to automatically prioritize the most effective MRs for testing a given program. We plan to add this functionality to MRpred. We also plan to incorporate information about fault categories when making this prioritization. Further, we plan to investigate techniques to automatically generate initial and follow-up test cases for given MRs so that the fault findings effectiveness can be further improved.

Chapter 8

Evaluating Hierarchical Domain-Specific Languages for Computational Science: Applying the Sprat Approach to a Marine Ecosystem Model

Arne N. Johanson, Wilhelm Hasselbring, Andreas Oschlies, and Boris Worm

In this chapter, we present a Model-Driven Software Engineering (MDSE) approach called *Sprat*, which adapts traditional software engineering practices in order to employ them in computational science. The approach is based on the hierarchical integration of so-called Domain-Specific Languages (DSLs) to facilitate the collaboration of scientists from different disciplines in the development of complex simulation software. We describe how multiple DSLs can be integrated to achieve a clear separation of concerns among the disciplines and how to apply Sprat during the different phases of the software life cycle.

To evaluate our approach, we discuss results from a case study in which Sprat has been utilized for the implementation of a coupled marine ecosystem model for spatially-explicit fish stock prediction. We report on the DSLs developed for this case study, how scientists benefit from them, and on lessons learned. In particular, we analyze the results from expert interviews conducted with both scientists and professional DSL developers.

The remainder of this chapter is structured as follows: in Section 8.1, we motivate our research and point out a communication gap between software engineering and computational science. This gap makes it necessary to *adapt* software engineering techniques and methods for them to be adopted by scientists. Section 8.2 explains why Model-Driven Software Engineering (MDSE) approaches and Domain-Specific Languages (DSLs) are good starting points for such adaptations. In Section 8.3, we introduce our Sprat Approach and describe the case study we use for its evaluation in Section 8.4. We report on results from this case study in Section 8.5. Conclusions and lessons learned are given in Section 8.6.

8.1 Motivation

When software engineers started to examine the software development practice in computational science, they noticed a "wide chasm" [296] between how these two disciplines view software development. Faulk et al. [293] describe this chasm between the two subjects using an allegory which depicts computational science as an isolated island that has been colonized but then was left abandoned for decades:

> "Returning visitors (software engineers) find the inhabitants (scientific programmers) apparently speaking the same language, but communication—and thus collaboration—is nearly impossible; the technologies, culture, and language semantics themselves have evolved and adapted to circumstances unknown to the original colonizers."

The fact that these two cultures are "separated by a common language" created a communication gap that inhibits knowledge transfer between them. As a result, modern software engineering practices are rarely employed in computational science.

So far, the most promising attempt to bridge the gap between computational science and software engineering seems to be education via workshop-based training programs focusing on Ph.D. students, such as the ones organized by Wilson [318] and Messina [306]. While the education approach does address the skill gap that is central to the "software chasm," education will not suffice alone: just exposing scientists to software engineering methods will not be enough because these methods often fail to consider the specific characteristics and constraints of scientific software development—i.e., the functioning of these methods is based on (often implicit) assumptions that are violated in the computational science context [288, 297]. We therefore conclude that—complementary to the education approach—we have to select suitable software engineering techniques and *adapt* them specifically to the needs of computational scientists.

8.2 Adapting Domain-Specific Engineering Approaches for Computational Science

The primary goal of scientists is *not* to create software, but to obtain novel scientific results, Software development is (just) a means to this end. At the same time, however, most scientists are very concerned about having full control over their applications and how these actually compute their results, which is why many prefer "older" programming languages with a relatively low level of abstraction from the underlying hardware (cf. [283, 288, 293, 310]).

Among the techniques and tools that software engineering has to offer, Model-Driven Software Engineering (MDSE) [284,315] and especially Domain-Specific Languages (DSLs) [294] are promising starting points for addressing the needs of computational scientists.

MDSE uses *models* expressed in *modeling languages* as the primary artifact in every stage of the software life cycle (implying that models are also implementation artifacts). *Transformations* are employed to map a source model to a target artifact which can either be a model again (*model-to-model* transformation) or an arbitrary textual artifact like source code (*model-to-text* transformation).

The modeling languages utilized in the context of MDSE are so-called *Domain-Specific Languages (DSLs)*. Like General-Purpose Languages (GPLs), such as C or Java, DSLs are programming languages. However, unlike GPLs, which are designed to be able to implement any program that can be computed with a Turing machine, DSLs limit their expressiveness to a particular application domain. By featuring high-level domain concepts that enable to model phenomena at the abstraction level of the domain and by providing a notation close to the target domain, DSLs can be very concise. The syntax of a DSL can be *textual* or *graphical* and DSL programs can be executed either by means of *interpretation* or through *generation* of source code in existing GPLs. A popular example of a textual DSL are regular expressions, which target the domain of text pattern matching and allow to model search patterns independently from any concrete matching engine implementation.

As with any other formal language, a DSL is defined by its *concrete* and *abstract syntax* as well as its *static* and *execution semantics*. While the concrete syntax defines the textual or graphical notation elements with which users of the DSL can express models, the abstract syntax of a DSL determines the entities of which concrete models can be comprised. These abstract model entities (abstract syntax) together with the constraints regarding their relationships (static semantics) can again be expressed as a model of all possible models of the DSL, which is therefore called the *meta-model* of the DSL.

Since DSLs are designed to express solutions at the abstraction level of the domain, they allow the scientists to care about what matters most to them: doing science without having to deal with technical, implementation-specific details. While they use high-level domain abstractions, they still stay in full control over their development process as it is them who directly implement their solutions in formal and executable (e.g., through generation) programming languages. Additionally, generation from a formal language into a low-level GPL permits to examine the generated code to trace what is actually computed.

DSLs can also help to reconcile the conflicting quality requirements of performance on the one hand and portability and maintainability on the other hand that are responsible for many of the difficulties experienced in scientific software development (cf. [288]). DSL source code is maintainable because it is often pre-structured and much easier to read than GPL code, which makes it almost self-documenting. This almost self-documenting nature of DSL source code and the fact that it can rely on an—ideally—well-tested generator for program translation ensure the reliability of scientific results based on the output of the software. Portability of DSL code is achieved by just replacing the generator for the language with one that targets another hardware platform. With DSLs, the high abstraction level does not have to result in performance losses because the domain-specificity first of all enables to apply—at compile time—domain-specific optimizations and greatly simplifies automatic parallelization.

In the way described above, DSLs integrated into a custom MDSE approach could help to improve the productivity of computational scientists and the quality of their software. A first indicator that supports this hypothesis can be found in the survey report of Prabhu et al. [308], who find that those scientists who program with DSLs "report higher productivity and satisfaction compared to scientists who primarily use general purpose, numerical, or scripting languages."

8.3 The Sprat Approach: Hierarchies of Domain-Specific Languages

In this section, we introduce *Sprat*, which is a MDSE approach that aims at enabling scientists from different disciplines to efficiently collaborate on implementing well-engineered simulation software without the need for extensive software engineering training. Its underlying idea is to provide a Domain-Specific Language (DSL) for each (sub-)discipline that is involved in the development project and to integrate these modeling languages in a hierarchical fashion. The hierarchical structure of the DSL integration is enabled by the typical architecture of scientific (simulation) software, which we discuss before introducing Sprat itself.

8.3.1 The Architecture of Scientific Simulation Software

Typical scientific simulation software can be implemented using the multi-layered software architecture pattern [286]. A software system conforms to this pattern if its components can be partitioned into a hierarchy of layers in which each layer corresponds to a particular level of abstraction of the system. In addition to that, every layer has to be implemented using only the abstractions of lower layers but never using abstractions from higher ones. Popular examples of the application of the layers pattern are networking protocols, which introduce layered levels of abstraction ranging from low-level bit transmission to high-level application logic.

We argue that the general structure of typical simulation software lends itself to the layers pattern and clarify this with an example: generally speaking, scientific simulation software employs algorithms to analyze scientific models—i.e., mathematical abstractions of the real world—by means of computation. The scientific models can be formalized using different mathematical frameworks, such as differential equations or agent-based models [295]. Based on the respective mathematical framework and on the aspects that the model is supposed to be examined for, a suitable analysis algorithm is chosen.

For example, an ocean model would usually be based on the physical laws of fluid dynamics which are formulated as Partial Differential Equations (PDEs). An implementation of this model would employ a suitable PDE solver algorithm and implement the concrete model equations using this solver.

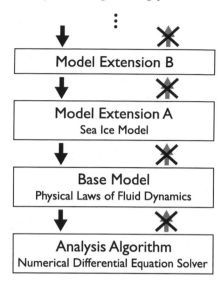

Figure 8.1: Usage relations in the layered architecture of scientific simulation software.

Note that an analysis algorithm is appropriate not only for the specific model in question but for at least a whole sub-class of models in the respective mathematical modeling framework. Therefore, the analysis algorithm can be implemented independently of any concrete model and can be arranged in a way that the model component makes use of the algorithm component but not the other way around.

If additional scientific effects are to be included in the simulation, they can usually be interpreted as extensions to a base model. If, for example, sea ice is supposed to be included in an ocean model, it can be represented as a layer over the entire sea surface which may contain ice of variable thickness [279]. This layer would then influence certain processes which are modeled in the basic fluid dynamics equations.

Such model extensions introduce higher levels of abstraction and can be implemented atop the existing base model, which remains independent of the extension components. In this way, multiple model extensions can be stacked on top of each other, which leads to a layered software architecture as depicted in Figure 8.1.

Alexander and Easterbrook [279] demonstrate that it is not only theoretically possible to employ the multi-layered architecture pattern in the engineering of scientific software but that is actually used by existing simulation software. For this purpose, they analyze the software architecture of eight global climate models that represent both ocean and atmosphere.

Regarding the boundaries between the different components of the climate models, Alexander and Easterbrook point out that they "represent both natu-

```
#pragma omp parallel for
for ( i =1;  i <N−1;  i++) {
    dt_u [ i ]    = rho [ i ];
    dt_rho [ i ] = ( v [ i +1] − v [ i −1]) / (2*dx );
    dt_v [ i ]   = ( rho [ i +1] − rho [ i −1]) / (2*dx );
}
```

Listing 8.1: Code snippet from a fictitious C implementation of a finite difference solver for the wave equation.

ral boundaries in the physical world (e.g., the ocean surface), and divisions between communities of expertise (e.g., ocean science vs. atmospheric physics)." Therefore, the hierarchically arranged components in simulation software also belong to distinct scientific (sub-)disciplines. This, of course, does not only hold true for climate models but also applies to general simulation software: the analysis algorithm, the base model, and all model extension components are separated from each other along the boundaries of different "communities of expertise."

We will make use of the possibility to partition scientific simulation software along discipline boundaries into hierarchically arranged layers by constructing a *DSL hierarchy* that mirrors this hierarchical structure.

8.3.2   Hierarchies of Domain-Specific Languages

Even though scientific simulation software can typically be engineered using a layered architecture (or actually features such an architecture), "code modularity remains a challenge" [279]. This challenge arises because high performance is required and old programming languages are used (see above). Schnetter et al. [312] demonstrate this with the simple example of a solver for the scalar wave equation in first-order form given as

$$\partial_t u = \rho \tag{8.1}$$

$$\partial_t \rho = \delta^{ij} \partial_i v_j \tag{8.2}$$

$$\partial_t v_i = \partial_i \rho. \tag{8.3}$$

An efficient parallel implementation in C of a finite difference solver for this equation in one dimension would very likely contain a loop like the one in Listing 8.1. It is clearly visible that different concerns are mixed within these few lines of code: the physical model to be simulated (wave equation), the numerical approximation algorithm (finite difference method), and its mapping to hardware resources (memory layout of the vectors, parallelization via OpenMP [289]). A real world application would, of course, be much more complex and would, thus, contain even more intertwined concerns such as memory layout and communication/synchronization for distributed comput-

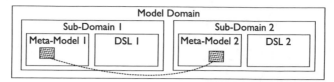

Figure 8.2: Horizontal integration of multiple DSLs. Figure adapted from [315].

ing nodes. Currently, with low-level programming languages such as C, there is no straightforward way to evade this problem without negatively affecting performance levels.

The aforementioned problems with the modularization of scientific simulation software impede the realization of a layered software architecture that would clearly separate the concerns of different scientific (sub-)disciplines. This makes the software unnecessarily hard to maintain and hinders the co-operation of experts focusing on different scientific aspects of the simulation. Furthermore, it makes it difficult for scientists with only basic programming skills to participate in the development effort at all.

In order to meet these challenges, we propose a software engineering approach called *Sprat*, which is specifically designed for interdisciplinary teams of scientists collaborating on the implementation of scientific (simulation) software. Sprat introduces a DSL for each (sub-)discipline involved in the development project and integrates the languages in a hierarchical fashion based on the layered architectural structure of scientific software outlined above.

8.3.2.1 Foundations of DSL Hierarchies

Typically, DSLs are integrated horizontally as depicted in Figure 8.2 (cf. [315]). In this way, a single domain can be divided into multiple sub-domains that share some common aspects of their respective domain meta-models. Through these shared concepts, the DSLs of the different sub-domains can interact with one another.

For our purpose, however, we need to integrate DSLs from completely different domains (such as numerical mathematics and fish stock modeling). To do so, we extend Stahl and Völter's [315] concept of a *domain-specific platform*. Instead of having a single, pre-implemented platform that already features domain-specific concepts, we introduce multiple, vertically-aligned domain-specific layers that are semantically oriented towards each other as illustrated in Figure 8.3. Each layer is associated with a different DSL which is used to implement a certain part (defined by domain boundaries) of the software system to be constructed. Together, these layers form what we call a *DSL hierarchy*. The layers establish a hierarchy in the sense that at least a portion of the application part associated with each layer forms the (domain-specific) implementation platform for the part on the next higher level. This means

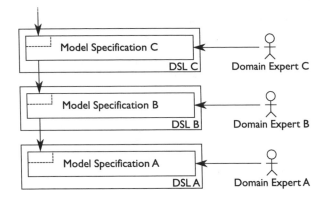

Figure 8.3: Multiple layers acting as domain-specific platforms for each other.

that each layer uses abstractions provided by the next lower hierarchy level but never uses abstractions from higher levels. For a description of how the levels of the hierarchy can interact and, thus, form domain-specific platforms for each other, see Section 8.3.2.2.

Each level in a DSL hierarchy is associated with a modeler role which uses the DSL of the level to model the application part of this level. Together, the application parts of all hierarchy levels form the whole scientific simulation application to be implemented. Note that we assign a *role* to each level and not a *person*. This implies that a single person can fulfill multiple roles in a DSL hierarchy and one role can be assumed by several persons at once.

By employing an individual DSL for each discipline that is involved in an interdisciplinary scientific software project, we achieve a clear separation of concerns. Additionally, this ensures that all participating scientists (who assume modeler roles) are working only with abstractions that they are already familiar with from their respective domain. Due to the high specificity of a well-designed DSL, the code of an implemented solution that uses this language can be very concise and almost self-documenting. This simplifies writing code that is easy to maintain and to evolve, which allows scientists to implement well-engineered software without extensive software engineering training.

8.3.2.2   An Example Hierarchy

To demonstrate what a DSL hierarchy looks like for an actual scientific software project, we depict in Figure 8.4 the DSL hierarchy for the development of the Sprat Marine Ecosystem Model, which is a PDE-based spatially-explicit model for the long-term prediction of fish stocks. For additional information concerning the different DSLs of the hierarchy and the Sprat Marine Ecosystem Model itself, refer to Section 8.4 below and [299, 300].

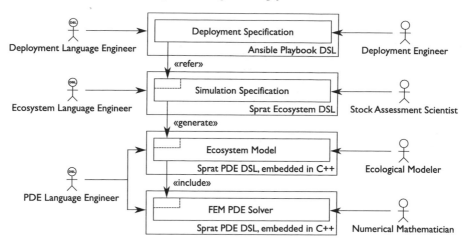

Figure 8.4: DSL hierarchy for the Sprat Marine Ecosystem Model.

The Sprat Marine Ecosystem Model is based on Partial Differential Equations (PDEs) and introduces fish into existing biogeochemical ocean models. Four different disciplines are involved in the implementation and application of the corresponding simulation software (see the right side of Figure 8.4). At the basis of the hierarchy, we find the role of the Numerical Mathematician who models a special-purpose PDE solver for the model equations. The solver is implemented using the Sprat PDE Solver DSL, which is embedded into C++.

Using the abstractions provided by the bottommost level, the Ecological Modeler implements the concrete equations to be solved for the ecosystem model. Since both the Numerical Mathematician and the Ecological Modeler work with the same abstractions (mathematical equations) to express their application parts, the ecosystem model is implemented with the same DSL as the PDE solver. The interaction between the first and the second layer is of the type *inclusion*: the higher level reuses existing abstractions from the lower level in the same DSL by including them into the model on the higher level.

To apply the simulation to a specific ecosystem (say, the Baltic Sea), it has to be parametrized by a fish stock assessment scientist for that particular ecosystem. For this purpose, the Stock Assessment Scientist creates an ecosystem simulation description using the external Sprat Ecosystem DSL. From such a description, information that is missing for a simulation to be complete is *generated* on the second hierarchy level.

While the first three layers complete the ecosystem simulation as such, it is still undefined how to build and execute the simulation in a (possibly distributed) compute environment. To formally describe this process, the Deployment Engineer models a deployment specification using the external Ansible Playbook DSL [280]. Such a specification interacts with the other levels of the

DSL hierarchy by *referring* to names of model artifacts without assuming any knowledge about the internal structure (i.e., the meta-model) of these models. This level of knowledge is sufficient to, for example, compile application parts.

One could argue that the deployment is a concern orthogonal to the implementation of the simulation and should, hence, not be included in the DSL hierarchy. We decided to incorporate the deployment into the hierarchy nonetheless because it allows us to have a single structure that can be used to abstractly describe to the scientists the whole development process of the simulation up to its execution. This is part of the effort to minimize the accidental complexity of the Sprat Approach (for a more detailed discussion of this aspect, see Section 8.3.4).

The last elements of Figure 8.4 which we have not discussed yet are the language engineer roles. Each DSL has a language engineer role assigned to it that is responsible for the design, implementation, and maintenance of the language. For a description of the individual tasks of a language engineer role and of how to assign this role, see Section 8.3.3.

As with any other approach for bridging the gap between software engineering and computational science, Sprat requires software engineers to assist scientists in the development of scientific software (in our case, language engineers have to design and implement DSLs). This can be problematic because positions for software engineers to provide development support in scientific research institutions have typically not been supported by funding agencies in the past [288]. The neglect of such positions by most funding bodies should be reconsidered, as it has been shown that investing in such positions can have a markedly positive impact [302]. In the meantime, Sprat minimizes the input that is needed from trained software engineers by letting the scientists stay in full control of all development activities of the scientific software itself (using the DSLs designed by professional language engineers; see below).

An overview on the meta-model of our concept of a DSL hierarchy is depicted in Figure 8.5. A detailed description of this meta-model is omitted here for lack of space but the above description of the example hierarchy serves to illustrate the general ideas.

8.3.3   Applying the Sprat Approach

This section describes the engineering process of the Sprat Approach, which builds upon the concept of hierarchies of DSLs introduced above. Sprat acknowledges that computational scientists want to have full control over the implementation of their simulation software. To mediate between the desire for independence on the one hand and the need for assistance on the other hand, the Sprat Approach allows the scientists to continue developing their simulations on their own but with programming languages specifically designed to help them create well-engineered software. Therefore, the Sprat Process, which is shown in Figure 8.6, involves both scientists and DSL engineers [303], with the latter playing a supporting role.

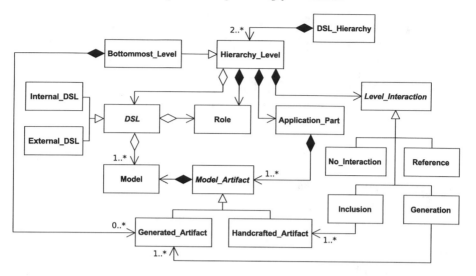

Figure 8.5: Meta-model for the concept of DSL hierarchies.

8.3.3.1 Separating Concerns

Scientists typically only have a "vague idea" [314] of the simulation software they need for answering their scientific questions. However, such a very general idea is sufficient to construct a DSL hierarchy for the software project. The first step in doing so is for the team of scientists to identify the scientific (sub-)domains that correspond to the classes of scientific effects that need to be modeled. In a second step, these domains are arranged hierarchically as described in Section 8.3.1.

8.3.3.2 Determining Suitable DSLs

Once the levels of the DSL hierarchy and their corresponding application parts have been established, the language engineers must determine whether or not suitable DSLs for the target domains already exist (adopting an existing DSL obviously requires much less effort than creating a new one). For this purpose, Mernik et al. [305] give a collection of patterns that can act as guidelines for deciding whether to develop a new DSL in a given situation. Note, however, that for this activity, the DSL engineers have to take into account a number of factors that are not commonly considered for DSL selection but are of special importance in the context of scientific software development:

1. Many computational scientists are reluctant to adopt "newer" technologies (cf. [293, 310]). Therefore, it has to be ensured that the technologies associated with candidate DSLs are accepted among the computational scientists who are supposed to use them.

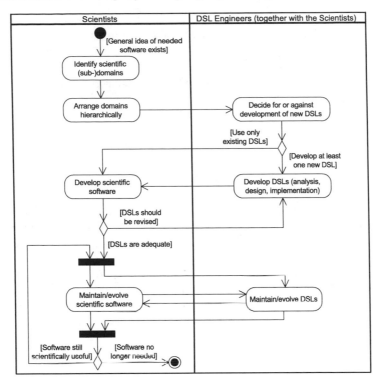

Figure 8.6: Engineering process of the Sprat approach.

2. The DSLs have to integrate well with the tools and workflows that the scientists are used to.

3. Candidate DSLs have to be easy to learn for domain specialists (the concrete syntax must appear "natural" to them) and offer good tool support. In this way, the scientists require only minimal training to use the languages.

4. As performance is a very important quality requirement in computational science, it must be made sure that the increased level of abstraction of a candidate DSL does not compromise the runtime performance of programs significantly. Additionally, the DSL should introduce as few dependencies as possible.

5. The language engineers must ensure that candidate DSLs can be integrated with each other vertically in a DSL hierarchy.

Clearly, the language engineers have to cooperate closely with the scientists and obtain feedback from them continuously to make sure that the selected DSLs actually meet the needs of the scientists and that the latter are really willing to use the languages. For this reason, it is important for the language engineers to know about and to respect the characteristics of software development in computational science.

If no suitable DSLs can be identified for some or all levels of the DSL hierarchy, the language engineers have to develop corresponding languages by themselves. In principle, the development of DSLs for computational science is not different from DSL engineering for other domains. Generally, the DSL development process can be divided into a domain analysis, a language design, and an implementation phase for which Mernik et al. [305] identify several patterns. A more detailed approach to DSL engineering that focuses on meta-modeling is given by Strembeck and Zdun [316]. Of course, for DSL development the language engineers have to pay special attention to the same factors that were already discussed above in the context of DSL selection for scientific software development. Again, it cannot be overemphasized that the language engineers have to work in close collaboration with the scientists all the time and that they have to respect (and at least partially embrace) the specific characteristics of scientific software development. For a DSL to be accepted by the target user community, the accidental complexity (both linguistic and technical) introduced along with it must be kept to a minimum.

Concerning the order in which the DSLs should be constructed, we generally propose to develop all languages of the language hierarchy at the same time. Preferably, the development of each DSL takes place in an incremental fashion using agile methods. This approach provides large flexibility because potential incompatibilities between different languages in the DSL hierarchy can be addressed early on. Since DSLs on higher levels of the hierarchy depend on those on lower ones, each development iteration for each language should begin on lower hierarchy levels moving on to higher ones.

8.3.3.3 Development and Maintenance

After DSLs have been assigned to or created for all hierarchy levels, the scientists start to implement the simulation software by assuming the different modeler roles of the DSL hierarchy. The Sprat Process does not impose any restrictions on this activity as this would very likely lead to the rejection of the whole approach (cf. [290]).

If it turns out during the development that some of the DSLs are insufficient for the implementation (e.g., missing elements in the meta-model or an overly technical concrete syntax), the languages have to be adapted by the language engineers. For externally developed DSLs, this very likely means that they have to be replaced by another DSL (possibly one developed "in-house"). This iterative process of the adaptation of the DSLs continues until the simulation software is "finished" in the sense that it can answer the scientific questions it was designed for (or the ones that emerged along the way during the implementation).

After reaching a state of relative maturity and stability, the simulation software enters its maintenance phase. In this phase, the number of changes applied to the software per unit of time is typically much lower than during the initial implementation phase. Note, however, that especially in computational science, the boundaries between the development and maintenance phase are rarely clear-cut.

During the maintenance phase, the simulation software is evolved in order to enable answering new scientific questions. Typically, the DSLs of the hierarchy should be able to support the changes to be introduced to the simulation. However, if previously ignored aspects of a domain have to be included in the simulation, also the DSLs have to be evolved in parallel to the scientific software.

New scientific questions could further make it necessary to add new levels to the DSL hierarchy because it may be required to model effects from totally different domains. In this case (which is not depicted in Figure 8.6 for reasons of clarity), one would have to start with the decision for or against the development of a new DSL for this level. The rest of the process for this specific hierarchy level would be the same as for the other levels.

After each maintenance iteration, when the new scientific questions could—or could *not*—be answered, the question arises whether it is still scientifically useful to maintain the simulation software. Depending on the answer to this question, either a new maintenance iteration is started or the software is not developed any further and the Sprat Process comes to its end.

8.3.4 Preventing Accidental Complexity

Segal [313] reminds us that software engineers "should not try to impose the full machinery of traditional software engineering on scientific software development." Any tool or development approach which assumes that scientific programmers will invest time and effort into mastering it is deemed to fail because "scientists tend to want results immediately" [308]. Therefore, Prabhu et al. [308] conclude that while educating scientists in software engineering methods is worthwhile, "a more promising approach is to develop solutions that are customized to the requirements of scientists" and "require little training." Such solutions have to adopt the frame of reference of the scientists and must necessarily make compromises with regard to their generality and formality [301]. If a tool confronts scientists with too many formal software engineering complexities—which might seem natural for a software engineer but are "accidental" from a scientist's perspective—the tool will inevitably face rejection [317].

The Sprat Approach achieves a compromise between formality and pragmatism by making two central concessions. First, we do not impose any restrictions on the concrete development activities of the scientific programmers, as discussed in Section 8.3.3.3. Second, we refrain from too much formality in the artifacts that are necessary for carrying out a scientific software development project with the Sprat Approach.

The only artifact that the scientists produce together with the language engineers to communicate the development process among themselves is a diagram of the DSL hierarchy. Therefore, *all* development aspects have to be represented in this diagram. This includes even concerns that could be modeled as orthogonal to the actual development of the software, such as the deployment process (cf. Figure 8.4). Thus, the hierarchy diagram represents a combination of different concerns and even mixes structural and procedural elements (e.g., *x* must be present before *y* can be deployed). This approach minimizes the complexity that the scientific programmers have to deal with but still enables meaningful reasoning about the software, its development process, and the different responsibilities of the personnel involved.

8.4   Case Study: Applying Sprat to the Engineering of a Coupled Marine Ecosystem Model

We evaluated the Sprat Approach by conducting a case study in which we applied Sprat to engineer a coupled marine ecosystem model that has been developed in collaboration with GEOMAR Helmholtz Centre for Ocean Research Kiel and Dalhousie University. In this section, we give a brief overview on the ecosystem model itself as well as on the DSLs used to implement it before discussing the results from our case study in Section 8.5. For a more in-depth description of the Sprat Marine Ecosystem Model and the DSLs utilized in its implementation, see [299, 300].

8.4.1   The Sprat Marine Ecosystem Model

The Sprat Marine Ecosystem Model is a PDE-based ecosystem model for long-term fish stock prediction that is coupled with existing biogeochemical ocean models. This online coupling allows to study the interactions of the different trophic levels in marine food webs.

Based on so-called population balance equations [309], the model's central system of PDE for $n \in \mathbb{N}$ fish species is given by

$$\frac{\partial}{\partial t} u^{[\kappa]} + \sum_{i=1}^{d} \frac{\partial}{\partial x_i} q_i^{[\kappa]} u^{[\kappa]} + \frac{\partial}{\partial r} g^{[\kappa]} u^{[\kappa]} = H^{[\kappa]} \qquad (8.4)$$

with $\kappa = 1, \ldots, n$. Here, $u : \mathbb{R}_{\geq 0} \times \Omega_x \times \Omega_r \mapsto \mathbb{R}^n$ represents the time-dependent mass distribution of fish in space and size/weight dimension. Thus, for every point in time $t \geq 0$, $u^{[\kappa]}$ assigns each point in space $x \in \Omega_x \subset \mathbb{R}^d$ and each possible size of a fish $r \in \Omega_r \subset \mathbb{R}_{>0}$ the average mass $u^{[\kappa]}(t, x, r)$ of individuals from species κ present with these coordinates. The $q_i^{[\kappa]}$ are spatial movement velocities and $g^{[\kappa]}$ is a growth velocity; all of them depend non-linearly on u. $H^{[\kappa]}$ is the forcing term that abstracts the sources and sinks of individuals (e.g., birth or fishing).

The DSL hierarchy for implementing this model with the Sprat Approach, which has already been presented in Section 8.3.2.2, employs three DSLs:

1. The Sprat PDE DSL for implementing the numerical solver and the equations of the Sprat Model.

2. The Sprat Ecosystem DSL for specifying ecosystem simulation experiments.

3. The Ansible Playbook DSL for describing the deployment of the Sprat Model in distributed High Performance Computing (HPC) environments.

The first two of these languages were developed by us while the third one was reused.

8.4.2   The Sprat PDE DSL

The Sprat PDE DSL is embedded into C++ via template meta programming techniques [278] and focuses on the implementation of special-purpose Finite Element Method (FEM) PDE solvers [285]. Since it targets developers of such algorithms rather than FEM practitioners, the language does not feature the most abstract concepts of FEM (say, variational forms) but concentrates on entities that allow to conveniently write mesh-based PDE solvers. From a technical perspective, the language is comprised of a set of header files written in C++11 that can be used by the application programmer with just a single include statement. These headers expose a set of classes and functions to implement the following three key features which are illustrated in Listing 8.2:

1. Lazily evaluated matrix-vector arithmetic with a natural and declarative syntax (see, e.g., Line 12)

2. Iterations over sets (see Lines 6–8)

3. Single Program, Multiple Data (SPMD) abstractions for parallelization (see Lines 14–15)

```
1   DistributedVector    u, q;
2   ElementVectorArray F_L;
3   ElementMatrixArray C;
4   ElementMatrix        D;
5
6   foreach_omp(tau, Elements(mesh), private(D), {
7       foreach(i, ElementDoF(tau), {
8           foreach(j, ElementDoF(tau), {
9               D(i, j) = max(i.globalIndex(), j.globalIndex());
10          })
11      })
12      F_L[tau] = C[tau]*q + D*u;
13  })
14  u *= u.dotProduct(q);
15  u.exchangeData();
```

Listing 8.2: Sprat PDE DSL code snippet.

8.4.3   The Sprat Ecosystem DSL

In order to apply the fish stock model implemented with the Sprat PDE DSL, it has to be parameterized for a specific marine ecosystem by a stock assessment scientist. For this purpose, we used Xtext [291, 292] to implement the external Sprat Ecosystem DSL that allows to specify the properties of the simulation run as well as the ecosystem and its fish species in an abstract and declarative way.

Figure 8.7 shows an example of a simulation description using the Sprat Ecosystem DSL in our Integrated Development Environment (IDE) for the language with custom syntax coloring. A simulation description consists of several top-level entities (Ecosystem, Output, Input, Species) that possess attributes which describe the entity. Most of these attributes have a constant numerical value given by an expression with a unit. If a unit is missing, the editor issues a warning and offers a quick fix that adds a unit of the correct quantity category to the expression. Unit conversions (e.g., from degree Fahrenheit to degree Celsius) are automatically carried out by the DSL. A keyword of the language is `record`, which can be used in the Output entity to let the user describe which data should be collected during a simulation run. This allows to aggregate the information already while the simulation is running and thus makes it unnecessary to store the potentially huge amount of all data generated by the simulation.

8.4.4   The Ansible Playbook DSL

Once the Sprat Model is fully parametrized by a Sprat Ecosystem DSL specification, a last piece of information is missing for a complete executable

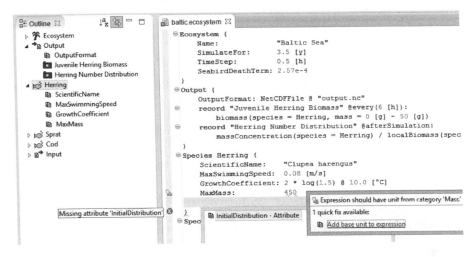

Figure 8.7: IDE for the Sprat Ecosystem DSL.

simulation: a description is needed of how to deploy it in a distributed HPC environment. For this purpose, we reuse the Ansible Playbook DSL [280], which describes configuration states that certain computer systems are supposed to be in. The user neither has to specify the initial state of the system nor the transformations that have to be applied to achieve the desired state. An example of the syntax of the DSL is given in Listing 8.3.

8.5   Case Study Evaluation

We employed a mixed-methods research design to evaluate the application of the Sprat Approach for the development of the Sprat Model. Specifically, we used online surveys, controlled experiments, performance benchmarking, and expert interviews to assess the quality of the DSLs and their impact on the development process. To save space, only results from the expert interviews that we conducted in order to evaluate the Sprat PDE DSL are discussed here. These results allow us to formulate some general lessons learned for developing DSLs for computational scientists.

8.5.1   Data Collection

We conducted semi-structured interviews [298] with eight experts which each lasted between one and two hours. The interviews were mostly carried

------

```
- hosts: localhost
connection: local
vars_files:
- ./openstack_config.yml

tasks:
- name: Make sure the cloud instances are running
nova_compute:
state:     present
hostname:  sprat{{ item }}
image_id:  "{{ os_image_id }}"
with_sequence: start=1 end={{ nInstances }}
```

Listing 8.3: Excerpt from the Ansible Playbook for deploying the Sprat Simulation on an OpenStack cloud.

out in a one-on-one fashion (with the exception of one interview in which we talked to two experts) in the expert's workplace.

Half of the sample were domain experts for PDE solvers and the other half were professional DSL developers. The domain experts were recruited by contacting professors of relevant research groups at Kiel University and GEOMAR Helmholtz Centre for Ocean Research Kiel. Candidates for the professional DSL developer group were selected from local industry. The actual involvement of these persons in DSL development was verified prior to conducting the interviews.

The group of domain experts consisted of one postdoc and three professors from research areas such as numerical analysis, optimization, and ocean modeling (all from different research groups). The professional DSL developers all had multiple years of experience with DSL design (one of them even authored a book on MDSE and DSLs) and were IT architects or consultants.

Two interview guides (one for the domain experts and one for the DSL developers) were developed based on four analysis dimensions deduced from our research question: *how do experts rate the functional and technical quality of the Sprat PDE DSL?* These analysis dimensions are:

1. Software development in computational science (only for the domain experts)

2. Learning material for DSLs

3. Meta-model and syntax of the Sprat PDE DSL

4. Technical implementation of the Sprat PDE DSL

Prior to the interviews, all interviewees were supplied with the source code of, code examples for, and a short written introduction to the Sprat PDE DSL in order to familiarize themselves with the language. Since we expected that not all of the interviewees would find the time to have a closer look at the language beforehand, we started each interview by briefly discussing the fundamental concepts of the language and by going through example algorithms implemented with the DSL. To make sure that the experts themselves had actually worked with the language, each interviewee was asked to solve tasks related to the supplied code examples during the interview (e.g., changing the mesh of a solver or altering the parallelization scheme of an algorithm).

8.5.2 Analysis Procedure

All interviews were taped and fully transcribed prior to the analysis. The transcripts were analyzed using the method of *qualitative content analysis* (specifically, *summarizing content analysis*) [304], for which we chose whole answers as our unit of analysis.

8.5.3 Results from the Expert Interviews

In the following, we describe selected aspects of the interview results. We present only results that address questions of DSL design for computational science in general and omit results that focus only on the quality of the specific DSL in question. This approach allows us to present some broader conclusions and lessons learned in Section 8.6.

8.5.3.1 Learning Material for DSLs

In this section, we discuss what kind of learning material the domain experts wish for in order to familiarize themselves with DSLs for computational science in general and with the Sprat PDE DSL in particular and how their requests differ from the ideas of the professional DSL developers.

All the scientists view commented example programs as the key element for the introduction to a new DSL for three reasons:

1. Example programs allow to judge quickly whether the DSL is suitable for the intended application and whether the scientists can imagine to work with it ("Is the code compact? Does it seem intuitive? Do I understand it?").

2. Examples make it easy to learn how a typical DSL program is structured.

3. Examples can be used as a basis for own programs without investing much time in reading other documentation artifacts.

Complementary to a set of commented examples, the interviewees would like to have a summary of the key concepts of the language which answers questions such as: What is the exact scope of the DSL? What is the performance of matrix-vector expressions? How is data managed with the language?

Additionally, they would like to have a specification of the data structures and interfaces of the DSL in order to understand how (possibly already existing) GPL code can be combined with the constructs of the language.

The DSL developers also suggest a combination of a summary and a complete language reference as learning material. However, they do not mention the importance of complete code examples (they rather seem to think of example snippets embedded into written text) and they generally put much more emphasis on the reference document than the scientists do: three out of four interviewed DSL developers name the reference first and talk about introductory material only when asked about it. For them, the basis of the reference document should be a formalized meta-model or the abstract syntax of the DSL, which is supposed to quickly give a top-down overview on the language. One of the interviewees mentions the reference of the Swift programming language [281] as exemplary in this respect. This reference is structured around grammar rules that are grouped according to which aspect of the language they belong to (expressions, types, etc.).

From the interviews, it can be seen that the domain scientists seem to favor a more practical and pragmatic approach to learning a DSL for computational science than DSL designers might think. The scientists emphasize the importance of complete documented code examples and they are interested in a reference only as a second step when it comes to more technical aspects of the implementation. In consequence, the utility of a formalized meta-model and lengthy grammar rule descriptions seems questionable for such an audience. When developing DSLs for computational scientists, DSL designers should reflect on their generally more formal and systematic approach to introducing others to such a language.

8.5.3.2 Concrete Syntax: Prescribed vs. Flexible Program Structure

One of the experts in DSL development suggests to enforce a common block structure for all Sprat PDE DSL programs. His motivation is to make sure that "as little nonsense as possible happens." When two of the domain experts are confronted with this idea in two subsequent interviews, they both express their fear that a prescribed code structure would take away too much control over their program and would make integration with existing code harder.

While software engineers working in the IT industry generally seem to focus their attention on consistency among solutions to facilitate reusability and maintainability, computational scientists favor loose structures that allow them to experiment and quickly obtain results. In order to be accepted by the scientists, a DSL for computational science (and especially for the HPC community) has to be pragmatic about the rigidity of prescribed structures and the level of abstraction it introduces. If one does not pay concessions to the need of computational scientists to freely experiment with a DSL, the language simply will not be adopted.

8.5.3.3 Internal vs. External Implementation

All except one of the domain experts favor an internal DSL over an external language for the level of abstraction that the Sprat PDE DSL aims for. They name several reasons for this:

1. An external DSL with a completely new syntax could be in conflict with concepts of programming languages such as Fortran and C that the experts have internalized. This could lead to confusion and an increased number of errors.

2. One expert already has negative experiences with external DSLs for implementing numerical algorithms. He says that such languages are often very good for the narrow domain they are designed for but commonly lack support for "everything else" in the large domain of computational science. In contrast to this, with an internal DSL, the user can seamlessly integrate DSL code with GPL code.

3. Another interviewee states that he does not believe that the increased flexibility of an external DSL offsets the added technical complexity of additional compiler runs and the need for other external tooling.

In spite of these reservations, none of the interviewees excludes the use of an external DSL with a code generator categorically, as long as this code generator is portable and available under an open source license.

The single domain expert who would actually prefer the Sprat PDE DSL to be an external language works with ocean models. He reports that in this scientific field, researchers are sometimes confronted with the problem of not being able to reproduce older simulation results once hardware platforms and compiler vendors/versions change. Therefore, he is interested in archiving source code that is as low-level as possible (e.g., already preprocessed Fortran code). With an internal language which uses template meta-programming techniques, such as the Sprat PDE DSL, this is not possible. Template meta-expressions are processed during compilation without yielding any intermediate low-level C++ code that could be archived. This lack of intermediate code also makes debugging of matrix-vector expressions hard because one cannot see what is actually executed during the evaluation of such an expression.

Since nobody excluded the use of an external DSL completely, a compromise would be possible: one could implement the Sprat PDE DSL as an external *language extension* to C or C++ using a framework such as the Meta Programming System (MPS) [287]. In this way, the requirements of both proponents, of those of an internal and of those of an external solution, could be met. All the features of the C/C++ GPL would be present while readable intermediate C/C++ code could be generated. It would even be possible to incorporate *interactive model-based compilation* techniques into the tooling that allow to trace in detail the transformations applied to DSL models during code generation [307]. However, further research has to be conducted in order to evaluate whether such an approach would actually be accepted in the community.

8.6   Conclusions and Lessons Learned

By assigning a DSL to each scientific (sub-)discipline that is involved in an interdisciplinary effort to develop complex simulation software, Sprat achieves a clear separation of concerns and enables scientists to produce maintainable, performant, and portable implementations by themselves without the need for extensive software engineering training. To evaluate the Sprat Approach, we applied it to the engineering of the Sprat Marine Ecosystem Model, which allows us to establish important lessons learned for the design of DSLs for computational science. These lessons learned, which stem mainly from the expert interviews conducted in the context of our case study, concern four areas of DSL design:

1. *Abstraction level of the meta-model*: the more related the application domain of a DSL is to computation, the more it needs to be possible for the users to influence how computations are executed (i.e., the closer to the underlying hardware platform the language must be). This especially allows full control over the runtime performance of solutions. In our experience, such languages are best implemented as internal DSLs embedded in relatively low-level programming languages, such as C++, which enables to reuse much of the existing language facilities of the host language.

2. *Concrete syntax*: the scientists participating in our study favor DSLs that do not prescribe too much structure of models because they want to have full control over their code and want to be able to experiment with it quickly and freely.

3. *DSL tooling*: in application domains not related to computing (such as biology) external DSLs with their own tooling are more likely to be accepted. The tooling should make sure that only scientifically reasonable DSL models are permitted and, otherwise, confront the user with error messages on the abstraction level of the domain (which would not be possible after generating code into programming languages with a lower abstraction level).

4. *Documentation*: professional DSL designers often focus on language references based on a formal meta-model or on the abstract syntax while

scientists favor code examples to get a fast overview on the capabilities of a DSL and to become productive quickly.

In the future, we plan to extend the Sprat Approach by including model-based software performance engineering and testing techniques [282, 311]. Since with Sprat, all implementation artifacts already are high-level models, these techniques would allow to increase the runtime performance and credibility of simulation results without considerable additional effort for the computational scientists.

Chapter 9

Providing Mixed-Language and Legacy Support in a Library: Experiences of Developing PETSc

Satish Balay, Jed Brown, Matthew Knepley, Lois Curfman McInnes, and Barry Smith

9.1   Introduction

This chapter explains how numerical libraries written in C can portably support its use from both modern and legacy versions of Fortran efficiently. This is done by examining, in a particular library, all the cross-language issues in mixing C and Fortran. Despite the chagrin of many computer scientists, scientists and engineers continue to use Fortran to develop new simulation codes, and the Fortran language continues to evolve with new standards and updated compilers. The need to combine Fortran and C code will also continue, therefore, will be no less important in future computing systems that include many-core processing with a hierarchy of memories and the integration of GPU systems with CPU systems all the way up to exascale systems. Thus, numerical analysts and other developers of mathematical software libraries must ensure that such libraries are usable from Fortran. To make the situation more complicated, depending on the age of the Fortran application (or the age of its developers), the Fortran source code may be Fortran 77, Fortran 90, Fortran 2003, or Fortran 2008 (possibly with TS 29113, required by MPI-3's "mpi_f08" module). In fact, the same Fortran application may include source files with the suffix .f that utilize Fortran 77 syntax and formatting (traditional fixed format), .F files that utilize some Fortran 90 or later language features but still have fixed format, and .F90 that use free format. Many Fortran application developers also resist utilizing the more advanced features of recent Fortran standards for a variety of reasons. Thus, any interlanguage Fortran library support must support both traditional Fortran dialects and modern features such as derived types. See [325] for a short history of Fortran.

The Babel project [321] was an ambitious effort to develop a language-independent object model that would allow scientific software libraries written in several languages to be utilized from any of the languages, much as Corba [326] was for business software. However, because of its extremely ambitious nature, the tools (Java) selected to develop the model, and insufficent funding for the large amount of development needed, the software could not fully serve application and library needs.

The Portable Extensible Toolkit for Scientific computation (PETSc) is a portable C software library for the scalable solution of linear, nonlinear, and ODE/DAE systems, and computation of adjoints (sometimes called sensitivities) of ODE systems. PETSc has been developed and supported at ANL for the past 20 years. PETSc has always supported a uniform Fortran interface [319], even in the very early phases of library development (see page 29 of) [323], [324]. PETSc is written using a C-based object model (in fact, that model inspired the Babel design) with a mapping of the objects and methods (functions) on the objects to Fortran as well as Python. This paper discussses only the Fortran mapping in PETSc.

9.2   Fortran-C Interfacing Issues and Techniques

Prior to the development of Fortran 2003, there was no standard within Fortran for interfacing with C code. That is, how can one call Fortran subroutines from C and C functions from Fortran in portable code as efficiently as possible. This means not needing to copy entire data structures between the two languages. Fortunately, since all Fortran compilers followed the same general set of protocols, one has always been able to portably mix Fortran and C code. The interlanguage issues that must be dealt with include the following.

Symbol names: Fortran compilers convert the symbol names to all capitals, all lower case, or all lower case with an underscore suffix. One variant is that symbols with an underscore get an additional underscore at the end of the symbol. In PETSc we handle this name mangling using the preprocessor, with code such as

```
#if defined(PETSC_HAVE_FORTRAN_CAPS)
#define matcreateseqaij_   MATCREATESEQAIJ
#elif !defined(PETSC_HAVE_FORTRAN_UNDERSCORE)
```

```
#define matcreateseqaij_   matcreateseqaij
endif
```

A terser, arguably better way of managing this is to use the paste $\#\#$ feature of the C preprocessor. First we define the macro FC_FUNC() based on the Fortran symbol format.

```
#if defined(PETSC_HAVE_FORTRAN_CAPS)
#define FC_FUNC(name,NAME) NAME ## _
#elif !defined(PETSC_HAVE_FORTRAN_UNDERSCORE)
#define FC_FUNC(name,NAME) name
#else
#define FC_FUNC(name,NAME) name ## _
#endif
```

Defining each symbol then takes only a single line, such as

```
#define matcreateseqaij_ FC_FUNC(matcreateseqaij,MATCREATESEQAIJ)
```

Character strings: Since Fortran strings are not null terminated, the Fortran compiler must generate additional code to indicate the length of each string. Most Fortran compilers include the string length (as an integer) as an additional argument at the end of the calling sequence; some compilers pass the length (as an integer) immediately after the character argument. In PETSc we handle this issue in the definition of our C stub function, again using the preprocessor #define, with code such as

```
void STDCALL vecsetoptionsprefix_(Vec *v,char* prefix
                        PETSC_MIXED_LEN(len),
                        PetscErrorCode *ierr
                        PETSC_END_LEN(len))
char *t;
FIXCHAR(prefix,len,t);
*ierr = VecSetOptionsPrefix(*v,t);
FREECHAR(prefix,t);
```

Here

```
#define FIXCHAR(a,n,b)
{
  if (a == PETSC_NULL_CHARACTER_Fortran) {
    b = a = 0;
  } else {
    while((n > 0) && (a[n-1] == ' ')) n--;
    *ierr = PetscMalloc((n+1)*sizeof(char),&b);
    if (*ierr) return;
    *ierr = PetscStrncpy(b,a,n+1);
```

```
    if (*ierr) return;
  }
}
```

allocates a null terminated version of the string to pass to C and

```
#define FREECHAR(a,b) if (a != b) PetscFreeVoid(b);
```

frees the temporary string. Depending on where the Fortran compiler places the `len` argument, either the `PETSC_MIXED_LEN(len)` or the `PETSC_END_-LEN(len)` macro simply removes the argument.

Stack management: Microsoft (and compilers for Microsoft systems) supports various ways that function arguments are pushed on the stack and if the caller or the callee removes the stack frame. Microsoft provides macros (used in the function prototypes in C) to indicate the convention that each function is using. Early Fortran compilers for Microsoft used the _ _stdcall call convention, while C and C++ did not; hence, C prototypes for each Fortran function required this annotation. Modern Intel Fortran compilers on Microsoft systems do not use the _ _stdcall call convention, and hence this annotation is needed only for older Fortran compilers on Microsoft systems. In PETSc we handle this issue by decorating the C function definition with STDCALL that becomes _ _stdcall only with older Fortran compilers for Microsoft systems.

Include files: Although the Fortran 77 standard did not provide for include files, most Fortran compilers support include files that use the C preprocessor (CPP) syntax; and for those systems that do not, one can always call the C preprocessor on the Fortran source and then call the Fortran compiler on the result. The use of include files with Fortran code makes possible many of the techniques utilized by PETSc (and discussed below). Full C/Fortran interoperability can be provided without requiring the use of Fortran include files, instead, for example, utilizing Fortran modules to contain the needed common data and values.

Enums: Since Fortran 77 provided no concept of the C enum, the established practice was to use

```
#define PetscEnum  integer
```

and then define each enum type with, for example,

```
#define InsertMode PetscEnum
```

The enumerated values are set by using the Fortran parameter statement, for example,

```
PetscEnum INSERT_VALUES
parameter (INSERT_VALUES=1)
PetscEnum ADD_VALUES
parameter (ADD_VALUES=2)
```

although care must be taken that the same integer values are used in the C and Fortran code. Recent versions of Fortran support enums via

```
ENUM   InsertMode
       ENUMERATOR :: INSERT_VALUE
       ENUMERATOR :: ADD_VALUE
   END ENUM
ENUM, BIND(C) :: InsertMode
```

which automatically ensures that the values assigned in Fortran match those in the C enum.

Compile and runtime constants: As demonstrated above, the Fortran parameter statement can be used to set compile-time constants that must match between C and Fortran. But what about runtime constants? These are traditionally handled by using common blocks whose entries are initialized from the C values when the package is initialized. For example, here is how PETSc handles the runtime value PETSC_COMM_WORLD. In a Fortran include file we define

```
MPI_Comm PETSC_COMM_WORLD
common /petscfortran/ PETSC_COMM_WORLD
```

Then after PETSC_COMM_WORLD is defined in C within `PetscInitialize()`, it calls the Fortran routine

```
      subroutine PetscSetCommonBlock(c1)
      implicit none
#include       <petsc/finclude/petscsys.h>
      integer c1
      PETSC_COMM_WORLD      = c1
      return
      end
```

to store the value in a Fortran common block. If one is willing to give up portability to pure Fortran 77 codes, then these values can be stored in a module rather than a common block. Initial communicating of Fortran runtime constants to C is handled similarly except that the Fortran code calls C with the required values. For example,

```
      subroutine PetscSetFromCommonBlock()
      implicit none
#include       <petsc/finclude/petscsys.h>
```

```
      call PetscSetFortranBasePointers(PETSC_NULL_CHARACTER,
          PETSC_NULL_INTEGER,PETSC_NULL_DOUBLE,PETSC_NULL_OBJECT,
          PETSC_NULL_FUNCTION)
      return
      end
```

passes the addresses within a common block to C.

```
      PetscChar(80)        PETSC_NULL_CHARACTER
      PetscInt             PETSC_NULL_INTEGER
      PetscFortranDouble   PETSC_NULL_DOUBLE
      PetscObject          PETSC_NULL_OBJECT
      external PETSC_NULL_FUNCTION
      common /petscfortran/ PETSC_NULL_CHARACTER,
                            PETSC_NULL_INTEGER,
                            PETSC_NULL_DOUBLE,
                            PETSC_NULL_OBJECT
```

The following C routine called from Fortran then puts the values of the Fortran common block addresses and external function into global C variables.

```
void STDCALL petscsetfortranbasepointers_(char *fnull_character
                                PETSC_MIXED_LEN(len),
                                void *fnull_integer,
                                void *fnull_double,
                                void *fnull_object,
                                void (*fnull_func)(void)
                                PETSC_END_LEN(len))
{
  PETSC_NULL_CHARACTER_Fortran = fnull_character;
  PETSC_NULL_INTEGER_Fortran   = fnull_integer;
  PETSC_NULL_DOUBLE_Fortran    = fnull_double;
  PETSC_NULL_OBJECT_Fortran    = fnull_object;
  PETSC_NULL_FUNCTION_Fortran  = fnull_func;
}
```

Note that since traditional Fortran has no concept of a common block variable declared as a function pointer, the PETSC_NULL_FUNCTION is simply declared with the external marker. This construct for managing null pointer usage in Fortran is needed because Fortran has no concept of a generic NULL. Instead, one needs a NULL for each data type; then in the C stub called from Fortran, the specific NULL data type is converted to the C NULL, for example,

```
void STDCALL matcreateseqaij_(MPI_Comm *comm,PetscInt *m,
                        PetscInt *n,PetscInt *nz,
                        PetscInt *nnz,Mat *newmat,
                        PetscErrorCode *ierr)
```

```
{
  if ((void*)(uintptr_t)nnz == PETSC_NULL_INTEGER_Fortran)
    { nnz = NULL; }
  *ierr = MatCreateSeqAIJ(MPI_Comm_f2c(*(MPI_Fint*)comm),*m,*n,
                                          *nz,nnz,newmat);
}
```

PETSc also has many runtime constants in the style of `MPI_COMM_WORLD`, such as `PETSC_VIEWER_STDOUT_WORLD`, which are handled similarly but are compile-time constants in Fortran. In Fortran they are defined as integers via the parameter statement.

```
      PetscFortranAddr PETSC_VIEWER_STDOUT_WORLD
      parameter (PETSC_VIEWER_STDOUT_WORLD = 8)
```

Then the C stub checks whether the input is one of these special values and converts to the appropriate runtime C value, for example,

```
#define PetscPatchDefaultViewers_Fortran(vin,v)
{
  if ((*(PetscFortranAddr*)vin) ==
                      PETSC_VIEWER_DRAW_WORLD_FORTRAN){
    v = PETSC_VIEWER_DRAW_WORLD;
  } else if ((*(PetscFortranAddr*)vin) ==
                      PETSC_VIEWER_DRAW_SELF_FORTRAN){
    v = PETSC_VIEWER_DRAW_SELF;
  } else if ((*(PetscFortranAddr*)vin) ==
                      PETSC_VIEWER_STDOUT_WORLD_FORTRAN){
    v = PETSC_VIEWER_STDOUT_WORLD;
  } else ...
  } else {
    v = *vin;
  }
}
void STDCALL vecview_(Vec *x,PetscViewer *vin,PetscErrorCode *ierr)
{
  PetscViewer v;
  PetscPatchDefaultViewers_Fortran(vin,v);
  *ierr = VecView(*x,v);
}
```

Pointers in traditional Fortran to C arrays: PETSc makes widespread use of array pointers in its API to allow efficient programmers access to "raw" data structures. For example,

```
double *x;
Vec v;
VecGetArray(v,&x);
```

gives users direct access to the local values with a vector. Traditional Fortran has no concept of an array pointer, which would severely limit the use of some of PETSc's functionality from traditional Fortran. Fortunately, again, despite there having been no Fortran standard for this type of functionality, it is still achievable and has been used in PETSc for over 20 years. In the user's Fortran code, an array of size one is declared as well as an integer long enough to access anywhere in the memory space from that array offset (`PetscOffset` is a 32-bit integer for 32-bit memory systems and a 64-bit integer for 64-bit memory systems).

```
Vec X
PetscOffset  lx_i
PetscScalar lx_v(1);
```

They then call, for example,

```
call VecGetArray(X,lx_v,lx_i,ierr)
call InitialGuessLocal(lx_v(lx_i),ierr)
call VecRestoreArray(X,lx_v,lx_i,ierr)
```

where `InitialGuessLocal` is defined, for example, as

```
subroutine InitialGuessLocal(x,ierr)
implicit none
PetscInt xs,xe,ys,ye
common /pdata/  xs,xe,ys,ye
PetscScalar      x(xs:xe,ys:ye)
PetscErrorCode ierr


!  compute entries in the local portion of x()
```

This approach uses the fact that traditional Fortran passes by pointer, as opposed to by value, and when passing array pointers does not distinguish between one and multidimensional arrays. The PETSc C routine that manages this is similar to the following code

```
void STDCALL vecgetarray_(Vec *x,PetscScalar *fa,size_t *ia,
                                     PetscErrorCode *ierr)
{
  PetscScalar *lx;
  *ierr = VecGetArray(*x,&lx); if (*ierr) return;
  *ierr = PetscScalarAddressToFortran(fa,lx,ia);
}
```

where

```
PetscErrorCode PetscScalarAddressToFortran(PetscScalar *base,
                                     PetscScalar *addr,
```

```
                                              size_t *ia)
{
  size_t   tmp1 = (size_t) base,tmp2;
  size_t   tmp3 = (size_t) addr;

  if (tmp3 > tmp1) {/* C address is larger than Fortran
    address */
    tmp2 = (tmp3 - tmp1)/sizeof(PetscScalar);
    *ia  = tmp2;
  } else {  /* Fortran address is larger than C address */
    tmp2 = (tmp1 - tmp3)/sizeof(PetscScalar);
    *ia  = -((size_t) tmp2);
  }
}
```

calculates the appropriate signed displacement between the Fortran (dummy) array and the actual C array. Although this may seem like a dangerous "pointer" trick, it has worked for over 20 years on all systems to which we have access. One caveat is that if the Fortran compiler contains support for array "out of bounds" checking, this feature must be turned off (for example, the IBM Fortran compiler has a command line option to turn on this checking).

Array pointers in F90 to C arrays: With Fortran 90 array pointers it became possible to simplify the Fortran user interface for routines such as VecGetArray() to

```
PetscScalar,pointer :: lx_v(:)
Vec X

call VecGetArrayF90(X,lx_v,ierr)
```

This is implemented in PETSc by the C stub

```
void STDCALL vecgetarrayf90_(Vec *x, F90Array1d *ptr,int *ierr
                       PETSC_F90_2PTR_PROTO(ptrd))
{
  PetscScalar *fa;
  PetscInt    len,one = 1;
  *ierr = VecGetArray(*x,&fa);       if (*ierr) return;
  *ierr = VecGetLocalSize(*x,&len); if (*ierr) return;
  *ierr = F90Array1dCreateScalar(fa,&one,&len,ptr
                       PETSC_F90_2PTR_PARAM(ptrd));
}
```

that calls the Fortran routine

```
subroutine F90Array1dCreateScalar(array,start,len1,ptr)
```

```
implicit none
#include <petsc/finclude/petscsys.h>
PetscInt start,len1
PetscScalar, target ::   array(start:start+len1-1)
PetscScalar, pointer :: ptr(:)
ptr => array
end subroutine
```

The Portland Group Fortran compiler passes additional information about each of the Fortran pointer arrays through final (hidden) arguments to the called functions. With this system the `PETSC_F90_2PTR_PROTO(ptrd)` is defined; on all other systems it generates nothing. The same general mechanism outlined above for PetscScalar one-dimensional arrays also works (with modification) for multiple-dimensional arrays as well as arrays of integers. One would think that with support for using F90 array features there would be no need to continue to support the F77 compatible `VecGetArray()`; yet, surprisingly large numbers of PETSc users continue to use the older version.

Portable Fortran source and include files: The Fortran standards provide a file format that is safe to use for all Fortran standards. This format uses exclusively the ! in the first column, only numerical values in the second to fifth column, a possible continuation character of & in the sixth column, Fortran commands in the seventh to 71st column, and a possible continuation character of & after the 72nd column. As long as this formatting is obeyed in the libraries' include files and source code, the code will compile with any Fortran compiler. Note that using C for the comment character or any symbol but the & for the continuation character will not be portable. A related issue with ensuring that code does not exceed the 71st column is that the CPP macro definitions in the Fortran include files may be longer than the name of the macro, thus pushing characters that appear to be with the 71st column past the 71st column. For example, depending on the Fortran compiler features and PETSc options, `PetscScalar` may be defined as `real(kind=selected_-real_kind(10))`, making user declarations such as

```
PetscScalar   ainput,broot,ccase,dnile,erank
```

illegal with the fixed format.

Representing C objects in Fortran: PETSc is designed around a collection of abstract objects that have a variety of back-end implementations. For example, the `Mat` object in PETSc that represents linear operators is represented in the users C code as

```
typedef struct _p_Mat*        Mat;
```

This representation allows encapsulating the details of the matrix implementations outside the scope of the user code. The actual `_p_Mat` C struct contains a variety of data records as well as function pointers that implement all the matrix functionality for a particular matrix implementation. We provide two ways of mapping the `Mat` object to Fortran. In the traditional approach we use the fact that all Fortran variables are passed by pointer (i.e., the address of the variable is passed to the subroutine). On the Fortran side the objects are then just

```
#define Mat PetscFortranAddr
```

where, as before, `PetscFortranAddr` is either a 32- or 64-bit integer depending on the size of the memory addresses. A drawback to this approach is that in Fortran all PETSc objects are of the same type, so that the Fortran compiler cannot detect a type mismatch. For example, calling `MatMult()` with a vector object would not be flagged as incorrect. Hence we provide an alternative configure time approach where each PETSc object family is defined by a Fortran derived type and utilizes modules.

```
use petscmat
type(Mat) A
```

The corresponding definition in the PETSc module is simply

```
type Mat
  PetscFortranAddr:: v
end type Mat
```

Again the simplicity of the Fortran pass-by-pointer argument handling means that what is actually passed to a C stub is again an integer large enough to hold the PETSc object (which is, of course, a pointer). In fact, this definition allows the same Fortran application to refer to a `Mat` in some files using the traditional approach (as an integer) and in other files using the modern approach (as a Fortran derived type). With Fortran 2003 one no longer needs to use an appropriately sized integer to hold the C pointer in Fortran. Instead, one can use the construct

```
use iso_c_binding
type(c_ptr) :: A
```

to directly hold the C object pointer, or one can use

```
use iso_c_binding
type Mat
  type(c_ptr) :: v
end type Mat
```

Handling function callbacks in Fortran: PETSc users writing in C employ function callbacks to utilize much of the functionality of PETSc. For example, to use the nonlinear solvers, the user provides a C function that defines the nonlinear system,

```
PetscErrorCode func(SNES snes,Vec x,Vec f,void* ctx)
{
  /* evaluate a mathematical function putting the result into ctx
}
```

In their main program, after they have created a PETSc nonlinear solver object (called a SNES), they call

```
SNESSetFunction(snes,r,func,ctx);
```

The SNES object stores the function pointer and function context. Then whenever the PETSc nonlinear solver object needs to evaluate the nonlinear function, it simply calls the function pointer with appropriate arguments. Since the function pointer is stored in the SNES object, multiple solvers can work independently each with its own user functions. The user interface for Fortran is almost identical to that used from C. The user provides a Fortran function, for example,

```
subroutine func(snes,x,f,ctx,ierr)
SNES snes
Vec x,f,
type(fctx) ctx
PetscErrorCode ierr
! evaluate a mathematical function putting the result into ctx
return
end
```

and in the main program has

```
call SNESSetFunction(snes,r,func,ctx);
```

The PETSc code that supports this interface is essentially[1] the following.

```
static struct {
  PetscFortranCallbackId function;
  PetscFortranCallbackId destroy;
  PetscFortranCallbackId jacobian;
} _cb;
static PetscErrorCode oursnesfunction(SNES snes,Vec x,Vec f,
                                                void *ctx)
{
  PetscObjectUseFortranCallback(snes,_cb.function,(SNES*,Vec*,
                             Vec*, void*,PetscErrorCode*),
                             (&snes,&x,&f,_ctx,&ierr)));
}
void STDCALL snessetfunction_(SNES *snes,Vec *r,
```

---

[1]The PGI Fortran compiler introduces an additional hidden pointer argument that we removed from this example to simplify the exposition.

```
                    void (STDCALL *func)(SNES*,Vec*,Vec*,
                    void*,PetscErrorCode*),void *ctx,
                    PetscErrorCode *ierr)
{
  *ierr = PetscObjectSetFortranCallback((PetscObject)*snes,
             PETSC_FORTRAN_CALLBACK_CLASS,&_cb.function,
             (PetscVoidFunction)func,ctx);
  if (!*ierr) *ierr = SNESSetFunction(*snes,*r,oursnesfunction,
                                                       NULL);
}
```

The routine `PetscObjectUseFortranCallback()` records the Fortran function pointer and context in the SNES object, which are then retrieved when the user's Fortran function is called.

In addition to introducing `type(c_ptr)` as discussed above for handling C objects (pointers) in Fortran, the 2003 standard introduced `type(c_funptr)` which represents a C function in Fortran. The standard also introduced Fortran function pointers and methods for converting between C and Fortran function pointers. Most important one can now directly declare a C function in the Fortran code and have the Fortran compiler automatically generate the stub code needed to call it from Fortran instead of requiring the user to manually provide the stub. This is done, for example, with

```
function MyCfunction(A) result(output) bind(C,name="cfunction")
  use iso_c_binding
  integer(c_int) :: A,output
end function
```

which declares a C function with a single C `int` input that returns an `int`. Fortran 2003 also provides `c_null_ptr` and `c_null_funptr` but still does not provide a generic NULL that has the flexibility to be passed anywhere a pointer is expected. The introduction of C bindings to the Fortran standard did not actually introduce any capability that was previously unavailable; it merely made the interface between C and Fortran simpler for those not familiar with the relatively straightforward issues outlined above.

Providing Fortran interface definitions: Since C provides function declarations that allow compile-time checking of argument types, Fortran 90 introduced interfaces that serve a similar purpose in Fortran.

9.3   Automatically Generated Fortran Capability

For a C package with only a handful of functions and data types, one can manually generate the appropriate Fortran function stubs (either using the traditional approach or with the C binding capability of Fortran 2003), Fortran interface definitions, and Fortran equivalent compile and runtime variables. However, for larger packages, especially those that evolve over time with more functionality, manually producing the capability and maintaining it is infeasible. Thus one must at least partially automate the process, much as SWIG [320] is used to generate Python stubs for C libraries. The PETSc team uses the Sowing package [322], developed by Bill Gropp for the MPICH package, to automatically generate much of the Fortran capability. Sowing generates both traditional Fortran stub functions and Fortran interface definitions for all C functions in the code that are "marked" by specific formatted comments. It does not handle character string arguments or function pointer arguments well, so those are handled in a partially manual manner. Since the traditional Fortran stub approach continues to work well for PETSc and is not a resource burden, we have not switched to using the Fortran 2003 C binding method for Fortran stubs. Thus we cannot say for sure that the Fortran 2003 C binding techniques would allow all the functionality from Fortran that PETSc's current techniques provide. Fully automatic generation of the C binding definitions, including proper support for NULL arguments and Fortran function pointers, would be a major exercise.

9.4   Conclusion

In PETSc, we have mapped all the C-based constructs needed by users, including enums, abstract objects, array pointers, null pointers, and function pointers (callbacks) to equivalent traditional Fortran and modern Fortran constructs, allowing Fortran PETSc users to utilize almost all the functionality of PETSc in their choice of Fortran standard. This support has substantially enlarged the user base for PETSc. We estimate that nearly one-third of our users work in Fortran, and we can provide them high quality numerical library support for modern algebraic solvers. As a result of automation of much of the process, the cost of PETSc Fortran support is significantly less than 10 percent of our development time. In addition, the Fortran support allows applications that are written partially in C and partially in Fortran, although we are not aware of many PETSc applications implemented in this way. Because of user and legacy demands, it is still important to support the full suite of F77, F90, F2003, F2011, and C interfaces. The advent of F2003 Fortran-C interoperability features, while a good addition, did not fundamentally change how PETSc supports Fortran users, nor did it allow us to discard outdated interfacing technology. Instead, it allowed us to enhance the Fortran support we already provided. The performance hit in using PETSc from Fortran rather than C for any nontrivial problems, consisting of only a small extra function call overhead, is negligible because of the granularity of the operations.

This material is based upon work supported by the U.S. Department of Energy, Office of Science, Advanced Scientific Computing Research, under Contract DE-AC02-06CH11357.

Chapter 10

HydroShare – A Case Study of the Application of Modern Software Engineering to a Large Distributed Federally-Funded Scientific Software Development Project

Ray Idaszak, David G. Tarboton (Principal Investigator), Hong Yi, Laura Christopherson, Michael J. Stealey, Brian Miles, Pabitra Dash, Alva Couch, Calvin Spealman, Jeffery S. Horsburgh, and Daniel P. Ames

Abstract

HydroShare is an online collaborative system under development to support the open sharing of hydrologic data, analytical tools, and computer models. With HydroShare, scientists can easily discover, access, and analyze hydrologic data and thereby enhance the production and reproducibility of hydrologic scientific results. HydroShare also takes advantage of emerging social media functionality to enable users to enhance information about and collaboration around hydrologic data and models.

HydroShare is being developed by an interdisciplinary collaborative team of domain scientists, university software developers, and professional software engineers from ten institutions located across the United States. While the combination of non–co-located, diverse stakeholders presents communication and management challenges, the interdisciplinary nature of the team is integral to the project's goal of improving scientific software development and capabilities in academia.

This chapter describes the challenges faced and lessons learned with the development of HydroShare, as well as the approach to software development that the HydroShare team adopted on the basis of the lessons learned. The chapter closes with recommendations for the application of modern software engineering techniques to large, collaborative, scientific software development projects, similar to the National Science Foundation (NSF)–funded HydroShare, in order to promote the successful application of the approach described herein by other teams for other projects.

10.1   Introduction to HydroShare

The HydroShare software development project is funded by the National Science Foundation (NSF) through its Software Infrastructure for Sustained Innovation program [333, 336]. Domain scientists, professional[1] software engineers, and academic software developers from ten academic institutions located across the United States[2] collaborate to develop HydroShare–an online,

---

[1]The term *professional*, as used here refers to an individual that has received formal education on software development and has applied this knowledge in a commercial or equivalent context.

[2]Brigham Young University, Caktus Group, Consortium of Universities for the Advancement of Hydrologic Science, Inc., Purdue University, Renaissance Computing Institute (RENCI) at the University of North Carolina at Chapel Hill, Tufts University, Institute for the Environment at the University of North Carolina at Chapel Hill, University of Texas at Austin, University of Virginia, and Utah State University.

collaborative system that extends the data-sharing capabilities of the Hydrologic Information System (HIS), which was developed by the Consortium of Universities for the Advancement of Hydrologic Sciences, Inc. (CUAHSI) [355]. HydroShare extends the data-sharing capabilities of HIS by broadening the classes of data that are accommodated, enabling the sharing of computer models and model components, and incorporating social media functionality in order to enhance communication and collaboration around hydrologic data and models [350, 351, 353].

In cooperation with CUAHSI, HydroShare is being used by the National Flood Interoperability Experiment (NFIE), which is a collaboration between the National Weather Service, government and commercial partners, and the academic community. NFIE is working to build a next-generation, high-resolution, near–real-time hydrologic simulation and forecasting model for the United States. With HydroShare, NFIE is able to better facilitate the flow of information between the federal, state, and local entities responsible for flood measurement, forecasting, and planning [338]. This near–real-time information also can be used by first responders during severe weather events to navigate to people in need of assistance [339].

The HydroShare project provides an example of the application of modern software engineering techniques to the development of scientific software. At the project's outset, most members of the HydroShare team did not fully understand the difference between software development and software engineering, nor were they familiar with iterative software methodology, code refactoring, continuous integration, or test-driven development (explained in Section 10.4.6). Much of the functionality of HydroShare–such as user interface, access control, social media incorporation, metadata handling, search and discovery, analytics, simulation, and storage capabilities–also was challenging for the team. While many members of the team had previous experience in the software development of hydrologic models, including models containing very complex algorithms and data structures, none of the models that had been developed by team members had the depth or complexity of the HydroShare software stack, and none required distributed code development and coordination across a large team. Thus, the team quickly realized the need to apply modern software engineering practices as part of the HydroShare experience. At the time of this writing, four years into the project, the team is now capable of applying advanced software engineering techniques to the development of HydroShare.

This chapter describes the approach, experience, and lessons learned when applying modern software engineering techniques to a large scientific software project, HydroShare. Recommendations are provided for how to integrate best practices in modern software engineering into large, collaborative research projects such as HydroShare. The overall intent is to support the advancement of science and expand the use of sustainable software engineering practices in academia. The goal is for other scientific software development teams to be able to adopt and adapt the techniques and practices described in this chapter.

10.2   Informing the Need for Software Engineering Best Practices for Science

Modern scientific research relies on software. Software enables scientists to collect data, perform analyses, run numerical and statistical models, and visualize data. With the aid of software, scientists are able to answer key research questions and test hypotheses that can revolutionize what is known about the world. Life-sustaining policies, products, and techniques–such as clinical therapies, pharmaceutical compounds, and solutions to environmental problems–derive from software-enabled scientific research.

Software such as HydroShare that supports data collection, analysis, and modeling is often used to accomplish research goals. Hannay, MacLeod, and Singer [349] have noted that scientists spend as much as 40% of their time using software. Often, existing software is ill-suited to a particular research project or, in the case of commercial software, prohibitively expensive. The result is that scientists often develop their own software–spending as much as 30% of their time doing so [349]–even though few incentives exist for software development in traditional tenure and promotion decision-making processes [352]. In other words, the time that an academic scientist spends developing software is not rewarded or recognized as a significant, independent accomplishment. Tenure and promotion, for example, are based on influential research, a successful publication record, the acquisition of grants, and teaching–not on whether one can author good software. Additionally, many funding agencies wish to see their funds going toward time spent on traditional research activities, not writing software.

While not incentivized, academic scientists continue to develop their own software. However, most academic scientists are not trained in software development or software engineering [342,345,359]. Software development courses, typically offered by computer science departments, are not required for most non-majors. Additionally, the training that scientists do receive from computer science departments often is perceived as overly general or abstract, and scientists may not see the relevance of such training [349]. As a result of the lack of training in software development and software engineering, the software that is developed by academic scientists often is not built to the development standards of the commercial sector. Software engineering best practices, such as documentation, versioning, and testing, may not be applied during the creation of academic scientific software. Furthermore, most academic software is developed to suit the needs of a specific research project and thus may not be applicable to other research projects or sustainable beyond the life of the initial project.

The lack of training in software development and software engineering can have dire consequences [346]. For instance, software that is developed without the use of proven software engineering techniques may lead to errors in the code. Even minor errors influence the validity of research findings; indeed, in some cases, papers have been retracted from scientific journals and careers have been ruined [357]. Paper retractions and irreproducible results due to poor-quality software impede the advancement of science and impart huge financial repercussions. Under the worst case scenario, programming errors can lead to the loss of lives if erroneous findings result in faulty medical technologies or misdirected policies on disaster response, to provide examples.

The detection of errors in academic software is extremely challenging, however. While manuscripts submitted for journal publication must undergo a peer review process, the software code that is used to generate the findings presented in manuscripts is rarely subjected to a peer review process or other measures of quality assurance. Yet, peer review and testing of software code are critical for the credibility of science and require software engineering best practices.

Of significance, the risk of introducing error into scientific research through the use of low-quality software provides a little recognized, but highly impactful, incentive for the adoption of software engineering best practices in academic scientific software development.

The HydroShare project addresses the challenges and highlights the benefits of the adoption of software engineering best practices through a collaborative scientific software project involving a large, geographically dispersed team of academic scientists, academic software developers, and professional software engineers.

10.3 Challenges Faced and Lessons Learned

This section describes the challenges faced and lessons learned when applying modern software engineering best practices to a software development project in hydrology. *Modern software engineering*, as used here refers to "the application of a systematic, disciplined, quantifiable approach to the development, operation, and maintenance of software; that is, the application of engineering to software" [330].

10.3.1 Cultural and Technical Challenges

Early on, the HydroShare team identified several overarching culture challenges. First, the team found that it is not a tradition to use modern software engineering best practices in the development of academic software due to a lack of incentives and a failure to recognize the benefits, as discussed above. The perception was that good software engineering practices are not needed to obtain scientific results and to publish scientific papers. Second, graduate students often develop software for their faculty advisors, yet graduate students have very short-term goals (i.e., graduate in the next couple of years), so software sustainability is not a high priority. Third, graduate students and their faculty advisors typically have not received formal training in software development, let alone software engineering. Fourth and lastly, the rigorous metadata requirements necessary for reproducible science make scientific software systems more complex than other types of software and thus require significant time to create unit tests. This presents a paradox, as the more complex software is, the more benefit one gets from having comprehensive unit tests.

The team also encountered more specific technical challenges. For example, as implementation of our HydroShare project began, the team quickly realized that most members were not familiar with Git, GitHub, or continuous integration (i.e., a development practice that requires developers to integrate code into a shared repository on a very frequent basis). The decision was thus made to assign only members at the lead technical institution the task of implementing initial beta release functionalities in order to expedite creation of the code infrastructure for subsequent collaborative development and continuous integration by the broader team members. However, this limited HydroShare beta release functionality to only those functionalities that could be implemented by the lead technical institution. This approach did expedite the initial release of the system, but the approach also precluded the ability for other team members to contribute to the development. For HydroShare, this trade-off was acceptable as the other team members used the additional time to get versed on continuous integration, Git, GitHub, and other specific technologies and approaches used in HydroShare software development.

Early on in the project, the team held several in-person meetings, as well as weekly team teleconferences, that served to achieve the development objectives, including the development of a data model (i.e., a conceptual model of how data elements relate to each other) and access control policies (i.e., policies to restrict access to data) and thorough consideration of how to accommodate hydrologic models within HydroShare. As implementation progressed and software engineering principles, such as code versioning (i.e., management of revisions to source code) and continuous integration, were diffused from the professional software engineers to the hydrologists, additional challenges emerged. For example, the distributed development team experienced difficulty achieving short-release cycles of continuous integration of the Django-based system using Git and GitHub. Django is a large, complex, open source, python-based web development framework, in which its customization model and content data are stored in databases [328]. Django proved to be difficult to manage via version control by a team with members of various skill levels. Specifically, the challenge was how to manage multiple, distributed development teams that were simultaneously checking out their own branch[3] of HydroShare, while

---

[3]A *branch* in GitHub lives separately from the production codebase, thus allowing for experimentation without affecting the *master branch* (or production codebase).

maintaining consistency in the back-end Django database. This led to multiple, complex code feature branches being checked out and worked on at the same time–without a sufficient number of intermediate merges.

Described below are two specific challenges–waiting too long between code merges and establishing a development environment–examined in greater depth, including the downstream challenges and lessons learned.

10.3.2   Waiting Too Long between Code Merges

To highlight the complications that may arise from waiting too long between code merges, this section considers a release of HydroShare in which two key items were addressed on different branches: base class refactoring and a change in the approach to access control. This presented a non-trivial challenge because of the intertwining of these two items, along with the need to preserve existing resources.

The HydroShare base class refactoring branch endeavored to promote the HydroShare Generic Resource type functionality from being abstract to fully defined. Being able to extend upon a fully defined resource opened the door for easier searching, indexing, and database querying that wouldn't otherwise be possible if the team had kept extending from the previously defined abstract model. Once this was implemented and tested for the Generic Resource type, the team then needed to apply this to all of the other HydroShare resource types in close coordination with the developers that had originally created them in order to ensure against loss of content, extended metadata, or other resource-specific attributes.

The HydroShare access control branch endeavored to implement an access control model that the team designed to best suit the hydrology research community [347]. However, this uniquely designed HydroShare access control model meant that it was necessarily non-standard and non-compliant with basic use of Django; thus, the team took extra care in how this change was implemented. The first, albeit incomplete, implementation of the HydroShare access control was integrated on top of Django's permission system for the sake of simplicity and the need to get an initial working version of HydroShare. To implement the full HydroShare access control, the team needed to decouple from Django's permission system and enforce a HydroShare-specific model, thereby adding additional system complexity.

To further complicate things, the HydroShare access control and base class refactoring had to be implemented on top of existing HydroShare resources in production use. The integrated rule-oriented data system (iRODS) [334] is used as a data management back-end to HydroShare. The challenge however, was migrating all of the existing HydroShare resources that were in use by users when the new resource and access control schema didn't fit the existing iRODS storage policies. Multiple steps and operations on the resources and database were required to properly migrate resources into the new models and access control schema. This proved to be quite a challenging endeavor.

Each of these items on their own presented a significant task; however, the summation of all of these branches into a single release required numerous dry-runs and small intermediate tests based on the results of the dry-runs before the team was confident that it was right. The team put as much time into testing and validation as they did into coding the changes themselves. The main lesson learned from this experience is that it is best to perform smaller, but more frequent merges, rather than a large release with multiple complex merges. With the former approach, the merge complexity will be reduced and time will be saved.

10.3.3   Establishing a Development Environment

Another major challenge for the development team was setting up the integrated development environment for individual developers. This presented a challenge mainly due to the many Docker containers [329] that the HydroShare system uses, as well as the fact that most of the developers did not have knowledge of Docker configuration, which was a relatively new technology at the beginning of the HydroShare project. This challenge was resolved by scripting the development environment, such that with few commands, the team could quickly set up the HydroShare development environment–something that had previously taken hours. As the development team was distributed, weekly videoconferences were used to train new HydroShare developers on how to set up the development environment.

The HydroShare software developers faced major challenges in code contribution in the early stages of the HydroShare project due to the size of the project and their inexperience, particularly when working in a distributed team environment. In addition, the team didn't have procedures in place for how to effectively contribute code using GitHub (also discussed in Section 10.4.8), which was new to many team members. In order to solve these challenges, the team created very detailed documentation specific to the project on how to push/pull to/from GitHub. In addition, hands-on training was provided to all software developers on best practices for using GitHub. In order to improve code quality, the team adopted the GitHub pull request feature for code review, whereby all code had to be code reviewed by an independent team member prior to merging the pull request. We found these practices to be extremely beneficial in providing the momentum to establish our software development environment.

10.4   Adopted Approach to Software Development Based on the Lessons Learned

This section conveys the approach to software development that was adopted for HydroShare based on the lessons learned early on in the project.

The approach includes the adoption of an iterative approach to software development that incorporates best practices in modern software engineering. Highlighted are several best practices in software engineering, including the use of virtual machines, code versioning, code reviews, and test-driven development. This section concludes with a discussion of the role and importance of communication and DevOps in facilitating effective multi-institutional collaboration.

10.4.1 Adopting Best Practices in Modern Software Engineering

One of the goals of the HydroShare Project is to continually adopt modern software engineering techniques to all scientific software development efforts. Although a scientist can author high-value software code, s/he approaches software development as a means to an end, with the end being new research findings. A software engineer, in contrast, approaches software development with code quality and sustainability as primary goals–not application. To a scientist, the research process is emphasized, and the final product is a set of scientific findings, which should be accurate, reproducible, and generalizable. To a software engineer, the coding process is emphasized, and the software code is the product, which should be error-free and reusable for solving other problems. In the same way that a scientist carefully designs a study to answer a research question or test a hypothesis, a software engineer carefully designs the code s/he will write to create new functionality. For example, software engineers use *design patterns*, or reusable and generalizable units of code that solve common software problems. Most scientists are not familiar with the concept of design patterns. Instead of combining reusable, tested units of code into new software, scientists often choose to write code from scratch in order to address a specific research need; after that need has been met, the software code is often tossed aside. Scientists are not as concerned about ensuring that the code is free of bugs because the code is not the object of interest, so code testing is not common practice. Software engineers, however, are trained to ensure that the code is free of bugs because quality code is the object of interest, so testing the code for accuracy is common practice.

One could argue that if scientists had lavish funding, they could hire professional software engineers to develop higher quality code over a more expeditious timeline. However, while an abundance of funding is always desirable, this would prevent the realization of certain opportunities. For HydroShare the involvement of hydrologists, including both graduate students and their faculty advisors, in software coding was extremely important for several reasons:

- As subject matter experts, the scientists were able to illuminate salient uses cases.

- As co-creators and owners of the software, the scientific community will be more likely to adopt the software and shepherd it throughout its lifetime.

- As graduate students, the incorporation of modern software engineering practices into their training is imperative in order to better prepare the next generation of hydrologists.

The key is that HydroShare should not be viewed simply as a software artifact, but also as a project that captures human and scientific capital for the advancement of transformative science through mature software engineering methodology. This is an important point. A lot of new ideas and thought processes have been created in the minds of the HydroShare team (i.e. human capital) as a result of this project, and these need to be kept concomitant with the software. Modern software engineering, in part, helps us achieve this.

10.4.2   Iterative Software Development

The Waterfall approach to software development emphasizes a discrete planning phase that includes gathering all possible requirements before the coding phase commences [340]. After a Waterfall phase is concluded, the rule-of-thumb is that that phase should not be revisited. This type of approach does not recognize or make allowances for the unknown and unpredictable. In other words, the Waterfall approach does not provide flexibility regarding changes in requirements, new needs or system uses, or changes in project focus.

Brooks [343] claims that software engineers should be open and ready to throw out unworkable ideas. "The only question is whether to plan in advance to build a throwaway, or to promise to deliver the throwaway to customers" [344]. When a distributed software development team endeavors to integrate several new and existing software systems at the onset of a project, complications can arise that preclude the ability of the team to efficiently and/or practically overcome those challenges. This is especially true in academic software development projects that have limited time and funding and include team members with varying levels of skill. With HydroShare, the team was not exempt from the "throwaway principle" and indeed had to completely discard a well-developed early version of the software due to unforeseen complications with the integration of disparate software systems. This was the result of several factors:

1. The decision to go with a seemingly appropriate technology, with much community adoption in other circles, was flawed at the beginning and made by a subset of the team without full consideration by the broader team. A more inclusive decision process would have led to better articulation regarding the platform requirements and a better outcome.

2. The system that was chosen, while having widespread community adoption in other circles, was one in which the team had no expertise. The

learning curve proved to be too high for them, at least on a practical level and given the time constraints.

3. The team's lack of expertise was magnified when the team members that made the decision to adopt the system left the project and a new lead development team came onboard without any prior knowledge of the selected technology or understanding of the previous team's activities; this challenge was exacerbated by lack of transition documentation to guide the new team.

The team has since adopted a more flexible iterative approach with HydroShare, one that embraces change. The conclusion is that one should expect to throw out an early version of a software product and learn from the experience. Also, one should realize that it is so much more efficient (and easier to accept) if this is part of the team's plan from the start, for when planning to throw out an early version of developed software, a team can view the experience as an exceptional opportunity to learn what works and what doesn't from the perspectives of software and technology integration, team communication, meeting productivity, and process efficiency. The HydroShare team also found it beneficial to encapsulate functionality in small, loosely coupled systems. For example, the distributed data management system used by HydroShare can work separately from the content management system, which can work separately from the web applications system, and so forth. In the first iteration, the team found that the integration of systems too tightly presents limitations. Unforeseen challenges arise in every software development project; the key is to plan for this early on and in every facet of the project–and expect to throw away at least one early product.

10.4.3　Virtual Machines

The HydroShare team uses virtual machines (VM) in testing and production in order to facilitate the distributed team's concurrent prototyping and development of the many diverse features of HydroShare. VMs can be created and spun-up very quickly, with configurable memory, processor, disk storage, and operating system to meet the diverse and evolving project and feature requirements. For features that are complex and highly susceptible to error, the HydroShare team creates a VM to test the feature. The team also creates feature-testing VMs for contextually-related features. For example, the group working on the search and filtering functionality has their own VM; the federated identity management group has its own VM; the user interface group has their own VM, and so on. Git (i.e., a revision control system) and GitHub (i.e., a hosting service for Git repositories) are used to manage and eventually merge the work on these VMs into a production release. Generally, a given branch of code that requires testing and feedback from the team is given its own VM. The exception is that some Git branches–especially those for general fixes–don't require deployment to a VM since they don't intertwine with other parts of the system and can be tested locally. Production VMs share an allocation of fifty terabytes of project disk space and another fifty terabytes of replicated disk space located four miles away in order to ensure fault tolerance and disaster recovery.

10.4.4 Code Versioning

Code versioning is a must for any modern software development project, academic or otherwise. There are several popular code versioning systems. The HydroShare team chose Git due to its ability to support distributed development workflows. Unlike other version control systems, Git allows developers to clone the main code repository on their local machines and develop and experiment with new code safely, in an independent environment completely separated from the main codebase. New code can then be submitted for inclusion into the main codebase after being reviewed and tested by other members of the team. This enforces code review, allows for experimentation within a safety net, and enables concurrent streams of development for a speedier process.

10.4.5 Code Reviews

With HydroShare, code reviews have opened up the reading of code and stimulated discussion around the structure of the code–something that was not happening before the team implemented the code review process. However, the team took a while to acclimate to the code review process, whereby the person who reviews the code is always different from the person who authors the code. For HydroShare, a code review includes an evaluation of:

- How well the new units of code address the associated use case;

- Code quality, in terms of clarity, concision, lack of redundancy, and thorough inline documentation;

- How easy the code's functionality is to use; and

- How the code fared in unit testing (i.e., tests of individual modules written for a particular function that together comprise a larger set of code).

The HydroShare team has found code reviews to be beneficial for encouraging discussion between scientists and software engineers around the structure of the code. These discussions have served as a vehicle for teaching software engineering best practices to the scientists involved in the project, particularly graduate students who are not required to take programming classes as part of their graduate work. In addition to these benefits, estimates suggest that rigorous code review can remove up to 90% of errors from a software product before any code testing is initiated [348] (code testing is discussed in next section).

The key point is that while it is necessary to establish regular code reviews early on, a period of acclimation should be expected.

10.4.6   Testing and Test-Driven Development

The testing of all code prior to release is extremely important for writing sustainable code – code that lasts over time because it has been tested for defects and performs consistently through new releases. There are a variety of tests that may be conducted during development, for example, unit testing, feature testing, regression testing, etc.

Unit testing is used to verify that the code does what it is expected to do without error. Ideally, using the software engineering concept of Test-Driven Development (TDD) [337], the test is written before the code is written. This forces the developer to think more carefully about the structure of the code, consider the best ways to satisfy the expectations of the unit of code, and plan for any error conditions *before the code is written.*

The HydroShare team has tied unit testing to Jenkins, which is an open source, continuous integration tool [335]. Jenkins is used to implement continuous integration by automating runs of unit tests for both new code submissions and nightly builds of the main codebase. Unit testing is beneficial because it allows developers to test new features within the context of the existing code prior to inclusion in the main codebase. This is done to verify that a new feature will not cause existing tests to fail after it is integrated into the main codebase. When many features are merged, they are tested together in order to ensure that their interactions do not cause failures. Roughly every two to three weeks, the development branch is merged into the production codebase (or master branch), which is the code that runs on the publicly visible HydroShare production site [332]. In this way, new functionality is both adequately reviewed and tested, as well as rapidly released.

While TDD provides an important model for software development, the HydroShare team implemented a hybrid approach by authoring some unit tests after functional HydroShare code was written. This approach was prompted by time constraints and the fact that TDD has a steep learning curve that may cause an initial decrease in developer productivity [356]. Indeed, even at this writing, the HydroShare team is still acclimating to the TDD process. Moreover, the HydroShare team does not yet use TDD for development of user interfaces, as the integration of emulated user interface actions, combined with all relevant user traversals of the HydroShare web page environment, is currently a prohibitively complex development endeavor for a project of the scale and complexity of HydroShare. Testing, combined with thorough initial design, has been shown to result in approximately 40% fewer defects compared to code developed with more ad-hoc testing [358]. The HydroShare team continues to strive toward more comprehensive use of TDD.

10.4.7   Team Communication

Invariably, a new project will commence with a series of meetings. Among the topics of those meetings should be the plan for both team communication and the software development infrastructure (i.e., the software and hardware used for development). With HydroShare, the establishment of communication protocols and development infrastructure early on in the project supported collaboration and productivity and likely will continue to serve the team well throughout the lifetime of the project.

For example, for weekly meetings of distributed team members, the team employs videoconferencing software with screen sharing capability. For communication outside of meetings, a team email list is used. HipChat [331], a synchronous chat tool, was adopted as a place solely for development-centric discussion, so as to avoid overloading subject matter experts (i.e., domain scientists who do not participate in development) with extraneous information or noise that only serves to distract from the research process. Furthermore, the team adopted a content management system to host all documents for the project, including meeting notes, presentations, use cases, architectural diagrams, API documentation, policies, etc. The team also uses email lists to disseminate community announcements (e.g., announce@hydroshare.org, support@hydroshare.org) and to allow people to obtain support for HydroShare. To describe the project to interested parties, the team has created public-facing web pages. Each of these activities has proven important to the success of HydroShare.

10.4.8 DevOps

In addition to effective communication among team members, close collaboration is essential. *Development Operations or DevOps* is an industry concept that can be defined as an approach to software development that emphasizes the importance of collaboration between all stakeholders [327]. DevOps recognizes that stakeholders (e.g., programmers, scientists) do not work in isolation. This principle was adopted for HydroShare; software developers and domain scientists work together, closely and continuously, in the development of the HydroShare code. For HydroShare, a software engineer was selected to fill the DevOps lead role because s/he must be a maestro of Git, GitHub, and coding, and few team scientist-developers were skilled with modern software engineering techniques at the start of the project. The appointment of an experienced software engineer as the DevOps lead allows the scientist-developers to learn tools such as Git as they develop and contribute code. The DevOps lead facilitates this learning process by writing task automation scripts in order to simplify and optimize code contributions in Git. With HydroShare, GitHub is used for issue tracking in order to drive new development or track defects (i.e. bugs). GitHub issues are also used to track the progress of code reviews, with developers giving a simple "+1" to indicate that the code has been reviewed and that the DevOps lead may proceed with a code merge. Task automation scripts help the DevOps lead groom the code repository and make Git's branching and merging processes more transparent. Together, these activities contribute to the DevOps lead's ability to successfully ensure continuous integration with automated testing. DevOps thus foster team collaboration on many levels over the course of a software development process.

10.5 Making Software Engineering More Feasible and Easier to Integrate into One's Research Activities

Many research projects do not have sufficient funding to support training in software development and the fundamentals of good software engineering [345]. Moreover, rigid or process-heavy software development approaches have been shown to be unappealing to scientists [345]. Thus, accepted software engineering approaches to the design, development, documentation, testing, and review of code, for example, may not be employed by scientists. The result is software that is not sustainable or usable by others.

In order to infuse the scientific community with good software engineering practices, it is important to make software engineering practices more appealing to scientists. One approach to encourage the adoption of modern software engineering practices is to emphasize the end result: software that is useful, high quality, and sustainable [341].

Through the HydroShare project, an approach has been identified to integrate software engineering best practices into a large, distributed scientific software development project in a manner that is feasible for scientists. Provided below are several specific recommendations for integrating software engineering practices into one's research activities.

First, an initial design specification should be completed at the very beginning of a project, followed by an iterative design review for continuous refinement throughout the project development cycle. This software engineering practice increases both software quality and productivity. The initial design should be just enough to get project development going. The design should be reviewed iteratively for continuous refinement as project development advances. The initial minimal set of specifications provides sufficient constraint and guidance for the first iteration of software development in order to ensure that no time is wasted in the present producing a specification that would be changed or abandoned later (especially if one plans to "throw one away" as covered in Section 10.4.2 herein). The design specification then evolves in conjunction with software development to best serve its purpose of guiding and planning software development in a most productive way. In practice, the project team needs to ensure that team members who are contributing to the system design communicate well with team members who are contributing to the system development throughout the project development cycle. This is in order to streamline the process in such a way as to produce an evolving design specification that is just enough to guide development of high-quality software.

Second, iterative software releases and the release of a prototype early in the development iteration are recommended in order to solicit feedback from end users. The software engineering practice of iterative software releases brings end users into the loop in such a way that their feedback can be integrated into the iterative software design and development process as early as possible, thereby ensuring the delivery of a software product with a large user base. It would be regrettable for any software project, especially large-scale, complex scientific projects that require several years of team development effort, to yield an end product with very few end users. The integration of end user feedback throughout the software development cycle via iterative software releases can prevent such a regrettable scenario from happening by addressing end user concerns in a timely manner. Early in the development process, the focus should be on simple designs that best fit the daily workflow of end users in order to ensure efficient delivery of an easy-to-use, high-quality end product.

Last, the adoption of software engineering practices is crucial to ensure software quality and sustainability, but these practices should be applied selectively to individual projects, so as not to hinder research productivity. Through the HydroShare experience three software engineering practices have been identified that warrant particular consideration for making software engineering more feasible and easier to integrate into one's research activities; namely, code refactoring, code review, and software testing. Code refactoring is needed on occasion in order to make changes to the underlying data structures and frameworks so that subsequent software development will be based on a better foundation, thereby resulting in improvements in software quality and development productivity. Because code refactoring can be very disruptive and may require a great deal of effort, careful consideration must be paid to the costs-benefits before adopting code refactoring. In certain circumstances, proof-of-concept prototyping will be needed in advance of any decision to adopt code refactoring in order to prove that the benefits outweigh the costs. While scientists often assume that output errors are the result of faulty theory rather than faulty software [354], the adoption of code review and software testing as precepts of sound software engineering in large-scale, scientific software development projects will help to minimize output errors and ensure that the final software product is high quality and sustainable.

10.6 Conclusion

The HydroShare project is a work in progress, and exploration, refinement, and implementation of the topics herein are by no means finished. Rather, the goal is to provide readers with insight into the HydroShare experience and lessons learned in order to minimize the learning curve and accelerate the development progress for other teams. The goal of this chapter is to provide readers with a basic understanding of why good software engineering for science is tantamount to the success and sustainability of a scientific research project and why poor software engineering will detract from research time, with more time spent managing poorly written code than actually conducting research. In the long run, good software engineering will foster research and one's research career by ensuring the validity of research findings, reducing the amount of time needed to maintain and extend code, and improving the ease at which new features can be adopted, thus supporting software reuse and sustainability.

Acknowledgments

Technical editorial and writing support was provided by Karamarie Fecho, Ph.D. This material is based upon work supported by the NSF under awards 1148453 and 1148090; any opinions, findings, conclusions, or recommendations expressed in this material are those of the authors and do not necessarily reflect the views of the NSF. The authors wish to thank many who have contributed to the HydroShare project, including but not limited to: Jennifer Arrigo, Larry Band, Christina Bandaragoda, Alex Bedig, Brian Blanton, Jeff Bradberry, Chris Calloway, Claris Castillo, Tony Castronova, Mike Conway, Jason Coposky, Shawn Crawley, Antoine deTorcey, Tian Gan, Jon Goodall, Ilan Gray, Jeff Heard, Rick Hooper, Harry Johnson, Drew (Zhiyu) Li, Rob Lineberger, Yan Liu, Shaun Livingston, David Maidment, Phyllis Mbewe, Venkatesh Merwade, Setphanie Mills, Mohamed Morsy, Jon Pollak, Mauriel Ramirez, Terrell Russell, Jeff Sadler, Martin Seul, Kevin Smith, Carol Song, Lisa Stillwell, Nathan Swain, Sid Thakur, David Valentine, Tim Whiteaker, Zhaokun Xue, Lan Zhao, and Shandian Zhe.

The authors wish to especially thank Stan Ahalt, Director of RENCI, and Ashok Krishnamurthy, Deputy Director of RENCI for their continued organizational and supplemental financial support of this project.

References

[1] J. C. Carver. First International Workshop on Software Engineering for Computational Science and Engineering. *Computing in Science Engineering*, 11(2):7–11, March 2009.

[2] J. C. Carver. Report: The Second International Workshop on Software Engineering for CSE. *Computing in Science Engineering*, 11(6):14–19, Nov 2009.

[3] Jeffrey C. Carver. Software engineering for computational science and engineering. *Computing in Science Engineering*, 14(2):8–11, March 2012.

[4] Jeffrey C. Carver, Neil Chue Hong, and Selim Ciraci. Software engineering for CSE. *Scientific Programming*, (591562):2, 2015.

[5] Jeffrey C. Carver and Tom Epperly. Software engineering for computational science and engineering [guest editors' introduction]. *Computing in Science Engineering*, 16(3):6–9, May 2014.

[6] S. H. D. Haddock and C. W. Dunn. *Practical Computing for Biologists*. Sinauer Associates, 2011.

[7] Sushil K. Prasad, Anshul Gupta, Arnold L. Rosenberg, Alan Sussman, and Charles C. Weems. *Topics in Parallel and Distributed Computing: Introducing Concurrency in Undergraduate Courses*. Morgan Kaufmann Publishers Inc., San Francisco, CA, USA, 1st edition, 2015.

[8] A. Scopatz and K. D. Huff. *Effective Computation in Physics*. O'Reilly Media, 2015.

[9] Agile methodology. http://agilemethodology.org/.

[10] IDEAS productivity: "How To" documents. https://ideas-productivity.org/resources/howtos/.

[11] Waterfall model. https://www.techopedia.com/definition/14025/waterfall-model.

[12] In L. I. Sedov, editor, *Similarity and Dimensional Methods in Mechanics*, pages 24–96. Academic Press, 1959.

[13] The FLASH code. http://flash.uchicago.edu/flashcode, 2000.

[14] A. Dubey, K. Weide, D. Lee, J. Bachan, C. Daley, S. Olofin, N. Taylor, P.M. Rich, and L.B. Reid. Ongoing verification of a multiphysics community code: FLASH. *Software: Practice and Experience*, 45(2), 2015.

[15] A. L. Atchley, S. L. Painter, D. R. Harp, E. T. Coon, C. J. Wilson, A. K. Liljedahl, and V. E. Romanovsky. Using field observations to inform thermal hydrology models of permafrost dynamics with ATS (v0.83). *Geosci. Model Dev. Discuss.*, 8:3235–3292, 2015.

[16] V. R. Basili, J. C. Carver, D. Cruzes, L. M. Hochstein, J. K. Hollingsworth, F. Shull, and M. V. Zelkowitz. Understanding the high-performance-computing community: A software engineer's perspective. *IEEE Software*, 25(4):29, 2008.

[17] M. Bauer, S. Treichler, E. Slaughter, and A. Aiken. Legion: Expressing locality and independence with logical regions. In *Proceedings of the International Conference on High Performance Computing, Networking, Storage and Analysis*, page 66. IEEE Computer Society Press, 2012.

[18] M. Berzins, J. Luitjens, Q. Meng, T. Harman, C. A. Wight, and J. R. Peterson. Uintah - a scalable framework for hazard analysis. In *TG '10: Proc. of 2010 TeraGrid Conference*, New York, NY, USA, 2010. ACM.

[19] M. Blazewicz, I. Hinder, D. M. Koppelman, S. R. Brandt, M. Ciznicki, M. Kierzynka, F. Löffler, E. Schnetter, and J. Tao. From physics model to results: An optimizing framework for cross-architecture code generation. *Scientific Programming*.

[20] A. C. Calder. Laboratory astrophysics experiments for simulation code validation: A case study. *Astrophysics and Space Science*, 298:25–32, July 2005.

[21] J. C. Carver. Software engineering for computational science and engineering. *Computing in Science & Engineering*, 14(2):8–11, 2012.

[22] J. C. Carver, R. P. Kendall, S. E. Squires, and D. E. Post. Software development environments for scientific and engineering software: A series of case studies. In *Software Engineering, 2007. ICSE 2007*, pages 550–559. IEEE, 2007.

[23] D. A. Case, V. Babin, J. Berryman, R. M. Betz, Q. Cai, D. S. Cerutti, T. E. Cheatham Iii, T. A. Darden, R. E. Duke, H. Gohlke, et al. Amber 2015. http://ambermd.org/, 2015.

[24] E. T. Coon, J. D. Moulton, and S. L. Painter. Managing complexity in simulations of land surface and near-surface processes. *Environmental Modelling & Software*, 78:134–49, 2016.

[25] G. Dimonte, D. L. Youngs, A. Dimits, S. Weber, M. Marinak, S. Wunsch, C. Garasi, A. Robinson, M. J. Andrews, P. Ramaprabhu, A. C. Calder, B. Fryxell, J. Biello, L. Dursi, P. MacNeice, K. Olson, P. Ricker, R. Rosner, F. Timmes, H. Tufo, Y.-N. Young, and M. Zingale. A comparative study of the turbulent Rayleigh–Taylor instability using high-resolution three-dimensional numerical simulations: The Alpha-Group collaboration. *Physics of Fluids*, 16:1668–1693, May 2004.

[26] A. Dubey, K. Antypas, M. K. Ganapathy, L. B. Reid, K. Riley, D. Sheeler, A. Siegel, and K. Weide. Extensible component-based architecture for FLASH, a massively parallel, multiphysics simulation code. *Parallel Computing*, 35(10-11):512–522, 2009.

[27] A. Dubey, A. C. Calder, C. Daley, R. T. Fisher, C. Graziani, G. C. Jordan, D. Q. Lamb, L. B. Reid, D. M. Townsley, and K. Weide. Pragmatic optimizations for better scientific utilization of large supercomputers. *International Journal of High Performance Computing Applications*, 27(3):360 373, 2013.

[28] A. Dubey and T. Clune. Optimization techniques for pseudospectral codes on MPPs. In *Proceedings of Frontiers 99*, 1999.

[29] A. Dubey, C. Daley, J. ZuHone, P. M. Ricker, K. Weide, and C. Graziani. Imposing a Lagrangian particle framework on an Eulerian hydrodynamics infrastructure in FLASH. *ApJ Supplement*, 201:27, Aug 2012.

[30] A. Dubey, D. Q. Lamb, and E. Balaras. Building community codes for effective scientific research on HPC platforms. http://flash.uchicago.edu/cc2012, 2012.

[31] A. Dubey, L. B. Reid, and R. Fisher. Introduction to FLASH 3.0, with application to supersonic turbulence. *Physica Scripta*, T132, 2008. Topical Issue on Turbulent Mixing and Beyond, results of a conference at ICTP, Trieste, Italy, August 2008.

[32] A. Dubey, A. Almgren, J. Bell, M. Berzins, S. Brandt, G. Bryan, P. Colella, D. Graves, M. Lijewski, F. Löffler, B. O'Shea, E. Schnetter, B. Van Straalen, and K. Weide. A survey of high level frameworks in block-structured adaptive mesh refinement packages. *Journal of Parallel and Distributed Computing*, 74(12):3217–3227, 2014.

[33] B. Fryxell, K. Olson, P. Ricker, F. X. Timmes, M. Zingale, D. Q. Lamb, P. MacNeice, R. Rosner, J. W. Truran, and H. Tufo. Flash: An adaptive mesh hydrodynamics code for modeling astrophysical thermonuclear flashes. *Astrophysical Journal, Supplement*, 131:273–334, 2000.

[34] J. E. Hannay, C. MacLeod, J. Singer, H. P. Langtangen, D. Pfahl, and G. Wilson. How do scientists develop and use scientific software? In

Proceedings of the 2009 ICSE Workshop on Software Engineering for Computational Science and Engineering, pages 1–8. IEEE Computer Society, 2009.

[35] M. A. Heroux and J. M. Willenbring. Barely sufficient software engineering: 10 practices to improve your cse software. In *Proceedings of the 2009 ICSE Workshop on Software Engineering for Computational Science and Engineering*, SECSE '09, pages 15–21, Washington, DC, USA, 2009. IEEE Computer Society.

[36] L. Hochstein and V. R. Basili. The ASC-alliance projects: A case study of large-scale parallel scientific code development. *Computer*, (3):50–58, 2008.

[37] L. V. Kale, E. Bohm, C. L. Mendes, T. Wilmarth, and G. Zheng. Programming petascale applications with Charm++ and AMPI. *Petascale Computing: Algorithms and Applications*, 1:421–441, 2007.

[38] J. O. Kane, H. F. Robey, B. A. Remington, R. P. Drake, J. Knauer, D. D. Ryutov, H. Louis, R. Teyssier, O. Hurricane, D. Arnett, et al. Interface imprinting by a rippled shock using an intense laser. *Physical Review E, Statistical, Nonlinear, and Soft Matter Physics*, 63(5 Pt 2):055401, 2001.

[39] Q. Meng, J. Luitjens, and M. Berzins. Dynamic task scheduling for the uintah framework. In *Proceedings of the 3rd IEEE Workshop on Many-Task Computing on Grids and Supercomputers (MTAGS10)*, 2010.

[40] D. Monniaux. The pitfalls of verifying floating-point computations. *ACM Transactions on Programming Languages and Systems (TOPLAS)*, 30(3):12, 2008.

[41] D. Moulton, M. Berndt, M. Buskas, R. Garimella, L. Prichett-Sheats, G. Hammond, M. Day, and J. Meza. High-level design of Amanzi, the multi-process high performance computing simulator. Technical report, ASCEM-HPC-2011-03-1, US Department of Energy, Washington, DC, 2011.

[42] J. D. Moulton, J. C. Meza, and M. Day et al. High-level design of Amanzi, the multi-process high performance computing simulator. Technical report, DOE-EM, Washington, DC, 2012.

[43] L. Nguyen–Hoan, S. Flint, and R. Sankaranarayana. A survey of scientific software development. In *Proceedings of the 2010 ACM-IEEE International Symposium on Empirical Software Engineering and Measurement*, ESEM '10, pages 12:1–12:10, New York, NY, 2010. ACM.

[44] P. K. Notz, R. P. Pawlowski, and J. C. Sutherland. Graph-based software design for managing complexity and enabling concurrency in multiphysics PDE software. *ACM Trans. Math. Softw.*, 39(1):1:1–1:21, November 2012.

[45] W. L. Oberkampf and C. J. Roy. *Verification and Validation in Scientific Computing*. Cambridge University Press, 2010.

[46] W. L. Oberkampf and T. G. Trucano. Verification and validation in computational fluid dynamics. *Progress in Aerospace Sciences*, 38(3):209–272, 2002.

[47] S. L. Painter, J. D. Moulton, and C. J. Wilson. Modeling challenges for predicting hydrologic response to degrading permafrost. *Hydrogeol. J.*, pages 1–4, 2013.

[48] S. G. Parker. A component-based architecture for parallel multi-physics PDE simulation. *Future Generation Comput. Sys.*, 22:204–216, 2006.

[49] J. C. Phillips, R. Braun, W. Wang, J. Gumbart, E. Tajkhorshid, E. Villa, C. Chipot, R. D. Skeel, L. Kale, and K. Schulten. Scalable molecular dynamics with namd. *Journal of Computational Chemistry*, 26(16):1781–1802, 2005.

[50] R. G. Sargent. Verification and validation of simulation models. In *Proceedings of the 30th Conference on Winter Simulation*, pages 121–130. IEEE Computer Society Press, 1998.

[51] J. Segal. When software engineers met research scientists: a case study. *Empirical Software Engineering*, 10(4):517–536, 2005.

[52] J. Segal and C. Morris. Developing scientific software. *Software, IEEE*, 25(4):18–20, 2008.

[53] The Enzo Collaboration, G. L. Bryan, M. L. Norman, B. W. O'Shea, T. Abel, J. H. Wise, M. J. Turk, D. R. Reynolds, D. C. Collins, P. Wang, S. W. Skillman, B. Smith, R. P. Harkness, J. Bordner, J.-H. Kim, M. Kuhlen, H. Xu, N. Goldbaum, C. Hummels, A. G. Kritsuk, E. Tasker, S. Skory, C. M. Simpson, O. Hahn, J. S. Oishi, G. C. So, F. Zhao, R. Cen, and Y. Li. Enzo: An Adaptive Mesh Refinement Code for Astrophysics. *ArXiv e-prints*, July 2013.

[54] D. Unat, J. Shalf, T. Hoefler, T. Schulthess, A. Dubey, et al. Programming abstractions for data locality. In *Workshop on Programming Abstractions for Data Locality (PADAL'14)*, 2014.

[55] Karen S. Ackroyd, Steve H. Kinder, Geoff R. Mant, Mike C. Miller, Christine A. Ramsdale, and Paul C. Stephenson. Scientific software development at a research facility. *IEEE Software*, 25(4):44–51, July/August 2008.

[56] Arne Beckhause, Dirk Neumann, and Lars Karg. The impact of communication structure on issue tracking efficiency at a large business software vendor. *Issues in Information Systems*, X(2):316–323, 2009.

[57] Jacques Carette. Gaussian elimination: A case study in efficient genericity with MetaOCaml. *Science of Computer Programming*, 62(1):3–24, 2006.

[58] Jacques Carette, Mustafa ElSheikh, and W. Spencer Smith. A generative geometric kernel. In *ACM SIGPLAN 2011 Workshop on Partial Evaluation and Program Manipulation (PEPM'11)*, pages 53–62, January 2011.

[59] Jeffrey C. Carver, Richard P. Kendall, Susan E. Squires, and Douglass E. Post. Software development environments for scientific and engineering software: A series of case studies. In *ICSE '07: Proceedings of the 29th International Conference on Software Engineering*, pages 550–559, Washington, DC, USA, 2007. IEEE Computer Society.

[60] CIG. Mineos. http://geodynamics.org/cig/software/mineos/, March 2015.

[61] CRAN. The comprehensive R archive network. https://cran.r-project.org/, 2014.

[62] CSA. Quality assurance of analytical, scientific, and design computer programs for nuclear power plants. Technical Report N286.7-99, Canadian Standards Association, 178 Rexdale Blvd. Etobicoke, Ontario, Canada M9W 1R3, 1999.

[63] Andrew P. Davison. Automated capture of experiment context for easier reproducibility in computational research. *Computing in Science & Engineering*, 14(4):48–56, July-Aug 2012.

[64] Andrew P. Davison, M. Mattioni, D. Samarkanov, and B. Teleńczuk. Sumatra: A toolkit for reproducible research. In V. Stodden, F. Leisch, and R.D. Peng, editors, *Implementing Reproducible Research*, pages 57–79. Chapman & Hall/CRC, Boca Raton, FL, March 2014.

[65] Paul F. Dubois. Designing scientific components. *Computing in Science and Engineering*, 4(5):84–90, September 2002.

[66] Paul F. Dubois. Maintaining correctness in scientific programs. *Computing in Science & Engineering*, 7(3):80–85, May-June 2005.

[67] Steve M. Easterbrook and Timothy C. Johns. Engineering the software for understanding climate change. *IEEE Des. Test*, 11(6):65–74, 2009.

[68] Ahmed H. ElSheikh, W. Spencer Smith, and Samir E. Chidiac. Semi-formal design of reliable mesh generation systems. *Advances in Engineering Software*, 35(12):827–841, 2004.

[69] ESA. ESA software engineering standards, PSS-05-0 issue 2. Technical report, European Space Agency, February 1991.

[70] Sergey Fomel. Madagascar Project Main Page. http://www.ahay.org/wiki/Main_Page, 2014.

[71] Carlo Ghezzi, Mehdi Jazayeri, and Dino Mandrioli. *Fundamentals of Software Engineering*. Prentice Hall, Upper Saddle River, NJ, USA, 2nd edition, 2003.

[72] GRASS Development Team. GRASS GIS bringing advanced geospatial technologies to the world. http://grass.osgeo.org/, 2014.

[73] Michael Heath. *Scientific Computing: An Introductory Survey*. McGraw-Hill Publishing Company, New York, NY, 2nd edition, 2002.

[74] Timothy Hickey, Qun Ju, and Maarten H. Van Emden. Interval arithmetic: From principles to implementation. *J. ACM*, 48(5):1038–1068, September 2001.

[75] Daniel M. Hoffman and Paul A. Strooper. *Software Design, Automated Testing, and Maintenance: A Practical Approach*. International Thomson Computer Press, New York, NY, 1995.

[76] IEEE. *Recommended Practice for Software Requirements Specifications, IEEE Std. 830*. IEEE, 1998.

[77] ISTI. Earthworm software standards. http://www.earthwormcentral.org/documentation2/PROGRAMMER/SoftwareStandards.html, September 2013.

[78] Jeffrey N Johnson and Paul F Dubois. Issue tracking. *Computing in Science & Engineering*, 5(6):71–77, 2003.

[79] Diane Kelly. Industrial scientific software: A set of interviews on software development. In *Proceedings of the 2013 Conference of the Center for Advanced Studies on Collaborative Research*, CASCON '13, pages 299–310, Riverton, NJ, USA, 2013. IBM Corp.

[80] Diane Kelly. Scientific software development viewed as knowledge acquisition: Towards understanding the development of risk-averse scientific software. *Journal of Systems and Software*, 109:50–61, 2015.

[81] Diane F. Kelly, W. Spencer Smith, and Nicholas Meng. Software engineering for scientists. *Computing in Science & Engineering*, 13(5):7–11, October 2011.

[82] Brian W. Kernighan and Rob Pike. *The Practice of Programming.* Addison-Wesley Professional, Reading, MA, 1999.

[83] Oleg Kiselyov, Kedar N. Swadi, and Walid Taha. A methodology for generating verified combinatorial circuits. In *Proceedings of the 4th ACM International Conference on Embedded Software*, EMSOFT '04, pages 249–258, New York, NY, USA, 2004. ACM.

[84] Donald E. Knuth. *Literate Programming.* CSLI Lecture Notes Number 27. Center for the Study of Language and Information, 1992.

[85] Adam Lazzarato, Spencer Smith, and Jacques Carette. State of the practice for remote sensing software. Technical Report CAS-15-03-SS, McMaster University, January 2015. 47 pp.

[86] Friedrich Leisch. Sweave: Dynamic generation of statistical reports using literate data analysis. In Wolfgang Härdle and Bernd Rönz, editors, *Compstat 2002 — Proceedings in Computational Statistics*, pages 575–580. Physica Verlag, Heidelberg, 2002. ISBN 3-7908-1517-9.

[87] Jon Loeliger and Matthew McCullough. *Version Control with Git: Powerful Tools and Techniques for Collaborative Software Development.* O'Reilly Media, Inc., 2012.

[88] Thomas Maibaum and Alan Wassyng. A product-focused approach to software certification. *IEEE Computer*, 41(2):91–93, 2008.

[89] NASA. Software requirements DID, SMAP-DID-P200-SW, release 4.3. Technical report, National Aeronautics and Space Agency, 1989.

[90] Nedialko S. Nedialkov. Implementing a Rigorous ODE Solver through Literate Programming. Technical Report CAS-10-02-NN, Department of Computing and Software, McMaster University, 2010.

[91] Suely Oliveira and David E. Stewart. *Writing Scientific Software: A Guide to Good Style.* Cambridge University Press, New York, NY, USA, 2006.

[92] Linda Parker Gates. Strategic planning with critical success factors and future scenarios: An integrated strategic planning framework. Technical Report CMU/SEI-2010-TR-037, Software Engineering Institute, Carnegie-Mellon University, November 2010.

[93] David L. Parnas. On the criteria to be used in decomposing systems into modules. *Comm. ACM*, 15(2):1053–1058, December 1972.

[94] David L. Parnas, P. C. Clement, and D. M. Weiss. The modular structure of complex systems. In *International Conference on Software Engineering*, pages 408–419, 1984.

[95] David L. Parnas and P.C. Clements. A rational design process: How and why to fake it. *IEEE Transactions on Software Engineering*, 12(2):251–257, February 1986.

[96] David Lorge Parnas. Precise documentation: The key to better software. In *The Future of Software Engineering*, pages 125–148, 2010.

[97] Matt Pharr and Greg Humphreys. *Physically Based Rendering: From Theory to Implementation*. Morgan Kaufmann Publishers Inc., San Francisco, CA, USA, 2004.

[98] Michael Pilato. *Version Control With Subversion*. O'Reilly & Associates, Inc., Sebastopol, CA, USA, 2004.

[99] Patrick J. Roache. *Verification and Validation in Computational Science and Engineering*. Hermosa Publishers, Albuquerque, NM, 1998.

[100] Padideh Sarafraz. Thermal optimization of flat plate PCM capsules in natural convection solar water heating systems. Master's thesis, McMaster University, Hamilton, ON, Canada, 2014. http://hdl.handle.net/11375/14128.

[101] Judith Segal. When software engineers met research scientists: A case study. *Empirical Software Engineering*, 10(4):517–536, October 2005.

[102] Judith Segal and Chris Morris. Developing scientific software. *IEEE Software*, 25(4):18–20, July/August 2008.

[103] W. Spencer Smith and Nirmitha Koothoor. A document driven method for certifying scientific computing software used in nuclear safety analysis. *Nuclear Engineering and Technology*, Accepted, October 2015. 42 pp.

[104] W. Spencer Smith, Yue Sun, and Jacques Carette. Comparing psychometrics software development between CRAN and other communities. Technical Report CAS-15-01-SS, McMaster University, January 2015. 43 pp.

[105] W. Spencer Smith, Yue Sun, and Jacques Carette. Statistical software for psychology: Comparing development practices between CRAN and other communities. *Software Quality Journal*, Submitted December 2015. 33 pp.

[106] W. Spencer Smith. Systematic development of requirements documentation for general purpose scientific computing software. In *Proceedings of the 14th IEEE International Requirements Engineering Conference, RE 2006*, pages 209–218, Minneapolis / St. Paul, MN, 2006.

[107] W. Spencer Smith, Nirmitha Koothoor, and Nedialko Nedialkov. Document driven certification of computational science and engineering software. In *Proceedings of the First International Workshop on Software Engineering for High Performance Computing in Computational Science and Engineering (SE-HPCCE)*, November 2013. 8 pp.

[108] W. Spencer Smith and Lei Lai. A new requirements template for scientific computing. In J. Ralyté, P. Ågerfalk, and N. Kraiem, editors, *Proceedings of the First International Workshop on Situational Requirements Engineering Processes – Methods, Techniques and Tools to Support Situation-Specific Requirements Engineering Processes, SREP'05*, pages 107–121, Paris, France, 2005. In conjunction with 13th IEEE International Requirements Engineering Conference.

[109] W. Spencer Smith, Lei Lai, and Ridha Khedri. Requirements analysis for engineering computation: A systematic approach for improving software reliability. *Reliable Computing, Special Issue on Reliable Engineering Computation*, 13(1):83–107, February 2007.

[110] W. Spencer Smith, John McCutchan, and Fang Cao. Program families in scientific computing. In Jonathan Sprinkle, Jeff Gray, Matti Rossi, and Juha-Pekka Tolvanen, editors, *7th OOPSLA Workshop on Domain Specific Modelling (DSM'07)*, pages 39–47, Montréal, Québec, October 2007.

[111] W. Spencer Smith and Wen Yu. A document driven methodology for improving the quality of a parallel mesh generation toolbox. *Advances in Engineering Software*, 40(11):1155–1167, November 2009.

[112] Daniel Szymczak, W. Spencer Smith, and Jacques Carette. Position paper: A knowledge-based approach to scientific software development. In *Proceedings of SE4Science'16*, United States, May 16 2016. In conjunction with ICSE 2016. 4 pp.

[113] L. Andries van der Ark. *mokken: Mokken Scale Analysis in R*, 2013. R package version 2.7.5.

[114] Hans van Vliet. *Software Engineering (2nd ed.): Principles and Practice*. John Wiley & Sons, Inc., New York, NY, USA, 2000.

[115] Judith S. VanAlstyne. *Professional and Technical Writing Strategies*. Pearson Prentice Hall, Upper Saddle River, NJ, sixth edition, 2005.

[116] Gregory V. Wilson. Where's the real bottleneck in scientific computing? Scientists would do well to pick some tools widely used in the software industry. *American Scientist*, 94(1), 2006.

[117] Gregory V. Wilson, D.A. Aruliah, C. Titus Brown, Neil P. Chue Hong, Matt Davis, Richard T. Guy, Steven H. D. Haddock, Kathryn D. Huff,

Ian M. Mitchell, Mark D. Plumblet, Ben Waugh, Ethan P. White, and Paul Wilson. Best practices for scientific computing. *CoRR*, abs/1210.0530, 2013.

[118] A. Arcuri, M. Z. Iqbal, and L. Briand. Random Testing: Theoretical Results and Practical Implications. *IEEE Trans. Software Engineering*, 38(2):258–277, 2012.

[119] J. M. Bové. Huanglongbing: A Destructive, Newly-Emerging, Century-Old Disease of Citrus. *Journal of Plant Pathology*, 88:7–37, 2006.

[120] F. Brayton, A. Levin, R. Tryon, and J. C. Williams. The Evolution of Macro Models at the Federal Reserve Board. In *Carnegie Rochester Conference Series on Public Policy*, pages 43–81, 1997.

[121] I. Burnstein. *Practical Software Testing: A Process-Oriented Approach*. Springer, New York, NY, 2003.

[122] F. T. Chan, T. Y. Chen, S. C. Cheung, M. F. Lau, and S. M. Yiu. Application of metamorphic testing in numerical analysis. In *IASTED International Conference on Software Engineering*, pages 191–197, 1998.

[123] N. J. Cunniffe, R. O. J. H. Stutt, R. E. DeSimone, T. R. Gottwald, and C. A. Gilligan. Optimizing and Communicating Options for the Control of Invasive Plant Disease When There Is Epidemiological Uncertainty. *PLOS Computational Biology*, 2015.

[124] O. Diekmann, J. A. P. Heesterbeek, and J. A. J. Metz. The Oracle Problem in Software Testing: A Survey. *Journal of Mathematical Biology*, 28(4):365–382, 1990.

[125] J. W. Duran. An Evaluation of Random Testing. *IEEE Trans. Software Engineering*, 10(4):438–444, 1984.

[126] A. Geller and S. J. Alam. A Socio-Political and -Cultural Model of the War in Afghanistan. *International Studies Review*, 12(1):8–30.

[127] M. F. C. Gomes, A. Pastore y Piontti, L. Rossi, D Chao, I. Longini, M. E. Halloran, and A. Vespignani. Assessing the International Spreading Risk Associated with the 2014 West African Ebola Outbreak. *PLoS Curr*, 2014.

[128] T. R. Gottwald. Current Epidemiological Understanding of Citrus Huanglongbing. *Annual Review of Phytopathology*, 48:119–139, 2010.

[129] J. E. Hannay, C. MacLeod, J. Singer, H. P. Langtangen, D. Pfahl, and G. Wilson. How Do Scientists Develop and Use Scientific Software? In *Soft. Eng. for Computational Science and Eng., ICSE*, 2009.

[130] N. Hansen. The CMA Evolution Strategy: A Comparing Review. In J. A. Lozano, P. Larrañaga, I. Inza, and E. Bengoetxea, editors, *Towards a New Evolutionary Computation (Studies in Fuzziness and Soft Computing)*, pages 75–102. Berlin, Germany: Springer, 2006.

[131] N. Hansen. CMA-ES Source Code. https://www.lri.fr/~hansen/cmaes_inmatlab.html, 2011. [Online]. Accessed 24 March 2016.

[132] N. Hansen, A. Auger, R. Ros, S. Finck, and P. Posik. Comparing Results of 31 Algorithms from the Black-Box Optimization Benchmarking BBOB-2009. In *Proc. 12th Genetic Evolutionary Computation Conf.*, pages 1689–1696, 2010.

[133] P. R. Harper and A.K. Shahani. Modelling for the Planning and Management of Bed Capacities in Hospitals. *Journal of the Operational Research Society*, 53(1):11–18, 2006.

[134] L. Hatton and A. Roberts. How Accurate is Scientific Software? *IEEE Trans. Software Engineering*, 20(10):785–797, 1994.

[135] S. Hettrick, M. Antonioletti, L. Carr, N. Chue Hong, S. Crouch, D. De Roure, I. Emsley, C. Goble, A. Hay, D. Inupakutika, M. Jackson, A. Nenadic, T. Parkinson, M. I. Parsons, A. Pawlik, G. Peru, A. Proeme, J. Robinson, and S. Sufi. UK Research Software Survey 2014. https://zenodo.org/record/14809, note = "[Online]. Accessed 24 March 2016".

[136] P.C. Jorgensen. *Software Testing: A Craftsman's Approach*. CRC Press, Boca Raton, FL, 4th edition, 2013.

[137] M. J. Keeling, M. E. J. Woolhouse, R. M. May, G. Davics, and B. T. Grenfell. Modelling Vaccination Strategies against Foot-and-Mouth Disease. *Nature*, 421:136–142, 2003.

[138] D. F. Kelly. A Software Chasm: Software Engineering and Scientific Computing. *IEEE Software*, 24(6):118–120, 2007.

[139] R. C. Martin. *Clean Code: A Handbook of Agile Software Craftsmanship*. Prentice Hall, Upper Saddle River, NJ, 2008.

[140] F. Massey. The Kolmogorov–Smirnov Test for Goodness of Fit. *Journal of the American Statistical Association*, 46(253):68–78, 1951.

[141] R. K. Meentemeyer, N. J. Cunniffe, A. R. Cook, J. A. N. Filipe, R. D. Hunter, D. M. Rizzo, and C. A. Gilligan. Epidemiological Modeling of Invasion in Heterogeneous Landscapes: Spread of Sudden Oak Death in California (1990–2030). *Ecosphere*, 2(2), 2011.

[142] Z. Merali. Computational science: Error, why scientific programming does not compute. *Nature*, 467(7317), 2010.

[143] H. Motulsky. Comparing Dose-Response or Kinetic Curves with Graph-Pad Prism. *HMS Beagle: The BioMedNet Magazine*, 34, 1998.

[144] D. Orchard and A. Rice. A Computational Science Agenda for Programming Language Research. In *Proc. International Conference on Computational Science*, pages 713–727, 2014.

[145] D. L. Parnas. On the Criteria to Be Used in Decomposing Systems into Modules. *Communications of the ACM*, 15(12):1053–1058, 1972.

[146] M. Parry, G. J. Gibson, S. Parnell, T. R. Gottwald, M. S. Irey, T. C. Gast, and C. A. Gilligan. Bayesian Inference for an Emerging Arboreal Epidemic in the Presence of Control. *Proc. National Academy of Sciences*, 111(17):6258–6262, 2014.

[147] A. Piccolboni. Quickcheck. `https://github.com/Revolution Analytics/quickcheck`, 2015. [Online]. Accessed 24 March 2016.

[148] K. Salari and P. Knupp. Code Verification by the Method of Manufactured Solutions. Technical Report SAND2000-1444, Sandia National Laboratories, June 2000.

[149] S. Shamshiri, J. M. Rojas, G. Fraser, and P. McMinn. Random or Genetic Algorithm Search for Object-Oriented Test Suite Generation? In *Proc. GECCO*, pages 1367–1374, 2015.

[150] J. A. Sokolowski and C. M. Banks. *Modeling and Simulation Fundamentals: Theoretical Underpinnings and Practical Domains*. Wiley, Hoboken, NJ, 4 edition, 2010.

[151] F. W. Thackeray and J. E. Findling. *Events That Formed the Modern World*. ABC CLIO, Santa Barbara, CA, 2012.

[152] J. Utts and R. Heckard. *Statistical Ideas and Methods*. Thomson, Belmont, CA, 2005.

[153] T. Weise. Global Optimization Algorithms - Theory and Application. `http://www.itweise.de/projects/book.pdf`, 2009. [Online]. Accessed 24 March 2016.

[154] E. J. Weyuker. On Testing Non-Testable Programs. *The Computer Journal*, 25(4):465–470, 1982.

[155] A. Dubey, K. Weide, D. Lee, J. Bachan, C. Daley, S. Olofin, N. Taylor, P.M. Rich, and L.B. Reid. Ongoing verification of a multiphysics community code: FLASH. *Software: Practice and Experience*, 45(2), 2015.

[156] Bamboo. https://www.atlassian.com/software/bamboo/.

[157] K. J. Bathe, editor. *Computational Fluid and Solid Mechanics*. Elsevier, 2001.

[158] K. Beck. *Test Driven Development*. Addison-Wesley, Boston, MA, 2003.

[159] K. Beck. *Extreme Programming (Second Edition)*. Addison-Wesley, 2005.

[160] Thirumalesh Bhat and Nachiappan Nagappan. Evaluating the efficacy of test-driven development: Industrial case studies. In *Proceedings of the 2006 ACM/IEEE International Symposium on Empirical Software Engineering*, ISESE '06, pages 356–363, New York, NY, USA, 2006. ACM.

[161] F. Brooks. *The Mythical Man-Month (second edition)*. Addison-Wesley, Boston, MA, 1995.

[162] CDash. www.cdash.org.

[163] E. Coon, J. D. Moulton, and S. Painter. Managing complexity in simulations of land surface and near-surface processes. Technical Report LA-UR 14-25386, Applied Mathematics and Plasma Physics Group, Los Alamos National Laboratory, 2014. To appear in *Environmental Modelling & Software*.

[164] CTest. https://cmake.org/Wiki/CMake/Testing_With_CTest.

[165] S. M. Easterbrook and T. C. Johns. Engineering the software for understanding climate change. *Computing in Science Engineering*, 11(6):65–74, Nov.-Dec. 2009.

[166] H. Erdogmus, M. Morisio, and M. Torchiano. On the effectiveness of the test-first approach to programming. *IEEE Transactions on Software Engineering*, 31(3):226–237, 2005.

[167] M. Feathers. *Working Effectively with Legacy Code*. Prentice-Hall, Upper Saddle River, NJ, 2004.

[168] M. Fowler. *Refactoring (Improving the Design of Existing Code)*. Addison Wesley, 1999.

[169] M. Gartner. *ATDD by Example: A Practical Guide to Acceptance Test-Driven Development*. Addison-Wesley, 2012.

[170] D. Goldberg. What every computer scientist should know about floating-point arithmetic. *ACM Computing Surveys*, March 1991.

[171] gtest. http://wiki.ros.org/gtest.

[172] *hypre*: High Performance Preconditioners. http://www.llnl.gov/CASC/hypre/.

[173] Parasoft Insure++. https://www.parasoft.com/product/insure/.

[174] Jenkins. https://jenkins-ci.org/.

[175] B. Koteska and A. Mishev. Scientific software testing: A practical example. In Z. Budimar and M. Hericko, editors, *Proceedings of the 4th Workshop of Software Quality, Analysis, Monitoring, Improvement, and Applications (SQAMIA 2015)*, Maribor, Slovenia, 8.-10.6.2015.

[176] X. S. Li, J. W. Demmel, J. R. Gilbert, L. Grigori, P. Sao, M. Shao, and I. Yamazaki. SuperLU Users' Guide. Technical Report LBNL-44289, Lawrence Berkeley National Laboratory, October 2014.

[177] S. McConnell. *Code Complete: Second Edition*. Microsoft Press, 2004.

[178] G. Miller. A scientist's nightmare: Software problem leads to five retractions. *Science*, 314(5807):1856–1857, 2006.

[179] J. Nocedal and S. Wright. *Numerical Optimization*. Springer, 1999.

[180] P. K. Notz, R. P. Pawlowski, and J. C. Sutherland. Graph-based software design for managing complexity and enabling concurrency in multiphysics PDE software. *Acm. T. Math. Software*, 39(1):1, 2012.

[181] M. Poppendieck and T. Poppendieck. *Implementing Lean Software Development*. Addison-Wesley, 2007.

[182] D. Post and L. Votta. Computational science demands and new paradigm. *Physics Today*, 58(1):35–41, 2005.

[183] J. Seward and N. Nethercote. Using valgrind to detect undefined value errors with bit-precision. In *Proceedings of the Annual Conference on USENIX Annual Technical Conference*, ATEC '05, pages 2–2, Berkeley, CA, USA, 2005. USENIX Association.

[184] A. K. Shuja and J. Krebs. *IBM Rational Unified Process Reference and Certification Guide: Solution Designer*. IBM Press, 2007.

[185] S. R. Slattery, P. P. H. Wilson, and R. P. Pawlowski. The Data Transfer Kit: A geometric rendezvous-based tool for multiphysics data transfer. In *International Conference on Mathematics & Computational Methods Applied to Nuclear Science & Engineering*, pages 5–9, 2013.

[186] SuperLU. http://crd-legacy.lbl.gov/~xiaoye/SuperLU/.

[187] D. Talby, A. Keren, O. Hazzan, and Y. Dubinsky. Agile software testing in a large-scale project. *Software, IEEE*, 23(4):30–37, 2006.

[188] The Trilinos Project. https://trilinos.org.

[189] H. Troger and A. Steindl. *Nonlinear stability and bifurcation theory: An introduction for engineers and applied scientists.* Springer, 1991.

[190] B. Turhan, L. Layman, M. Diep, H. Erdogmus, and F. Shull. How effective is test-driven development? In *Making Software: What Really Works and Why We Believe It*, pages 207–217. O'Reilly, 2010.

[191] xUnit. http://xunit.github.io/.

[192] Boris Beizer. *Software Testing Techniques.* Dreamtech Press, 2003.

[193] David L. Donoho, Arian Maleki, Inam Ur Rahman, Morteza Shahram, and Victoria Stodden. Reproducible research in computational harmonic analysis. *Computing in Science and Engineering*, 11(1):8–18, 2009.

[194] Steve M. Easterbrook and Timothy C. Johns. Engineering the software for understanding climate change. *Computing in Science and Engineering*, 11(6):64–74, 2009.

[195] Rob Gray and Diane Kelly. Investigating test selection techniques for scientific software using Hook's mutation sensitivity testing. *Procedia Computer Science*, 1(1):1487–1494, 2010.

[196] Daniel Hook. Using Code Mutation to Study Code Faults in Scientific Software. Master's thesis, Queen's University, Kingston, ON, Canada, April 2009. Available at http://hdl.handle.net/1974/1765.

[197] Daniel Hook and Diane Kelly. Mutation sensitivity testing. *Computing in Science and Engineering*, 11(6):40–47, 2009.

[198] Upulee Kanewala and James M. Bieman. Testing scientific software: A systematic literature review. *Information and Software Technology*, 56(10):1219–1232, 2014.

[199] Nicholas Jie Meng. A Model for Run-time Measurement of Input and Round-off Error. Master's thesis, Queen's University, Kingston, ON, Canada, September 2012. Available at http://hdl.handle.net/1974/7508.

[200] Glenford J Myers, Corey Sandler, and Tom Badgett. *The Art of Software Testing.* John Wiley & Sons, 2011.

[201] William L. Oberkampf, Timothy G. Trucano, and Charles Hirsch. Verification, validation, and predictive capability in computational engineering and physics. In *Proceedings of Foundations '02, a Workshop on Modeling and Simulation Verification and Validation for the 21st Century*, Laurel, MD, USA, October 2002. Johns Hopkins University.

[202] Rebecca Sanders and Diane Kelly. The challenge of testing scientific software. In *CAST '08: Proceedings of the 3rd Annual Conference of the Association for Software Testing*, pages 30–36, Toronto, ON, Canada, 2008. Association for Software Testing.

[203] Rebecca Sanders and Diane Kelly. Dealing with risk in scientific software development. *IEEE Software*, 25(4):21–28, 2008.

[204] A framework to write repeatable Java tests. available at http://junit.org, Accessed: 12-20-2015.

[205] A Unit Testing Framework for C. available at http://cunit. source-forge.net, Accessed: 12-10-2015.

[206] A Unit Testing Framework for FORTRAN. available at https:// rubygems.org/gems/funit/versions/0.11.1, Accessed: 20-12-2015.

[207] Cube 4.x series, 2015. Version 4.3.2, available at http://www.scalasca. org/software/cube-4.x/download.html, Accessed: 06-10-2015.

[208] D. Babic, L. Martignoni, S. McCamant, and D. Song. Statically-directed dynamic automated test generation. pages 12–22, 2011.

[209] G. B. Bonan. The land surface climatology of the NCAR land surface model coupled to the NCAR community. *Climate Model. J. Climate*, 11·1307–1326.

[210] C. Cadar, D. Dunbar, and D. Engler. Klee: Unassisted and automatic generation of high-coverage tests for complex systems programs. pages 209–224, 2008.

[211] D. Wang, W. Wu, T. Janjusic, Y. Xu, C. Iversen, P. Thornton, and M. Krassovisk. Scientific functional testing platform for environmental models: An application to community land model. *International Workshop on Software Engineering for High Performance Computing in Science*, 2015.

[212] R. E. Dickinson, K. W. Oleson, G. Bonan, F. Hoffman, P. Thornton, M. Vertenstein, Z. Yang, and X. Zeng. The community land model and its climate statistics as a component of the community climate system model. *J. Clim.*, 19:2302–2324, 2006.

[213] M. Feathers. *Working Effectively with Legacy Code*. Prentice-Hall, 2004.

[214] A. Knüpfer, C. Rössel, D. Mey, S. Biersdorf, K. Diethelm, D. Eschweiler, M. Gerndt, D. Lorenz, A. D. Malony, W. E. Nagel, Y. Oleynik, P. Saviankou, D. Schmidl, S. Shende, R. Tschüter, M. Wagner, B. Wesarg, and F. Wolf. Score-P - A Joint Performance Measurement Run-Time Infrastructure for Periscope, Scalasca, TAU, and Vampir. *5th Parallel Tools Workshop*, 2011.

[215] A. Knüpfer, H. Brunst, J. Doleschal, M. Jurenz, M. Lieber, H. Mickler, M. S. Müller, and W. E. Nagel. The Vampir Performance Analysis Tool-Set. In M. Resch, R. Keller, V. Himmler, B. Kramer, and A. Schulz, editors, *"Tools for High Performance Computing", Proceedings of the 2nd International Workshop on Parallel Tools for High Performance Computing*, Stuttgart, Germany, July 2008. Springer-Verlag.

[216] A. Kolawa and D. Huizinga. *Automated Defect Prevention: Best Practices in Software Management.* Wiley-IEEE Computer Society Press, 2007.

[217] K. Oleson, D. Lawrence, B. Gordon, M. Flanner, E. Kluzek, J. Peter, S. Levis, S. Swenson, P. Thornton, and J. Feddema. Technical description of version 4.0 of the community land model (clm). 2010.

[218] M. Pezze and M. Young. *Software Testing and Analysis: Process, Principles and Techniques.* Wiley, 2007.

[219] D. Wang, Y. Xu, P. Thornton, A. King, C. Steed, L. Gu, and J. Schuchart. A functional test platform for the community land model. *Environ. Model. Softw.*, 55(C):25–31, May 2014.

[220] Z. Yao, Y. Jia, D. Wang, C. Steed, and S. Atchley. In situ data infrastructure for scientific unit testing platform. *Proceeding Computer Science*, 80:587–598, Dec. 31, 2016.

[221] U. Kanewala and J. M. Bieman, "Testing scientific software: A systematic literature review," *Information and Software Technology*, vol. 56, no. 10, pp. 1219–1232, 2014. [Online]. Available: http://www.sciencedirect.com/science/article/pii/S0950584914001232

[222] T. Clune and R. Rood, "Software testing and verification in climate model development," *Software, IEEE*, vol. 28, no. 6, pp. 49–55, Nov.–Dec. 2011.

[223] P. Dubois, "Testing scientific programs," *Computing in Science Engineering*, vol. 14, no. 4, pp. 69–73, Jul.–Aug. 2012.

[224] W. Wood and W. Kleb, "Exploring XP for scientific research," *Software, IEEE*, vol. 20, no. 3, pp. 30–36, May–June.

[225] G. Miller, "A scientist's nightmare: Software problem leads to five retractions," *Science*, vol. 314, no. 5807, pp. 1856–1857, 2006. [Online]. Available: http://www.sciencemag.org/content/314/5807/1856.short

[226] E. J. Weyuker, "On testing non-testable programs," *The Computer Journal*, vol. 25, no. 4, pp. 465–470, 1982. [Online]. Available: http://comjnl.oxfordjournals.org/content/25/4/465.abstract

[227] U. Kanewala and J. Bieman, "Using machine learning techniques to detect metamorphic relations for programs without test oracles," in *Proc. 24th IEEE International Symposium on Software Reliability Engineering (ISSRE)*, Pasadena, California, USA, Nov. 2013, pp. 1–10.

[228] A. Bertolino, "Software testing research and practice," in *Abstract State Machines 2003*, ser. Lecture Notes in Computer Science, E. Börger, A. Gargantini, and E. Riccobene, Eds. Springer Berlin Heidelberg, 2003, vol. 2589, pp. 1–21. [Online]. Available: http://dx.doi.org/10.1007/3-540-36498-6_1

[229] S. M. Easterbrook, "Climate change: a grand software challenge," in *Proceedings of the FSE/SDP Workshop on Future of Software Engineering Research*, ser. FoSER '10. New York, NY, USA: ACM, 2010, pp. 99–104. [Online]. Available: http://doi.acm.org/10.1145/1882362.1882383

[230] C. Murphy, M. S. Raunak, A. King, S. Chen, C. Imbriano, G. Kaiser, I. Lee, O. Sokolsky, L. Clarke, and L. Osterweil, "On effective testing of health care simulation software," in *Proc. 3rd Workshop on Software Engineering in Health Care*, ser. SEHC '11. New York, NY, USA: ACM, 2011, pp. 40–47.

[231] J. C. Carver, R. P. Kendall, S. E. Squires, and D. E. Post, "Software development environments for scientific and engineering software: A series of case studies," in *Proceedings of the 29th International Conference on Software Engineering*, ser. ICSE '07. Washington, DC, USA: IEEE Computer Society, 2007, pp. 550–559. [Online]. Available: http://dx.doi.org/10.1109/ICSE.2007.77

[232] D. Kelly, S. Smith, and N. Meng, "Software engineering for scientists," *Computing in Science Engineering*, vol. 13, no. 5, pp. 7–11, Sep.–Oct. 2011.

[233] M. T. Sletholt, J. Hannay, D. Pfahl, H. C. Benestad, and H. P. Langtangen, "A literature review of agile practices and their effects in scientific software development," in *Proceedings of the 4th International Workshop on Software Engineering for Computational Science and Engineering*, ser. SECSE '11. New York, NY, USA: ACM, 2011, pp. 1–9. [Online]. Available: http://doi.acm.org/10.1145/1985782.1985784

[234] R. Sanders and D. Kelly, "The challenge of testing scientific software," in *Proc. of the Conference for the Association for Software Testing (CAST)*, Toronto, July 2008, pp. 30–36.

[235] C. Murphy, G. Kaiser, and M. Arias, "An approach to software testing of machine learning applications," in *Proc of the 19th International Conference on Software Engineering and Knowledge Engineering (SEKE)*, Boston, MA, USA, Jul. 2007, pp. 167–172.

[236] T. Y. Chen, J. W. K. Ho, H. Liu, and X. Xie, "An innovative approach for testing bioinformatics programs using metamorphic testing." *BMC Bioinformatics*, vol. 10, pp. 24–36, 2009.

[237] D. Kelly and R. Sanders, "Assessing the quality of scientific software," in *Proc of the First International Workshop on Software Engineering for Computational Science and Engineering*, 2008.

[238] J. Pitt–Francis, M. O. Bernabeu, J. Cooper, A. Garny, L. Momtahan, J. Osborne, P. Pathmanathan, B. Rodriguez, J. P. Whiteley, and D. J. Gavaghan, "Chaste: Using agile programming techniques to develop computational biology software," *Philosophical Transactions of the Royal Society A: Mathematical, Physical and Engineering Sciences*, vol. 366, no. 1878, pp. 3111–3136, 2008. [Online]. Available: http://rsta. royalsocietypublishing.org/content/366/1878/3111.abstract

[239] J. E. Hannay, C. MacLeod, J. Singer, H. P. Langtangen, D. Pfahl, and G. Wilson, "How do scientists develop and use scientific software?" in *Proceedings of the 2009 ICSE Workshop on Software Engineering for Computational Science and Engineering*, ser. SECSE '09. Washington, DC, USA: IEEE Computer Society, 2009, pp. 1–8. [Online]. Available: http://dx.doi.org/10.1109/SECSE.2009.5069155

[240] J. Segal, "Scientists and software engineers: A tale of two cultures," in *PPIG 2008: Proceedings of the 20th Annual Meeting of the Pschology of Programming Interest Group*, J. Buckley, J. Rooksby, and R. Bednarik, Eds. Lancaster, UK: Lancaster University, 2008, proceedings: 20th annual meeting of the Psychology of Programming Interest Group; Lancaster, United Kingdom; September 10–12 2008. [Online]. Available: http://oro.open.ac.uk/17671/

[241] A. J. Abackerli, P. H. Pereira, and N. Calônego Jr., "A case study on testing CMM uncertainty simulation software (VCMM)," *Journal of the Brazilian Society of Mechanical Sciences and Engineering*, vol. 32, pp. 8–14, Mar. 2010.

[242] L. Nguyen–Hoan, S. Flint, and R. Sankaranarayana, "A survey of scientific software development," in *Proceedings of the 2010 ACM-IEEE International Symposium on Empirical Software Engineering and Measurement*, ser. ESEM '10. New York, NY, USA: ACM, 2010, pp. 12:1–12:10. [Online]. Available: http://doi.acm.org/10. 1145/1852786.1852802

[243] M. A. Heroux, J. M. Willenbring, and M. N. Phenow, "Improving the development process for CSE software," in *Parallel, Distributed and Network-Based Processing, 2007. PDP '07. 15th EUROMICRO International Conference on*, Feb. 2007, pp. 11–17.

[244] D. Kelly, R. Gray, and Y. Shao, "Examining random and designed tests to detect code mistakes in scientific software," *Journal of Computational Science*, vol. 2, no. 1, pp. 47–56, 2011. [Online]. Available: http://www.sciencedirect.com/science/article/pii/S187775031000075X

[245] D. Kelly, S. Thorsteinson, and D. Hook, "Scientific software testing: Analysis with four dimensions," *Software, IEEE*, vol. 28, no. 3, pp. 84–90, May–Jun. 2011.

[246] P. E. Farrell, M. D. Piggott, G. J. Gorman, D. A. Ham, C. R. Wilson, and T. M. Bond, "Automated continuous verification for numerical simulation," *Geoscientific Model Development*, vol. 4, no. 2, pp. 435–449, 2011. [Online]. Available: http://www.geosci-model-dev.net/4/435/2011/

[247] S. M. Easterbrook and T. C. Johns, "Engineering the software for understanding climate change," *Computing in Science Engineering*, vol. 11, no. 6, pp. 65–74, Nov.–Dec. 2009.

[248] D. E. Post and R. P. Kendall, "Software project management and quality engineering practices for complex, coupled multiphysics, massively parallel computational simulations: Lessons learned from ASCI," vol. 18, no. 4, pp. 399–416, Winter 2004. [Online]. Available: http://hpc.sagepub.com/content/18/4/399.full.pdf+html

[249] M. D. Davis and E. J. Weyuker, "Pseudo-oracles for non-testable programs," in *Proceedings of the ACM '81 Conference*, ser. ACM '81. New York, NY, USA: ACM, 1981, pp. 254–257. [Online]. Available: http://doi.acm.org/10.1145/800175.809889

[250] L. Hatton, "The T experiments: Errors in scientific software," *IEEE Computational Science Engineering*, vol. 4, no. 2, pp. 27–38, Apr.– Jun. 1997.

[251] T. Chen, J. Feng, and T. H. Tse, "Metamorphic testing of programs on partial differential equations: A case study," in *Computer Software and Applications Conference, 2002. COMPSAC 2002. Proceedings. 26th Annual International*, pp. 327–333.

[252] S. Brilliant, J. Knight, and N. Leveson, "Analysis of faults in an n-version software experiment," *Software Engineering, IEEE Transactions on*, vol. 16, no. 2, pp. 238–247, 1990.

[253] P. C. Lane and F. Gobet, "A theory-driven testing methodology for developing scientific software," *Journal of Experimental & Theoretical Artificial Intelligence*, vol. 24, no. 4, pp. 421–456, 2012. [Online]. Available: http://www.tandfonline.com/doi/abs/10.1080/0952813X.2012.695443

[254] R. Sanders and D. Kelly, "Dealing with risk in scientific software development," *IEEE Software*, vol. 25, no. 4, pp. 21–28, Jul.–Aug. 2008.

[255] D. Hook and D. Kelly, "Testing for trustworthiness in scientific software," in *Software Engineering for Computational Science and Engineering, 2009. SECSE '09. ICSE Workshop on*, May 2009, pp. 59–64.

[256] L. Hochstein and V. Basili, "The ASC-Alliance projects: A case study of large-scale parallel scientific code development," *Computer*, vol. 41, no. 3, pp. 50–58, March.

[257] J. Mayer, A. A. Informationsverarbeitung, and U. Ulm, "On testing image processing applications with statistical methods," in *Software Engineering (SE 2005), Lecture Notes in Informatics*, 2005, pp. 69–78.

[258] M. Cox and P. Harris, "Design and use of reference data sets for testing scientific software," *Analytica Chimica Acta*, vol. 380, no. 2–3, pp. 339–351, 1999. [Online]. Available: http://www.sciencedirect.com/science/article/pii/S0003267098004814

[259] Z. Q. Zhou, D. H. Huang, T. H. Tse, Z. Yang, H. Huang, and T. Y. Chen, "Metamorphic testing and its applications," in *Proc. 8th International Symposium on Future Software Technology (ISFST 2004)*. Xian, China: Software Engineers Association, 2004, pp. 346–351.

[260] X. Xie, J. W. Ho, C. Murphy, G. Kaiser, B. Xu, and T. Y. Chen, "Testing and validating machine learning classifiers by metamorphic testing," *Journal of Systems and Software*, vol. 84, no. 4, pp. 544–558, 2011.

[261] S. Yoo, "Metamorphic testing of stochastic optimisation," in *Proc. Third International Conference on Software Testing, Verification, and Validation Workshops (ICSTW)*, Apr. 2010, pp. 192–201.

[262] T. Chen, J. Feng, and T. Tse, "Metamorphic testing of programs on partial differential equations: A case study," in *Proc. 26th International Computer Software and Applications Conference on Prolonging Software Life: Development and Redevelopment*, ser. COMPSAC '02. Washington, DC, USA: IEEE Computer Society, 2002, pp. 327–333.

[263] T. Y. Chen, T. H. Tse, and Z. Q. Zhou, "Fault-based testing without the need of oracles," *Information and Software Technology*, vol. 45, no. 1, pp. 1–9, 2003.

[264] T. Y. Chen, S. C. Cheung, and S. M. Yiu, "Metamorphic testing: A new approach for generating next test cases," Department of Computer Science, Hong Kong University of Science and Technology, Hong Kong, Tech. Rep. HKUST-CS98-01, 1998.

[265] C. Murphy, G. Kaiser, L. Hu, and L. Wu, "Properties of machine learning applications for use in metamorphic testing," in *Proc of the 20th International Conference on Software Engineering and Knowledge Engineering (SEKE)*, Redwood City, CA, USA, Jul. 2008, pp. 867–872.

[266] J. Mayer and R. Guderlei, "On random testing of image processing applications," in *Quality Software, 2006. QSIC 2006. Sixth International Conference on*, Oct. 2006, pp. 85–92.

[267] C. Murphy, K. Shen, and G. Kaiser, "Using JML runtime assertion checking to automate metamorphic testing in applications without test oracles," in *Proc. 2009 International Conference on Software Testing Verification and Validation*, ser. ICST '09. Washington, DC, USA: IEEE Computer Society, 2009, pp. 436–445.

[268] R. Guderlei and J. Mayer, "Statistical metamorphic testing – testing programs with random output by means of statistical hypothesis tests and metamorphic testing," in *Proc. 7th International Conference on Quality Software (QSIC)*, Portland, Oregon, USA, Oct. 2007, pp. 404–409.

[269] U. Kanewala, J. M. Bieman, and A. Ben-Hur, "Predicting metamorphic relations for testing scientific software: A machine learning approach using graph kernels," *Software Testing, Verification and Reliability*, 2015, in press.

[270] F. E. Allen, "Control flow analysis," *SIGPLAN Not.*, vol. 5, no. 7, pp. 1–19, Jul. 1970. [Online]. Available: http://doi.acm.org/10.1145/390013.808479

[271] R. Vallee–Rai and L. J. Hendren, "Jimple: Simplifying Java bytecode for analyses and transformations," 1998.

[272] R. I. Kondor and J. Lafferty, "Diffusion kernels on graphs and other discrete structures," in *Proc. 19th International Conf. on Machine Learning*, 2002, pp. 315–322.

[273] T. Gärtner, P. Flach, and S. Wrobel, "On graph kernels: Hardness results and efficient alternatives," in *Learning Theory and Kernel Machines*, ser. Lecture Notes in Computer Science, B. Schölkopf and M. Warmuth, Eds. Springer Berlin Heidelberg, 2003, vol. 2777, pp. 129–143.

[274] J. Huang and C. Ling, "Using AUC and accuracy in evaluating learning algorithms," *IEEE Transactions on Knowledge and Data Engineering*, vol. 17, no. 3, pp. 299–310, Mar. 2005.

[275] J. H. Andrews, L. C. Briand, and Y. Labiche, "Is mutation an appropriate tool for testing experiments?" in *Proceedings of the 27th International Conference on Software Engineering*, ser. ICSE '05. New York, NY, USA: ACM, 2005, pp. 402–411.

258   *References*

[276] Y. Jia and M. Harman, "An analysis and survey of the development of mutation testing," *IEEE Transactions on Software Engineering*, vol. 37, pp. 649–678, 2011.

[277] Y.-S. Ma and J. Offutt, "Description of method-level mutation operators for java," November 2005. [Online]. Available: http://cs.gmu.edu/~offutt/mujava/mutopsMethod.pdf

[278] David Abrahams and Aleksey Gurtovoy. *C++ Template Metaprogramming: Concepts, Tools, and Techniques from Boost and Beyond.* Addison Wesley, 2004.

[279] Kaitlin Alexander and Stephen M. Easterbrook. The software architecture of climate models: A graphical comparison of CMIP5 and EMICAR5 configurations. *Geoscientific Model Development Discussions*, 8(1):351–379, 2015.

[280] Ansible Incorporated. Ansible documentation. http://docs.ansible.com, 2015.

[281] Apple Incorporated. The Swift programming language – language reference. https://developer.apple.com/library/ios/documentation/Swift/Conceptual/Swift_Programming_Language/AboutTheLanguageReference.html, 2015.

[282] Simonetta Balsamo, Antinisca Di Marco, Paola Inverardi, and Marta Simeoni. Model-based performance prediction in software development: A survey. *Software Engineering*, 30(5):295–310, 2004.

[283] Victor R. Basili, Daniela Cruzes, Jeffrey C. Carver, Lorin M. Hochstein, Jeffrey K. Hollingsworth, Marvin V. Zelkowitz, and Forrest Shull. Understanding the high-performance-computing community: A software engineer's perspective. *IEEE Software*, 25(4):29–36, 2008.

[284] Marco Brambilla, Jordi Cabot, and Manuel Wimmer. *Model-driven software engineering in practice.* Number 1 in Synthesis Lectures on Software Engineering. Morgan & Claypool, 2012.

[285] Susanne Brenner and L. Ridgway Scott. *The Mathematical Theory of Finite Element Methods.* Springer, 3 edition, 2008.

[286] Frank Buschmann, Regine Meunier, Hans Rohnert, Peter Sommerlad, Michael Stal, Peter Sommerlad, and Michael Stal. Pattern-oriented software architecture, volume 1: A system of patterns, 1996.

[287] Fabien Campagne. *The MPS Language Workbench: Volume I.* Fabien Campagne, 2014.

[288] Jeffrey C. Carver, Richard P. Kendall, Susan E. Squires, and Douglass E. Post. Software development environments for scientific and engineering software: A series of case studies. In *Proceedings of the 29th International Conference on Software Engineering (ICSE 2007)*, pages 550–559. IEEE, 2007.

[289] Leonardo Dagum and Ramesh Menon. OpenMP: An industry standard API for shared-memory programming. *Computational Science & Engineering*, 5(1):46–55, 1998.

[290] Stephen M. Easterbrook and Timothy C. Johns. Engineering the software for understanding climate change. *Computing in Science & Engineering*, 11(6):65–74, 2009.

[291] Sven Efftinge, Moritz Eysholdt, Jan Köhnlein, Sebastian Zarnekow, Robert von Massow, Wilhelm Hasselbring, and Michael Hanus. Xbase: Implementing domain-specific languages for Java. In *Proceedings of the 11th International Conference on Generative Programming and Component Engineering*, pages 112–121. ACM, 2012.

[292] Moritz Eysholdt and Heiko Behrens. Xtext: Implement your language faster than the quick and dirty way. In *Proceedings of the ACM International Conference Companion on Object-Oriented Programming Systems Languages and Applications Companion*, pages 307–309. ACM, 2010.

[293] Stuart Faulk, Eugene Loh, Michael L. Van De Vanter, Susan Squires, and Lawrence G. Votta. Scientific computing's productivity gridlock: How software engineering can help. *Computing in Science & Engineering*, 11:30–39, 2009.

[294] Martin Fowler. *Domain-Specific Languages*. Addison-Wesley, 2010.

[295] Volker Grimm and Steven F. Railsback. *Individual-based Modeling and Ecology*. Princeton University Press, 2005.

[296] Jo ErsKine Hannay, Hans Petter Langtangen, Carolyn MacLeod, Dietmar Pfahl, Janice Singer, and Greg Wilson. How do scientists develop and use scientific software? In *Software Engineering for Computational Science and Engineering, 2009. SECSE'09. ICSE Workshop on*, pages 1–8. IEEE, 2009.

[297] Dustin Heaton and Jeffrey C. Carver. Claims about the use of software engineering practices in science: A systematic literature review. *Information and Software Technology*, 67:207–219, 2015.

[298] Siw Elisabeth Hove and Bente Anda. Experiences from conducting semi-structured interviews in empirical software engineering research. In *11th IEEE International Software Metrics Symposium (METRICS 2005)*, pages 1–10. IEEE, 2005.

260   *References*

[299] Arne N. Johanson and Wilhelm Hasselbring. Hierarchical combination of internal and external domain-specific languages for scientific computing. In *Proceedings of the 2014 European Conference on Software Architecture Workshops*, ECSAW'14, pages 17:1–17:8. ACM, 2014.

[300] Arne N. Johanson and Wilhelm Hasselbring. Sprat: Hierarchies of domain-specific languages for marine ecosystem simulation engineering. In *Proceedings TMS SpringSim'14*, pages 187–192. SCS, 2014.

[301] Diane Kelly. A software chasm: Software engineering and scientific computing. *IEEE Software*, 24(6):118–120, 2007.

[302] Sarah Killcoyne and John Boyle. Managing chaos: Lessons learned developing software in the life sciences. *Computing in Science & Engineering*, 11(6):20–29, 2009.

[303] Anneke Kleppe. *Software Language Engineering: Creating Domain-Specific Languages Using Metamodels*. Addison-Wesley, 2008.

[304] Philipp Mayring. *Qualitative Inhaltsanalyse: Grundlagen und Techniken*. Beltz, 12 edition, 2015.

[305] Marjan Mernik, Jan Heering, and Anthony M. Sloane. When and how to develop domain-specific languages. *ACM Computing Surveys (CSUR)*, 37(4):316–344, 2005.

[306] Paul Messina. Gaining the broad expertise needed for high-end computational science and engineering research. *Computing in Science & Engineering*, 17(2):89–90, 2015.

[307] Christian Motika, Steven Smyth, and Reinhard von Hanxleden. Compiling SCCharts – a case-study on interactive model-based compilation. In *Leveraging Applications of Formal Methods, Verification and Validation. Technologies for Mastering Change*, pages 461–480. Springer, 2014.

[308] Prakash Prabhu, Thomas B. Jablin, Arun Raman, Yun Zhang, Jialu Huang, Hanjun Kim, Nick P. Johnson, Feng Liu, Soumyadeep Ghosh, Stephen Beard, Taewook Oh, Matthew Zoufaly, David Walker, and David I. August. A survey of the practice of computational science. In *State of the Practice Reports*, SC'11, pages 19:1–19:12. ACM, 2011.

[309] Doraiswami Ramkrishna. *Population Balances: Theory and Applications to Particulate Systems in Engineering*. Academic Press, 2000.

[310] Rebecca Sanders and Diane F. Kelly. Dealing with risk in scientific software development. *Software, IEEE*, 25(4):21–28, 2008.

[311] Ina Schieferdecker. Model-based testing. *IEEE Software*, 29(1):14–18, 2012.

[312] Erik Schnetter, Marek Blazewicz, Steven R. Brandt, David M. Koppel-man, and Frank Löffler. Chemora: A PDE-solving framework for modern high-performance computing architectures. *Computing in Science & Engineering*, 17(2):53–64, 2015.

[313] Judith Segal. Models of scientific software development. In *Proceedings of the First International Workshop on Software Engineering for Computational Science and Engineering, SECSE'08*, pages 1–7, 2008.

[314] Judith Segal and Chris Morris. Developing scientific software. *Software, IEEE*, 25(4):18–20, 2008.

[315] Thomas Stahl and Markus Völter. *Model-Driven Software Development: Technology, Engineering, Management*. Wiley, 2006.

[316] Mark Strembeck and Uwe Zdun. An approach for the systematic development of domain-specific languages. *Software: Practice and Experience*, 39(15):1253–1292, 2009.

[317] Gregory V. Wilson. Where's the real bottleneck in scientific computing? *American Scientist*, 94(1):5–6, 2006.

[318] Gregory V. Wilson. Software carpentry: Lessons learned. *F1000Research*, 3:1–11, 2014.

[319] Satish Balay, Shrirang Abhyankar, Mark F. Adams, Jed Brown, Peter Brune, Kris Buschelman, Lisandro Dalcin, Victor Eijkhout, William D. Gropp, Dinesh Kaushik, Matthew G. Knepley, Lois Curfman McInnes, Karl Rupp, Barry F. Smith, Stefano Zampini, and Hong Zhang. PETSc Users Manual. Technical Report ANL-95/11 - Revision 3.6, Argonne National Laboratory, 2015.

[320] David M. Beazley. SWIG: An easy to use tool for integrating scripting languages with C and C++. In *Proceedings of the 4th USENIX Tcl/Tk Workshop*, pages 129–139, 1996.

[321] Thomas G. W. Epperly, Gary Kumfert, Tamara Dahlgren, Dietmar Ebner, Jim Leek, Adrian Prantl, and Scott Kohn. High-performance language interoperability for scientific computing through Babel. *International Journal of High Performance Computing Applications*, page 1094342011414036, 2011.

[322] William D. Gropp. Users manual for bfort: Producing Fortran interfaces to C source code. Technical Report ANL/MCS-TM-208, Argonne National Laboratory, IL (United States), 1995.

[323] William D. Gropp and Barry F. Smith. Simplified linear equation solvers users manual. Technical Report ANL–93/8, Argonne National Laboratory, IL (United States), 1993.

[324] William D. Gropp and Barry F. Smith. Scalable, extensible, and portable numerical libraries. In *Proceedings of the Scalable Parallel Libraries Conference*, pages 87–93, Mississippi State University, 1994. IEEE.

[325] Michael Metcalf. The seven ages of fortran. *Journal of Computer Science & Technology*, 11, 2011.

[326] Object Management Group. Common Object Request Broker Architecture (CORBA). http://www.corba.org, 2007.

[327] DevOps. https://en.wikipedia.org/wiki/DevOps.

[328] Django. https://www.djangoproject.com/.

[329] Docker. https://www.docker.com/.

[330] Guide to the Software Engineering Body of Knowledge (SWEBOK), V3. http://www.computer.org/web/swebok/v3-guide/.

[331] HipChat. https://www.hipchat.com/.

[332] HydroShare. http://www.hydroshare.org/.

[333] Implementation of NSF CIF21 Software Vision (SW-Vision). http://www.nsf.gov/si2/.

[334] iRODS. http://irods.org/.

[335] Jenkins. https://jenkins.io/.

[336] NSF collaborative HydroShare award numbers 1148453 and 1148090. http://www.nsf.gov/awardsearch/showAward?AWD_ID=1148453 and http://www.nsf.gov/awardsearch/showAward?AWD_ID=1148090.

[337] Test-Driven Development (TDD). https://www.agilealliance.org/glossary/tdd.

[338] National Flood Interoperability Experiment. http://www.caee.utexas.edu/prof/maidment/giswr2014/Synopsis/GISWRSynopsis12.pdf, 2014.

[339] Graduate students take part in National Flood Interoperability Experiment Summer Institute to develop new tools. http://www.tuscaloosanews.com/article/20150607/NEWS/150609776?p=2&tc=pg/, 2015.

[340] S. Ahalt, L. Band, L. Christopherson, R. Idaszak, C. Lenhardt, B. Minsker, M. Palmer, M. Shelley, M. Tiemann, and A. Zimmerman. Water Science Software Institute: Agile and open source scientific software development. *IEEE Computing in Science and Engineering (CiSE)*, 6(3):18–26, 2014.

[341] R. Bartlett, M. Heroux, and W. Willenbring. Overview of the TriBITS Lifecycle Model : A Lean/Agile Software Lifecycle Model for Research-based Computational Science and Engineering Software. In *Proceedings of the First Workshop on Maintainable Software Practices in e-Science*. Part of the IEEE International Conference on eScience, 2012.

[342] V. R. Basili, J. C. Carver, D. Cruzes, L. M. Hochstein, J. K. Hollingsworth, F. Shull, and M. V. Zelkowitz. Understanding the high-performance computing community: A software engineer's perspective. In *Software*, pages 29–36. IEEE, 2008.

[343] F. P. Brooks. *The Mythical Man Month: Essays on Software Engineering, Anniversary Edition (2nd Edition)*. Addison-Wesley Professional, 1995.

[344] Ibid Brooks. p. 116.

[345] J. C. Carver, R. P. Kendall, S. E. Squires, and D. E. Post. Software development environments for scientific and engineering software: A series of case studies. In *29th International Conference on Software Engineering (ICSE)*, pages 550–559. Minneapolis, MN: IEEE, 2007.

[346] Engineering Committee on Science, National Academy of Engineering Public Policy, National Academy of Science, and Institute of Medicine of the National Academies *On Being a Scientist: A Guide to Responsible Conduct in Research*. Washington, DC: National Academies Press, 2009.

[347] A. Couch, D. G. Tarboton, R. Idaszak, J. S. Horsburgh, H. Yi, and M. J. Stealey. A Flexible File Sharing Mechanism for iRODS. In *iRODS User Group Meeting 2015 Proceedings*, pages 61–68, 2015.

[348] R. L. Glass. Frequently Forgotten Fundamental Facts about Software Engineering. *IEEE Software*, page 110, 2001.

[349] J. E. Hannay, C. MacLeod, and J. Singer. How do scientists develop and use scientific software? In *ICSE Workshop on Software Engineering for Computational Science and Engineering*, pages 1–8. Vancouver, Canada: IEEE, 2009.

[350] J. Heard, D. G. Tarboton, R. Idaszak, J.S. Horsburgh, D. Ames, A. Bedig, A. M. Castronova, A. Couch, P. Dash, C. Frisby, T. Gan, J. Goodall, S. Jackson, S. Livingston, D. Maidment, N. Martin, B. Miles, S. Mills, J. Sadler, D. Valentine, and L. Zhao. An Architectural Overview of Hydroshare, A Next-Generation Hydrologic Information System. In *11th International Conference on Hydroinformatics, HIC 2014*. CUNY Academic Works, 2014.

[351] J. S. Horsburgh, M. M. Morsy, A. M. Castronova, J. L. Goodall, T. Gan, H. Yi, M. J. Stealey, and D. G. Tarboton. Hydroshare: Sharing Diverse Environmental Data Types and Models as Social Objects with Application to the Hydrology Domain. *Journal of the American Water Resources Association (JAWRA)*, pages 1–17, 2015.

[352] J. Howison and J. D. Herbsleb. Scientific software production: Incentives and collaboration. In *Proceedings of the ACM 2011 Conference on Computer Supported Cooperative Work*, pages 513–522. Hangzhou, China: ACM, 2011.

[353] J. M. Sadler, D. P. Ames, and S. J. Livingston. Extending HydroShare to enable hydrologic time series data as social media. *Journal of Hydroinformatics*, 18(2):198–209, 2015.

[354] R. Sanders and D. Kelly. Dealing with risk in scientific software development. In *Software*, pages 21–28. IEEE, 2008.

[355] D. G. Tarboton, J. S. Horsburgh, D. Maidment, T. Whiteaker, I. Zaslavsky, M. Piasecki, J. L. Goodall, D. Valentine, and T. Whitenack. Development of a community hydrologic information system. In *18th World IMACS Congress and MODSIM09 International Congress on Modelling and Simulation*, pages 988–994. R. S. Anderssen, R. D. Braddock, and L. T. Newham (Ed.), 18th Modelling and Simulation Society of Australia and New Zealand and International Association for Mathematics and Computers in Simulation, 2009.

[356] B. Turhan, L. Layman, M. Diep, H. Erdogmus, and F. Shull. How Effective Is Test-Driven Development? In *Making Software: What Really Works and Why We Believe It*, pages 207–217. O'Reilly, 2010.

[357] R. Van Noorden. Science publishing: The trouble with retractions. *Nature*, 478:26–28, 2011.

[358] L. Williams, M. Maximilien, and M. Vouk. Test-Driven Development as a Defect-Reduction Practice. In *Proceedings of the 14th International Symposium on Software Reliability Engineering*, page 34, 2003.

[359] G. V. Wilson. Where's the real bottleneck in scientific computing? *American Scientist*, 94(1):5–6, 2006.

Index